D1569811

SEDENTISM AND MOBILITY IN
A SOCIAL LANDSCAPE

SEDENTISM

AND

MOBILITY

IN A

SOCIAL

LANDSCAPE

MESA VERDE & BEYOND

Mark D. Varien

The University of Arizona Press   Tucson

The University of Arizona Press
© 1999 The Arizona Board of Regents
First Printing

⊚ This book is printed on acid-free, archival-quality paper.
Manufactured in the United States of America

04   03   02   01   00   99   6   5   4   3   2   1

Library of Congress Cataloging-in-Publication Data
Varien, Mark.
Sedentism and mobility in a social landscape : Mesa Verde and
beyond / Mark D. Varien.
p. cm.
Includes bibliographical references (p.) and index.

ISBN 0-8165-1904-8 (acid-free, archival-quality paper)
1. Pueblo Indians—Antiquities. 2. Land settlement patterns,
Prehistoric—Colorado—Mesa Verde National Park. 3. Residential
mobility—Colorado—Mesa Verde National Park. 4. Sand Canyon
Pueblo (Colo.) 5. Duckfoot Site (Colo.) I. Title.
  E99.P9 V384 1999   98-40106
  307.2'09788'27—ddc21   CIP

British Library Cataloguing-in-Publication Data
A catalogue record for this book is available from the British Library.

All royalties will be donated to the Ian Thompson Celebration Fund
at the Crow Canyon Archaeological Center in Cortez, Colorado.

Publication of this book is made possible in part by the proceeds of
a permanent endowment created with the assistance of a Challenge
Grant from the National Endowment for the Humanities, a federal
agency.

In memory of
Ian "Sandy" Thompson,
who knew and loved the Four Corners
country as well as anyone who ever lived

CONTENTS

ILLUSTRATIONS

TABLES

ACKNOWLEDGMENTS

Many people and institutions contributed to the successful completion of this book, which is a revised version of my Ph.D. dissertation. Financial support from the Department of Anthropology at Arizona State University (ASU) and the Crow Canyon Archaeological Center made the research possible. I was fortunate to have a remarkable committee at ASU. My chair, Dr. Keith Kintigh, provided wise counsel throughout graduate school and insightful guidance in the development of my dissertation research. I am grateful for his advice and friendship. The other members of my committee include Dr. Katherine Spielmann and Dr. Barbara Stark from ASU, Dr. Jeffrey Dean from the University of Arizona, and Dr. William (Bill) Lipe from Washington State University. Each member of the committee provided detailed comments that shaped this research as it progressed, and any success the book achieves is due largely to their efforts.

Three people deserve special thanks. Dr. Dee Ann Story was instrumental in my becoming an archaeologist by supervising my undergraduate and graduate research at the University of Texas. When I conduct fieldwork, it is as if Dee Ann is looking over my shoulder, and I will forever try to live up to the meticulous standards she set for archaeological data collection. Bill Lipe supervised my work at the Dolores Archaeological Program and at Crow Canyon. I am grateful for all he has taught me about Mesa Verde–region archaeology, for the professional opportunities he has given me, and for the intellectual inspiration he provides. Finally, Ian "Sandy" Thompson became a mentor and friend as soon as I came to Crow Canyon in 1987. As executive director at Crow Canyon, Sandy recognized that the Sand Canyon Project Site Testing Program could make a significant contribution to archaeological method and theory, and he structured the institutional backing that ensured that the project realized this potential. More importantly, he committed an enormous amount of intellectual energy to understanding the empirical, methodological, and theoretical issues involved in this research. He became a leading figure in Mesa Verde region archaeology in his own right and a valued colleague in our collaborative research into Mesa Verde–region settlement patterns. Sandy also served as an unofficial committee member, reading, editing, and commenting on each draft of the manuscript.

This book took shape in the remarkable climate of scholarship I found at ASU. I would like to thank all of my professors, especially Dr. George Cowgill and Dr. Michelle Hegmon for their courses in social theory, and my fellow graduate students. Jim Potter deserves special recognition; we discussed our respective research problems continually, producing a rich collaboration and a valued friendship. Brett Hill also deserves special recognition for his friendship and the expert advice he provided as a consultant on the geographic information systems analyses presented in this book.

I owe a deep debt of gratitude to all of my colleagues at Crow Canyon who helped develop this research. My work on this project and my absence from the institution undoubtedly increased the work load on others who continued to run the center's research and education programs. Everyone on the Crow Canyon staff deserves mention, but space, unfortunately, permits me to mention only a few. Kristin Kuckelman served as codirector of the Sand Canyon Project Site Testing Program, which provided much of the data on which this dissertation is based. Ricky Lightfoot provided support in many areas, not least of which was his excellent research into household organization at the Duckfoot site. Melita Romasco, laboratory director, provided artifact output crucial to the completion of this research, as did computer consultants Lynn Udick, Art Rohr, and Lee Gripp. Maggie Thurs, material culture analyst, also provided computer support, including entry of the tree-ring data used in this report. Chris Pierce, material culture specialist, was particularly helpful in thinking through issues related to cooking pot breakage and discard. Bill Lipe, Richard Wilshusen, and Sandy Thompson all served as research director while my graduate studies and dissertation research developed, and each made important contributions to this research. I am grateful to Ginnie Dunlop and Neal Morris, who helped produce the final figures, and Theresa Titone, who assisted in the production of this manuscript. The remainder of my colleagues at Crow Canyon provided continuous support and constructive criticism as my research developed, and I am grateful to all of them for their love and support.

The research developed in this book owes an intellectual debt to many colleagues. Tim Kohler has been a key figure in developing accumulations research as a tool for estimating occupation span. Research by Eric Blinman and Dean Wilson on Mesa Verde–region pottery assemblages was crucial to my studies, and Eric offered many helpful suggestions for modeling cooking pot accumulations. Richard Wilshusen, who has been an exceptional friend and colleague for over two decades, and Sarah Schlanger provided a model for abandonment studies that was particularly influential in my work. Andrew Fowler and John Stein were the first to open my eyes to the changing face of Puebloan communities between A.D. 1000 and 1300. The research of Mike Adler and Carla Van West on Mesa Verde–region settlement patterns paved the way for my studies. Crow Canyon sponsored a working conference on accumulations research that was attended by Barbara Mills, Michael Schiffer, and Sarah Schlanger, along with several of the Crow Canyon research staff. The ideas discussed at that conference were critical to the development of my application of these methods, and the conference participants outlined a publication on accumulations research that was eventually coauthored by Barbara Mills and me. Jim Eder, Patricia Gilman, Sue Kent, Steve Lekson, Glenn Stone, and Tom Rocek all reviewed an early version of my critique of sedentism and mobility studies, and their comments were a great help in the further development of these ideas. Finally, thanks go to Tim Kohler and Pat Gilman for their comments on this manuscript and to Jane Kepp for her excellent work in editing this book.

Compilation of the community center database resulted from the collaborative effort of many archaeologists working in the Mesa Verde region, and I have publicly acknowledged their contribution elsewhere. However, the following individuals agreed to review this database one more time in preparation for this research: Kristie Arrington, David Breternitz, Jerry Fetterman, Steve Fuller, Linda Honeycutt, Winston Hurst, and Jim Judge. I thank them for being so generous with their knowledge of the region.

The Site Testing Program excavations took place on both private and public land. I am indebted to the following landowners who granted Crow Canyon permission to work on or travel through their property: Troy and Shorlene Oliver and their family; Roy and Lillian Retherford and their daughters Glenna Harris and Guyrene McAfee; and Catherine Stanley and her son Stanton Stanley. The generosity of these people, who gave a great deal and asked for nothing in return, cannot be overstated. The Bureau of Land Management (BLM) was also a partner in this research, and I am grateful to Sally Wisely, then the San Juan Resource Area manager, Kristie Arrington, BLM archaeologist, and the entire staff of the Anasazi Heritage Center.

I am thankful for the funding I received to conduct this research. A grant from the Colorado Historical Society funded the cooking-pot sherd accumulation rate study. A grant from the Ballantine Family Fund and another from the ASU Graduate Research Support Office funded the geographic information systems analysis of Mesa Verde–region settlement patterns. The William D. Lipe Fund at Crow Canyon provided funding for the production of the final figures. Finally, a research and development grant from the ASU Department of Anthropology funded the compilation of the tree-ring database.

Completion of this research required the patience, love, and support of many individuals. Nancy Mahoney was an emotional and intellectual anchor during the production of this book, and I am grateful for her loving support. I am also grateful for the unconditional love provided by my family: parents Richard and Merrill, brother Richard, and sister Anne, who would have been so proud of me. I love you all.

SEDENTISM AND MOBILITY IN
A SOCIAL LANDSCAPE

SEDENTISM

AND

MOBILITY

IN

HORTICULTURAL

AND

AGRICULTURAL

SOCIETIES

Existing research on mobility is based on the study of "simple" hunter-gatherer groups practicing high-frequency residential movement: that is, groups moving several times a year. Concepts developed through this hunter-gatherer research are useful, but they are ultimately inadequate for studying population movement in societies where residential moves occur on a supra-annual basis, sometimes only once in one or two generations. In addition, hunter-gatherer models focus on the environmental and ecological determinants of mobility. Research into mobility should acknowledge the importance of the environment, but it must also examine the social determinants of mobility and recognize that all decisions to move or stay are conditioned by the social context in which they occur.

Examination of settlement patterns in the Mesa Verde region demonstrates that sedentism and mobility are not opposing concepts but separate strategies that were employed simultaneously. The analyses that follow examine household residential mobility and show that the frequency of household movement varied between once every generation and once every three generations, and later residential sites had longer occupation spans than earlier sites. An analysis of community movement demonstrates that it, too, varied in frequency, but it occurred less often than household movement—between approximately once every century and once every three centuries. In the center of the Mesa Verde region communities moved short distances and had longer occupation spans, whereas on the periphery of the region communities moved farther and had shorter histories.

This variation in household and community movement can be understood only by considering the changing social context in the region. A key feature of this social context was the historical development of communities. For the purpose of this study, a community is defined as a group of individuals who live in proximity to one another within a geographically limited area, who have face-to-face interaction on a regular basis, and who share access to resources in their local sustaining areas. The communities examined in this study each consist of a relatively permanent community center—a densely settled area usually associated with public architecture— and an associated, less densely settled residential area. In the analyses that follow, I identify the 27 largest and most persistent communities that developed in the Mesa Verde region between A.D. 950 and 1300.

During this period, the social context of the region changed in two ways. First, communities in the center of the region became increasingly numerous, creating greater competition for resources. Second, the area encompassed by the Mesa Verde regional settlement system, as defined by the largest and most permanent communities, shrank through time, which increasingly isolated the Mesa Verde–region settlement system from those in adjacent regions. Identification of these persistent communities and analyses of their distribution reveal a third level of settlement structure that characterized the social context of the Mesa Verde region: supracommunity clusters with overlapping catchments.

This changing social context provides the structure in which residential mobility occurred. One important aspect of this ever-changing structure was the development of land tenure systems, which were produced and reproduced through the practices of individuals acting within and upon their historically derived structure. Residential mobility is a practice central to the development of land tenure systems, and land tenure appears to change from usufruct to the heritable transfer of land between generations during the years from A.D. 950 to 1300. Thus, residential mobility is modeled as a social process in which behavior is both enabled and constrained by the existing structure. Through the practice of residential mobility, the settlement system in the Mesa Verde region was simultaneously reproduced and transformed.

THE ANALYSES

The analyses that follow use data from the Duckfoot and Sand Canyon Projects (Lightfoot 1994; Lightfoot and Etzkorn 1993; Lipe 1992), both of which examine ancient households and communities in the Mesa Verde region. Duckfoot, a ninth-century hamlet with four pit structures and 19 surface rooms, is an unusually strong case study because it is well preserved, precisely dated, and almost completely excavated. The Sand Canyon Project documents changes in settlement patterns and community organization during a 350-year period using a diverse sample of well-dated sites from a single settlement system (Lipe 1992; Varien et al. 1996). Research includes environmental archaeology (Adams 1992), full coverage survey (Adler 1990, 1992), and the excavation of 15 sites from two adjacent communities (Bradley 1992; Huber 1993; Varien 1998). In addition, the Sand Canyon Project produced an inventory of all known community centers in the Mesa Verde region dating between A.D. 950 and 1300 (Varien et al. 1996).

These data are used to examine the sedentism and mobility of a number of social units at different spatial scales. The frequency and distance of population movement is examined for individuals, households, and communities. Mobility of these social units is examined at three spatial scales, those of residential sites, localities, and regions.

Residential sites have discrete spatial boundaries and contain the structures and middens associated with relatively long-term occupation. Localities are areas that are larger than an individual residential site but smaller than a region. The boundaries of each locality include many residential sites that comprised a community or a group of communities and the immediate sustaining area that provided the bulk of the subsistence resources for the community. Despite its long history of use in settlement archaeology (Willey and Phillips 1958:18), locality remains a relatively weak and arbitrary concept, and the term *study area* might be reasonably substituted. Locality is used in this study because the Sand Canyon locality has been defined and appears frequently in Sand Canyon Project research publications (Lipe 1992). Finally, the Mesa Verde region, as defined in this study, is an area of approximately 14,000 square kilometers (5,000 square miles) within which there are distinct architectural and ceramic traditions.

Residential sites were occupied by individuals, households, and—in the case of the largest sites—entire communities. Households are defined in behavioral terms on the basis of a redundant set of activities that are inferred from the distribution of architectural and artifactual evidence (Wilk and Netting 1984). Behaviorally, communities consisted of many households that lived in close proximity to one another and had regular face-to-face interaction. This regular face-to-face interaction resulted in the need for some decision making above the level of the household, especially with regard to the shared use of local social and natural resources. The archaeological definition of community boundaries is difficult because residential settlement patterns in the Mesa Verde region changed from dispersed to aggregated between A.D. 950 and 1300. The problem of defining community boundaries is addressed by using the clustering of residential settlement and, in most cases, the presence of public architecture (Adler and Varien 1994).

Analyzing Household Residential Mobility

Accumulations research (Varien and Mills 1997) is used to examine the frequency of household movement by measuring the length of site occupation. This research examines the rate at which cooking-pot sherds accumulate at sites, establishing an average annual accumulation rate per household for cooking-pot sherds and developing confidence intervals associated with this rate. The accumulation rate is then used to measure the length of occupation at 13 excavated sites within the Sand Canyon locality, documenting the frequency of residential movement at these sites. There is considerable variation in the frequency of household movement at any point in time and increasing residential sedentism through time. Variation in the frequency of residential movement is evidence that these moves were stimulated by a variety of processes, including social factors, and the change in the frequency of residential movement over time is interpreted in terms of changing patterns of land tenure, which were stimulated by greater competition for resources.

Estimating the length of site occupation is critical not only for studies of mobility but also for accurate estimation of population size and, therefore, for any theory that requires knowledge of population size (Nelson, Kohler, and Kintigh 1994; Powell 1988). Moreover, accumulations research is critical for understanding the formation of archaeological assemblages (Schiffer 1987; Varien and Mills 1997).[1] Its methods are relevant to problems faced by archaeologists working in all parts of the world.

Analyzing Community Movement

The frequency of community movement *within* a locality is addressed in this book using three analyses. First, the treatment of pit structure roofs at the time of structure abandonment is examined to determine whether timbers were salvaged or abandoned as de facto refuse (Cameron 1990, 1991; Wilshusen 1986, 1988a). When timbers were salvaged, a short-distance move to the next occupied site is inferred, and the continuity of community occupation is assumed. The abandonment of timbers as de facto refuse is interpreted as evidence for a long-distance move and community mobility. Second, the density of artifacts in the fill of abandoned pit structures is calculated (Montgomery 1993; Reid 1973). High artifact density in fill is interpreted as evidence for continued use of a site and community sedentism. Third, wood procurement events are examined (Ahlstrom, Dean, and Robinson 1991; Schlanger and Wilshusen 1993), and the continuous harvesting of timbers is interpreted as evidence for community sedentism.

These analyses demonstrate that most Mesa Verde–region communities occupied their sustaining localities continuously for over a century and perhaps as long as three centuries. Previous studies of mobility have not distinguished between the frequency of household movement and the movement of entire communities. Documenting differences between household and community mobility provides a more robust and accurate picture of population movement, and this perspective permits the interpretation of mobility within a social framework.

Analyzing Sedentism and Mobility at a Regional Scale

At the regional scale, I examine how the rugged terrain of the Mesa Verde region impeded travel on foot, thereby conditioning interaction and structuring community boundaries. Next, the changing social landscape of the

Mesa Verde region is described, because the movement of individuals, households, and communities was negotiated in this landscape. Analyses of the distribution of Mesa Verde communities show how competition for resources increased between A.D. 950 and 1300. Finally, the frequency and geographic scale of community movement is documented, both within the region and between the Mesa Verde region and adjacent areas.

The Mesa Verde–region social landscape is reconstructed by examining the chronology, distribution, and physiographic location of community centers. The analyses build on previous studies (Adler and Varien 1994; Varien et al. 1996) but for the first time incorporate digital elevation models and geographic information systems (GIS) technology to examine how the physiography affected population movement and the formation of the Mesa Verde–region social landscape. In addition, every tree-ring date from the Mesa Verde region—almost 10,000 dates—is analyzed to examine movement of large numbers of people into and out of the Mesa Verde region.

The analyses presented in the following pages examine mobility for a variety of social units at a range of spatial scales. Integrating these various scales is critical to fully understanding the sedentism and mobility of ancient societies, but such integration has been largely absent in previous studies of population movement, especially in the study of mobility among agriculturalists in the ancient Southwest. Also absent from previous studies is an adequate evaluation of social factors that influence mobility and the social context in which this population movement occurred. The empirical studies developed here are used to evaluate existing models and to develop a new, more appropriate model of population movements among Southwestern agriculturalists.

THE PROBLEM

Conventional wisdom maintains that ancient societies in the Southwest were sedentary after the introduction of agriculture. At the core of this conventional interpretation is the assumption that the appearance of cultigens produced a dependence on agriculture and that agriculture, along with the subsequent appearance of pottery and more substantial architecture, signaled the beginning of a sedentary way of life. Two additional factors contributed to the paradigmatic bias that saw ancient Southwestern groups as sedentary: the use of historic-period pueblos as analogs for ancient settlements and emphasis on the excavation of large sites (Lekson 1990). The conventional interpretation was challenged in the 1970s (Dean 1970) and 1980s (Gilman 1987, 1988; Lekson 1990; Powell 1983) and was so thoroughly questioned that Whalen and Gilman (1990) dubbed mobility the "idea of the 1980s" in Southwestern archaeology.

A number of trends can be identified in recent literature on mobility in the Southwest. First, the site is the spatial scale of most new studies, and, in the tradition of hunter-gatherer models, the question addressed is whether site occupation was seasonal or year-round. Ecofacts, artifacts, features, architecture, and cross-cultural research are used to evaluate this question (Gilman 1987; Jewett and Lightfoot 1986; Kent 1991a, 1992; Kent and Vierich 1989; Lightfoot and Jewett 1984; Plog 1986; Powell 1983; Rocek 1988). Emphasis on documenting the season of occupation has resulted in a focus on small sites in most recent studies (Powell 1990). The examination of small sites means that the household, or some small residential group, is typically the social scale of the research. Less often, larger sites and community mobility are considered (Dean 1969; Kintigh 1985; Nelson and LeBlanc 1986).

Second, when year-round occupation is acknowledged, it is now typically seen as short-term sedentism (Nelson and Anyon 1996; Nelson and LeBlanc 1986) or shifting sedentism (Lekson 1996). Long-term sedentism, or "deep-sedentism" (Lekson 1990), is seen as having been limited to the protohistoric period. Thus, communities are rarely seen as having histories, and historical interpretation is not emphasized in the explanation of regional change.

Third, climatic factors (Carmichael 1990; Schlanger 1988; Schlanger and Wilshusen 1993) and resource depletion (Kohler 1992a, 1992b; Kohler and Matthews 1988; Lekson 1993, 1996; Plog 1986) are the variables most often cited as causing mobility. Finally, sedentism versus mobility is treated as an either/or phenomenon.

Eder (1984) points out that sedentism and mobility are not either-or phenomena, nor are they on opposite ends of a continuum. He argues that sedentariness is a threshold property that applies to social groups, and that mobility is a continuous variable best seen at the level of individuals. This distinction is helpful because it emphasizes that individuals practice mobility in every society—even if their society has crossed a threshold definition of what it means to be sedentary. Seeing mobility as a property only of individuals, however, may cloud the issue by failing to acknowledge that individuals often move in groups.

"Sedentism" is not easily defined. For Plog (1990:180), sedentism refers to "groups in which all major segments of the population—infant, adolescent, and adults as well as males and females—use facilities and structures within a village during all seasons of the year." Plog stresses the word "use" as opposed to "reside" in this definition because he regards agriculturalists who use both field houses and more permanent habitations as sedentary (Plog 1990:181). Others (Kelly 1992:49; Rafferty 1985:115) use a definition of sedentism offered by Rice (1975:97) in which at least part of the population remains at the same residential site throughout the entire year. These categorical definitions separate sedentism as a threshold property from mobility as a continuous variable, and sedentism is seen as a property of groups rather than individuals.

But defining sedentism as a threshold property remains problematic. For example, in the definitions proposed by Plog and Rice it is impossible to distinguish between the relative sedentariness of groups once they have crossed the threshold definition. As Rocek (1996) notes, the problem of defining sedentism and mobility is more than just terminological; it is a multivariate problem conditioned by variables that are interwoven. The problem should not be addressed with another definition of sedentism but rather by recognizing that all human societies are mobile, that this mobility is multidimensional, and that a society can be described as being increasingly sedentary as the frequency of its residential moves decreases.

Part of the problem is that the concepts used to examine sedentism and mobility have developed entirely from studies of hunter-gatherer, not agrarian, societies (Binford 1980, 1982, 1990; Kelly 1983; Yellen 1977). Mobility strategies in hunter-gatherer studies are typically defined as "seasonal movements of hunter-gatherers across the landscape" (Kelly 1983:277). Binford's (1980) distinction between residential and logistical mobility—the latter referring to task-specific movement to and from a residential site—is one of the most useful concepts from hunter-gatherer mobility studies. High-frequency residential movement characterizes the most mobile groups. When residential moves decrease in frequency, logistical mobility is increasingly emphasized. When groups are residentially fixed for the entire year they are typically regarded as sedentary, and all mobility is seen as logistically organized. Thus, hunter-gatherer mobility studies are largely limited to the study of seasonal movement. Ecological factors are seen as conditioning these short-term economic decisions. Given this intellectual history, it is no surprise that Southwestern archaeologists have largely focused on the narrow issue of whether individual archaeological sites were occupied seasonally or year-round and have looked to ecological factors to explain mobility.

Logistically organized mobility for the purpose of procuring seasonally available resources was clearly important in the agricultural and mixed economies of the ancient Southwest. But documenting the logistical mobility of these societies does not tell us about their sedentariness. Understanding the sedentariness of a group requires consideration of two aspects of mobility that have been given almost no attention. These poorly understood aspects of mobility are (1) the frequency with which households move their primary residence and (2) the frequency with which communities relocate within regions. The low-frequency residential movement of households and communities—called "long-term" or "territorial" mobility by Kelly (1992) and "supra-annual" mobility by Mills (1994)—characterizes the settlement systems of agriculturalists, groups with mixed economies, and sedentary/complex hunter-gatherers. At present, methods and theories for studying the low-frequency residential movement of households and communities are grossly underdeveloped, and this low-frequency movement cannot be understood using the temporal and social scales of existing hunter-gatherer models.

Ancient Southwestern societies with agriculture were simultaneously mobile and sedentary. That is, as groups became more residentially stable, their logistical mobility became increasingly complex (Binford 1978a, 1980; Eder 1984). Failure to acknowledge that groups can exhibit a high degree of mobility at one scale even as they become more sedentary at another caused archaeologists to talk past one another during the debates of the 1980s. In addition, increasing residential sedentism does *not* mean that residential mobility decreases in importance. This is particularly true in agricultural societies where people often claim access to their primary means of production—agricultural land—by moving onto the land they cultivate.

But refining our understanding of mobility and sedentism is not an end in itself. Interest in characterizing the mobility and sedentism of ancient societies has been sustained because sedentism and mobility are crucial to understanding the economic and social organization of societies and the development of political complexity (Keeley 1988; Price and Brown 1985). Anthropology has long been concerned with these issues, and archaeology has made many important contributions to them (Fried 1967; Service 1971). Within this tradition, numerous organizational models have been proposed for ancient societies in the American Southwest, resulting in vigorous and sometimes acrimonious debate (Graves, Longacre, and Holbrook 1982; Graves and Reid 1984; Lightfoot 1984; Upham 1982; Upham and Plog 1986). These debates remain unresolved because the empirical evidence needed to address fundamental questions, including accurately determining the length and continuity of site occupation, is lacking. This limits our ability to establish the contemporaneity of sites (Ammerman 1981; Dewar 1991) and undermines any attempt at population and demographic reconstruction (Dean et al. 1985:542; Nelson, Kohler, and Kintigh 1994; Powell 1988), both of which are essential to understanding the social, economic, and political organization of any ancient society.

There is an important link between the subsistence economy, sedentism, and the development of social complexity and inequality. Studies of hunter-gatherers have demonstrated that agricultural dependence is not necessary for the development of social complexity (Arnold 1993; Brown 1985; Charles and Buikstra 1983; Keeley 1988; Price and Brown 1985). However, the studies that uncouple social complexity from domesticated food production explicitly do *not* separate complexity and sedentism (Ames 1981:799; Brown 1985:201; Keeley 1988:397). It appears that it is the degree to which resource procurement can be *intensified* that conditions the degree of sedentism, as well as the types of mobility strategies practiced, regardless of whether the resources are wild foods or cultigens. Intensification and increased sedentism are, in turn, related to changes in a number of practices that structure economies, including storage, trade, territoriality, male and female work patterns, gender inequality, fertility, and household size (Kelly 1992).

Understanding sedentism and mobility is therefore central to understanding a suite of problems of more general anthropological interest.

THE DUCKFOOT AND SAND CANYON ARCHAEOLOGICAL PROJECTS

This study concentrates on the Mesa Verde region in southwestern Colorado and southeastern Utah (fig. 1.1). The study area is bounded roughly by the La Plata River on the east, the Mancos and San Juan Rivers on the south, Cedar Mesa on the west, the Abajo Mountains on the northwest, and the Dolores River and La Plata Mountains on the northeast. Archaeologically, this is one of the most intensively studied areas in the world. Numerous large-scale survey and excavation projects have been conducted there, and occupations dating to each of the Pecos classification periods (Kidder 1927) have been thoroughly excavated and interpreted.

Data for this study include four principal sources: the Duckfoot Project; the Sand Canyon Archaeological Project; a database with information on all known large sites dating between A.D. 950 and 1300; and a database of all tree-ring-dated sites in the Mesa Verde region. The Crow Canyon Archaeological Center, a nonprofit education and research institution located in Cortez, Colorado, sponsored the compilation of these data.

Duckfoot is an extremely well-preserved, well-dated habitation site occupied by three households between A.D. 850 and 880. The intensive excavations have been reported in detail (R. Lightfoot 1992a, 1992b, 1993; Lightfoot and Etzkorn 1993), and Lightfoot's (1994) study of household organization and site formation processes at Duckfoot is the basis for determining the rate at which households discard cooking pots. Development of this discard rate also utilizes comparative material from the Dolores Archaeological Program (Breternitz 1993).

The A.D. 900 to 1300 period has been studied since the late 1800s, but the Sand Canyon Project represents the most recent and thorough investigation. Sand Canyon Project excavations were conducted in the Sand Canyon locality, an area of approximately 200 square kilometers that lies 15 kilometers (9 miles) northwest of Cortez, Colorado (fig. 1.2). Near the center of the locality are two of the largest sites in the Mesa Verde region, Sand Canyon Pueblo and Goodman Point Pueblo, both dating to the 1200s.

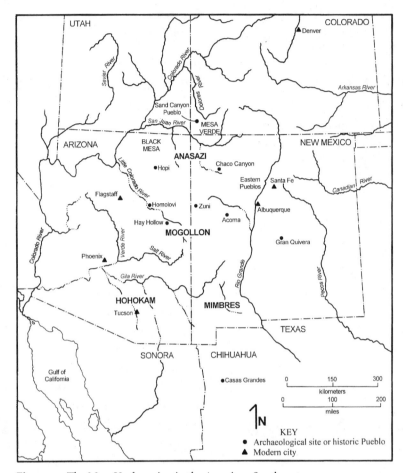

Figure 1.1 The Mesa Verde region in the American Southwest.

Sand Canyon Project research included a ten-year (1984–1993) excavation project conducted at Sand Canyon Pueblo proper (Bradley 1992, 1993). A second intensive excavation project was conducted at Green Lizard, a small site that was partly contemporary with Sand Canyon Pueblo (Huber 1993; Huber and Lipe 1992). Intensive survey has been completed in the locality, in both upper and lower Sand Canyon (Adler 1990, 1992; Gleichman and Gleichman 1992). The four-year Sand Canyon Project Site Testing Program was designed to bridge the intensive excavations and the intensive

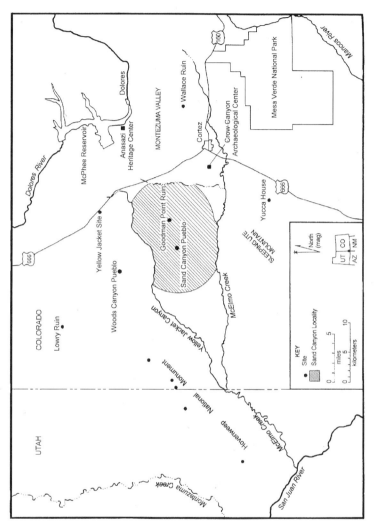

Figure 1.2 The Sand Canyon locality within the Mesa Verde region.

survey. Using a stratified random sampling procedure, crews excavated at 13 sites that varied in size, setting, and period of occupation (Varien 1998; Varien, Kuckelman, and Kleidon 1992). A number of projects have been conducted by the Environmental Archaeology Program of the Sand Canyon Project (Adams 1992), and a major effort at modeling ancient climate and agriculture in southwestern Colorado has been completed (Van West 1994; Van West and Lipe 1992). In addition, oral history has focused on historic-period homesteading and agricultural practices in the Sand Canyon locality (Connolly 1992). Finally, the Crow Canyon Archaeological Center sponsored a conference on settlement throughout much of the Southwest during the 1150 to 1350 period, placing the results of the Sand Canyon Project in a larger regional and macroregional context (Adler 1996a; Varien et al. 1996).

KEY TERMS

A number of terms need definition. These include terms for the social groups and spatial units used in the analyses. In addition, the concepts of mobility and sedentism are briefly discussed.

Households

For the purpose of this study, a household is defined as a group of individuals who share a single residence and who cooperate regularly in a number of basic economic and social activities. This perspective recognizes that the form and composition of households—including patterns of coresidence—can vary considerably, both within and between societies (Wilk 1984). This position follows a 30-year trend in which households have come to be viewed behaviorally rather than being categorized into types according to their composition (Dean 1969, 1970; Hammel 1984; Lightfoot 1994; Lowell 1988, 1991; Netting, Wilk, and Arnould 1984; Rohn 1965; Wilk and Netting 1984; Wilk and Rathje 1982; Yanagisako 1979). In other words, households are studied in terms of what they do, not on the basis of the kin relations among the household members. Understanding variation in household form and composition remains a worthwhile field of inquiry but one that is best approached by understanding the household in behavioral terms.

This behavioral perspective provides a better basis for the comparative analysis of household organization; indeed, it developed as researchers confronted the considerable variation that exists in household composition within and between societies. As an analytic unit, the household bridges the gap between the typological classification of ideal family types that was the focus of early studies and the highly variable groups actually observed in ethnographic situations (Wilk and Netting 1984).

Wilk and Netting (1984) have been particularly clear on how to recognize the household as a behavioral unit. My reading of Wilk and Netting does not see them simply arguing for a functional definition of households. Instead, the term *function* could be replaced with *practice*. Wilk and Netting argue for understanding households first in terms of the practices of household members. Then the interplay between practice and the structure of a particular group can be examined to better understand the variation in household composition and form.

To examine household practice, Wilk and Netting (1984) recommend focusing on five overlapping activity systems: production, distribution, transmission, reproduction, and coresidence. Production and distribution form the economic base of the household, transmission refers to the role of households in relegating ownership of resources among individuals and between generations, reproduction refers to biological and social reproduction, and coresidence refers to the group that regularly occupies the house.

Lightfoot (1994) adopted this approach in his study of household organization at the Duckfoot site, looking at the dominant activities and their patterned association. For production he examined the construction of houses and the location of tools of production, for distribution he focused on the location of storage facilities, and for coresidence he examined the spaces available for sleeping and the patterned repetition of activity areas across the site. He concluded that the architectural expression of the household at Duckfoot was a pit structure and its associated surface rooms.

Having conducted this analysis of activities, Lightfoot returned to the question of household composition, concluding that Duckfoot households probably comprised extended families that incorporated more than one infrahousehold group. These infrahousehold groups might have been nuclear families or a variety of possible dyads (Lightfoot 1994:158), or they could have been individuals who were not kin-related but who nevertheless resided together in a particular house. The point is that the composition of extended family households is variable *and* fluid.

Lightfoot (1994:147) went on to examine the worldwide ethnographic literature, concluding that despite variation in household composition and form, variation in average household size is relatively limited: most households range between 4.2 and 7.0 persons. This may be due to census data's being collected by residence and to limits on the number of people who reside together regardless of whether they have larger extended-family social ties. Lightfoot's finding does not resolve all the problems one faces in trying to define households behaviorally, but it is good news for archaeologists who want to use residence as a basis for comparative analyses (e.g., the accumulations research in chapters 4 and 5) and as means of estimating population size.

The unit pueblo is interpreted as the archaeological correlate for most households in the Mesa Verde region between A.D. 750 and 1300. The unit pueblo is the recurring association of a pit structure or kiva, a roomblock, and a trash area (Prudden 1903). This patterned association was present by late Pueblo I times, when Duckfoot was occupied, and—despite important architectural changes—continued in generally similar form until Puebloans abandoned the region for residential settlement at approximately A.D. 1290 (Lipe 1989:55). The unit pueblo as the architectural expression of a household is therefore equivalent to the pit structure suite that Lightfoot (1994) sees as representing extended family households at Duckfoot.

Equating a unit pueblo with a household differs from some traditional interpretations because it does not interpret kivas as having been used exclusively for specialized ritual activities, and it does not see kivas as having been used by numerous households, or what is sometimes termed a minimal lineage (Steward 1937). Addressing the first point, recent analyses indicate that many Mesa Verde–region kivas were used for both domestic and ritual activities (Adler 1989; Cater and Chenault 1988; Lipe 1989; Lipe and Hegmon 1989). Regarding the second point, the room-to-kiva ratio is especially high in the cliff dwellings on Mesa Verde, and there kivas have been interpreted as integrating multiple households (Rohn 1965, 1971). However, the room-to-kiva ratio at tested sites in the Sand Canyon locality is approximately 5:1 (Varien 1998), which is less than the 9:1 average reported by Lipe (1989:56) for the Pueblo III period in the Mesa Verde region as a whole. This low room-to-kiva ratio in the Sand Canyon locality is consistent with the interpretation that kivas were used by relatively small social groups.

In a recent study of household organization, Ortman (n.d.) analyzed the location and frequency of grinding bins at Pueblo III and Pueblo IV sites in many regions of the Southwest. Like Lightfoot's research, Ortman's study moves from an analysis of activities, or practice, to inferences about household composition. For the Mesa Verde region he documents that a single grinding facility (which includes one or more mealing bins in a spatially discrete location) is typically associated with a unit pueblo. He also reports the range of variation in the number of mealing bins in these grinding facilities and uses the number of bins to make inferences about the size and composition of Mesa Verde–region households. He documents considerable variation in the form and composition of households but concludes that most Mesa Verde–region Pueblo III households were main-tained by extended families—an interpretation similar to that made by Lightfoot for Pueblo I households.

These analyses support the interpretation that unit pueblos—and their equivalent architectural suites in larger pueblos—are appropriate archaeo-logical correlates for Mesa Verde–region households in most cases. House-holds varied considerably in composition and form, but most unit pueblos appear to represent relatively large households. Understanding the variable and fluid nature of the household is an important problem that needs to be addressed by future research, but current research indicates that variation in size of the coresidential household group may have been relatively limited.

Community

For the purpose of this study, a community consists of many households that live close to one another, have regular face-to-face interaction, and share the use of local social and natural resources. There are temporal, geographic, demographic, and social dimensions of community organiza-tion that help us recognize ancient communities in the archaeological record. The temporal dimension is straightforward: community members must reside within the community most of the time in order to interact on a regular basis. The geographic dimension means that the territory occupied by a community must be small enough to permit regular, face-to-face interaction. The demographic dimension means that there are upper and lower limits to the population size of the community. On the low end, the community is larger than individual households or groups of households that form a corporate group. On the high end, cross-cultural data suggest that there are upper limits to the size of communities in politically nonstratified societies. Perhaps most important is the social dimension. By interacting on a regular basis in a geographically limited area, community members *share access* to local resources. These resources include both productive natural resources—land, water, raw materials for tool manufacture, and wild foods—and social resources—the labor, experience, skills, creativity, and intellect of fellow community members.

In what follows, I examine these dimensions in an effort to build the social theory of ancient agrarian communities and to construct bridging arguments that link this theory to the archaeological remains used to identify ancient communities.

Communities are composed of individuals, and the membership of communities, like that of households, is fluid. The individuals that make up a community typically live with other individuals in residential sites, forming the households discussed earlier. It is tempting to describe communities as entities, thereby reifying the concept and implying that communities somehow act. But it is important to remember that it is people, and not communities, who act. Community members *do* develop institutions (e.g., kin groups, sodalities, ceremonialism, and land tenure), but it is the practices of individuals that produce and reproduce these institutions. And it is the practices of individuals that create the material remains that archaeologists use to identify the community. Because all communities are historically situated—they occur in a particular time and space—this perspective on communities as collections of individual actors is not simply a manifestation of methodological individualism (Watkins 1968). Individual actors do not behave independently of historically contingent forces.

The temporal placement of individuals in history results in behavior that is both enabled and constrained by conditions specific to a particular point in time. Examples of historical circumstances that enable and constrain individual behavior include the mode of production (including both the social relations of production and the means of production) specific to a society, the external environmental conditions in which people lived, and the customs and ideology of a society, which are embodied as an individual's *habitus* (Bourdieu 1990).

The geographic dimension in which individual community members are situated includes their proximity to natural resources, to other community members, and to the members of neighboring communities. The geographic dimension of historical contingency is particularly important because communities are *both people and place.* That is, communities are places where individuals interact on a regular basis (Murdock 1949). Regular face-to-face interaction should not be glossed as a familiarity that results simply from seeing one another frequently. Instead, it should be understood in terms of how interaction in the context of copresence is fundamental to the production and reproduction of society (Giddens 1984:64–72). Some degree of spatial proximity is a prerequisite for this regular interaction. The spatial dimension also encompasses the built environment, consisting of both residential and public architecture found within the community, and the way in which this built environment affects interaction in the context of copresence.

The social dimension includes historical conditions, which combine the dimensions of time and space. These historical conditions provide the "structure," or the rules and resources that people draw upon as they pursue their socially defined self-interest (Giddens 1984). Intracommunity and intercommunity relationships were an important part of the structure of ancient society in the Mesa Verde region. Just as our understanding of households is informed by analyzing the practices of household members within the confines of their residence, our understanding of communities is informed by analyzing the practices of community members within the larger context of the community and the regional social landscape. In cross-cultural analyses, Adler (1990, 1996b) found that communities in politically nonstratified societies were critical to the creation and perpetuation of land tenure rights in the context of a larger regional landscape that included many other—often competing—communities.

Thus, behaviors organized at the level of the household shape the labor inputs of agricultural systems, but behaviors organized at the scale of the community shape the negotiation of rights to land (Brush and Turner 1987). The community can therefore be seen as a territorial unit whose members recognize shared access to the productive resources of the vicinity, even though those resources may be allocated to individual users (Adler and Varien 1994:84). The institutions that facilitate this social process thereby play an important role in economic organization that encompasses individuals, households, and larger corporate groups. Decision making at the level of the community is often required to resolve disputes between community members over access to resources (Brush and Turner 1987). This illustrates the political dimension of the practices that occur within communities, and institutions develop to facilitate this political activity.

There is still much to learn about the organization and boundaries of ancient Southwestern communities, but I agree with Lekson (1991:42) that "if the unit house is the fundamental element of Anasazi architecture, the community is the fundamental unit of Anasazi settlement." This is especially true for the Mesa Verde region, where archaeological survey has consistently shown that residential sites do not occur in isolation but rather are grouped together into settlement clusters (Adler 1990; Fetterman and Honeycutt 1987; Greubel 1991; Neily 1983; Rohn 1977). Because settlement is clustered at a number of inclusive levels, there arises the question, which level of settlement clustering represents a community? Cross-cultural research indicates that there is an upper limit to the population of communities in politically nonstratified societies. In a worldwide sample that included examples from the American Southwest, Adler (1990, 1994; Adler and Varien 1994) found that such communities did not exceed 1,500 people; other researchers place the limit at approximately 2,000 people (Forge 1972; Kosse 1990; Lekson 1984). Population estimates for the settlement clusters identified as Mesa Verde–region communities should be at or below these levels. Thus, there are population thresholds as well as spatial thresholds that help us recognize the upper limits for the size of Mesa Verde–region communities.

In accordance with the perspective that institutionalized economic and political behavior characterized community organization, Adler (1990) and Adler and Varien (1994) looked for evidence of activities that integrated individuals and households within the larger social context of communities. They focused on the role of public architecture. Cross-culturally, the public structures used by entire communities tend to have the largest floor areas and the most specialized uses of any buildings in the community (Adler 1989; Adler and Wilshusen 1990). These cross-cultural patterns help us identify particular buildings in the Mesa Verde region as public architecture. To identify communities and their boundaries, Adler and Varien (1994) combined the spatial clustering of residential sites and the presence of public architecture in those clusters.

This combination of settlement clustering and public architecture is used to identify communities in the analyses that follow. Lipe (1994:5) takes a similar perspective in defining what he calls "first-order, face-to-face communities." He notes that these first-order communities can form alliances with other, similar communities, but he keeps these alliances conceptually distinct from the first-order communities themselves. He further argues that these alliances need not exhibit formal political hierarchies or a regional polity, which implies that the supracommunity alliances may not be as persistent through time as the first-order communities that make them.

It is likely that further research into the definition of community boundaries and the nature of community organization in the Mesa Verde region will document a wide range of settlement configurations. The geographic and demographic scales of communities will almost certainly vary across space and through time. Some settlement clusters may be smaller than others and lack public architecture, or they may have unrecognized types of public space. Ultimately, analyses of this variability will be essential to a full understanding of Mesa Verde–region society, but in this book I examine only communities that meet the criteria of having a settlement cluster with an associated community center.

Residential Sites, Localities, and Regions

Residential sites, localities, and regions are the spatial units used to study households and communities. Residential sites have distinct boundaries and contain structures and middens used by one or more households. The residential sites examined in the analyses that follow are interpreted as the primary residences for their households. A locality, as defined by Willey and Phillips (1958:18), is typically a spatial unit larger than a residential site and smaller than a region. In this study, locality refers to the area immediately surrounding a community or cluster of communities. It is the area from which a community derived the bulk of its sustaining resources (Lipe 1992:3), and it is therefore roughly analogous to the catchment areas discussed in chapter 7. In the case of the Sand Canyon Project, locality boundaries were drawn at the beginning of our investigation into community organization to ensure that research was conducted at a scale appropriate to a study of one or a few multisite communities (Lipe 1992:2).

The Mesa Verde region encompasses the sustaining areas for many communities whose combined interaction produced distinct regional architectural and pottery traditions. Recent evaluation of traditionally defined archaeological regions in the Southwest demonstrates that there was considerable variation in the patterns of interaction *within* these areas (Duff n.d.). This is no doubt true for the Mesa Verde region, but as a whole it displays relative homogeneity of material remains when they are compared with remains found in surrounding regions.

Mobility and Sedentism

Three tendencies continue to characterize analyses of mobility and sedentism, even as greater variation in mobility strategies is recognized. First, mobility and sedentism continue to be conceptualized as lying at either end of a unilineal continuum. Second, a paradigm is used that stresses classification and typology as a means for dealing with the variation. Finally, research fails to integrate the appropriate social and spatial scales. The result is that newly recognized variation in mobility strategies simply fills our classificatory continuum with ever more numerous types of mobility.

This study focuses on the low-frequency residential movement of households and communities in agricultural societies. This low-frequency movement has been ignored because sedentism has been defined as a threshold reached when groups remain in one place for an entire year. After people cross this arbitrary threshold, the mobility that remains to be studied is logistical movement, and the only recognized type of residential movement is long-distance migration. The low-frequency residential movement of households and communities has been lost in the netherworld of our classificatory continuum, somewhere between the residential movements of collectors and the migrations of larger groups. The low-frequency residential movement of households and communities in agricultural societies should not be seen as another "type" of mobility that fills this unilineal continuum. Instead, mobility is variable and multidimensional, and low-frequency residential movement is only one dimension of the mobility practiced by these groups. Mobility in the Mesa Verde region occurred simultaneously at a number of social, temporal, and geographic scales; seasonal, logistically organized mobility was undoubtedly important in these societies as well.

With regard to sedentism, threshold definitions do not allow us to distinguish among the relative sedentariness of groups. This problem can be addressed by focusing on the frequency of their residential moves. Thus sedentism, unlike mobility, is unidimensional and can be conceptualized as forming a continuum.

MOBILITY AS A SOCIAL PROCESS

Modeling mobility as a social process requires social theory; the concepts of structure, agency, and practice (Bourdieu 1990; Giddens 1984; Ortner 1984) are essential to the social theory used to interpret mobility and sedentism in the Mesa Verde region. In addition, considering mobility as part of a society's mode of production is important in understanding population movement in social terms (Halperin 1989).

Structure, Agency, and Practice

"Structure" is similar to what has been traditionally termed culture, society, or even "the system," but structure, as used in recent social theory, differs from the traditional view. In the traditional view, structure included the roles, rules, norms, and institutions of a society; individuals learned the rules and norms and passively assumed the roles defined by institutions. This view has been criticized because it sees an individual's behavior as a simple predetermined enactment of these rules, norms, and roles (Ortner 1984:150) and because little attention is paid to how structure is produced, reproduced, and transformed. My use of the term *structure* follows that of Giddens (1984) and refers to the rules and resources that people draw upon in their daily interactions.

Recent theories do not view structure as a given. Instead, the origin and transmission of structure is viewed as an important problem in its own right. The attempt to understand how structure is produced, reproduced, and transformed has resulted in a different perspective on the relationship between structure and individuals. Rather than viewing individuals as passive receptacles of culture who enact rules and norms, recent studies view them as conscious, strategic actors or agents. As strategic actors, individuals *are* enculturated and socialized, and this *does* constrain their perceived options for behavior, as described in Bourdieu's concept of *habitus* (Bourdieu 1990). But within the parameters set by this *habitus,* individuals also consciously develop strategies for manipulating the structure, and this, in part, accounts for how the structure is both reproduced *and* transformed. Recent studies also stress that perceptions of the structure vary among individuals in a society; this variation can be along age, gender, ethnic, or factional lines, producing not one but many structures. The complex relationship between structure and agency has come to be one of the chief problems examined by social theory (Giddens 1979, 1984; Ortner 1984:145).

Attempts to examine the relationship between structure and agency have been termed "practice theory" (Bourdieu 1990) or "structuration theory" (Giddens 1984). These studies stress that structure and agency are not a dichotomy but two sides of a reflexive relationship. The daily practice of strategic actors produces and reproduces the structure. That is, structure develops as a historical process that serves both to constrain and to enable an individual's behavior, but it is the regular action and interaction of individuals that produce and reproduce the structure.

Incorporating the concepts of structure and agency into archaeological theory does not mean tracing specific individuals and their specific actions in the past (Cowgill 1993a, 1996) but recognizing that the archaeological record is the aggregated residue of the actions of strategic actors—a residue that is, of course, transformed by formation processes (Shennan 1993). In Cowgill's words (1993a:556), this entails "seeing ancient remains as the outcome of behavior by conscious, knowing actors, negotiating and strategizing in pursuit of diverse aims."

Important problems remain for any social theory that uses the concepts of structure and agency. Not the least of these is gaining a better understanding of what motivates actors in their "diverse aims" (Cowgill 1993a; Ortner 1984). One theory of motivation is what Ortner (1984:151) terms "interest theory," which sees actors as pursuing their self-interest in an individualistic and "rational" manner. That actors operate in particular environmental, technological, and social contexts (Cowgill 1993a, 1993b; Earle 1991) means that rationality refers to behavior that is sensible from a means-to-ends perspective. This is different from the rationality that characterizes some formal models in which optimizing behavior is deliberately viewed as unaffected by cultural constraints. This culturally constituted, pragmatic rationality is one aspect of motivation, but it is not the only thing that motivates strategic actors (Cowgill 1993a; Ortner 1984:151).

As Cowgill (1993a) points out, humans also display nonrational propensities, which he divides into universal and local nonrational propensities. These propensities are not *ir*rational, but they are motivations that produce behaviors that cannot be understood solely in terms of self-interest. Universal nonrational propensities include motivations that are grounded in our nervous systems and influenced by our genetic makeup (Cowgill 1993a:558). They are also influenced by the social learning that occurs in particular cultural contexts, resulting in local nonrational propensities (Cowgill 1993a:559).

A second problem facing social theory is understanding how structure is transformed. Some critics have argued that Bourdieu's concepts of *habitus* and practice are no more than a sophisticated version of functionalism, meaning that individuals learn *habitus* and then through practice reproduce *habitus* (Jenkins 1992). Such a view, critics argue, cannot explain why and how change occurs. Practice theory (Bourdieu 1990), structuration theory (Giddens 1984), and other models of structure and agency (e.g., Sahlins 1981) avoid this problem. Structure provides the context for action, but people simultaneously manipulate their structure, using the resources that are available to them, and this serves to change structure. In addition, individual behavior generated by a historically constituted structure encounters a present that is never an exact replica of history. The ever-changing present is shaped by external forces (e.g., environmental change or expansionist societies) and internal forces (e.g., ambition, creativity, innovation, social contradictions, and the unintended consequences of human action). This dialectic, in which strategic actors reflexively draw on a historically constituted structure to act within an ever-changing present, provides the context in which change occurs. Archaeology is unique among the social sciences in its ability to view the long-term interplay between structure and practice and to understand how structure is both reproduced and transformed.

Structure, Agency, and Practice in Mesa Verde–Region Mobility Patterns

How do the concepts of structure, agency, and practice apply to mobility patterns in the Mesa Verde region? The residential movement documented by this research, in which the relatively high-frequency movement of households occurred in a social landscape characterized by relatively persistent communities, is best understood by using this conceptual framework. Residential movement was a practice by which individuals and households gained access to their primary means of production: land and labor. Residential mobility, therefore, was one aspect of the group's mode of production and was strategic in the sense that it enabled individuals and households to gain access to the most important resources necessary for production. Households, and the individuals that comprised households, were strategic actors that negotiated residential movement through a historically constituted structure: the social landscape defined by the communities that developed over centuries in the Mesa Verde region.

Cowgill (1993a:559) discusses how local rules are a part of the structural context in which strategic actors operate. By local rules, Cowgill means widely shared (at least along age, gender, class, and factional lines) ideas about how things are to be done, ideas that can range from obligatory laws to less binding standards of "proper" behavior. It may be misleading to think of these as "rules" because there is so much variation in how widely they are shared, the degree to which they are followed, and the extent to which they are or are not articulated. Nevertheless, in the jargon of modern social theory, these local rules are contained in one's *habitus* and expressed through practice.

Regardless of the terms used, local rules are an aspect of structure that would have affected residential mobility. Particularly relevant to residential mobility are practices related to land tenure, resource access systems, and marriage and residence rules. The issue is whether these aspects of structure can be recognized in the archaeological record; I argue that they can. The geographic and demographic scales of communities can be measured and used to make inferences about the mobility of individuals that resulted from the formation of new households at marriage. Residential mobility can be monitored by measuring site occupation span, and inferences can be made about land tenure systems based on the frequency of residential movement and the nature of the regional social landscape in which that movement occurred. Thus we can monitor the interplay between one aspect of structure—land tenure systems—and the practice of residential mobility over centuries.

2

ANTHROPOLOGICAL

PERSPECTIVES

ON

SEDENTISM

AND

MOBILITY

In most existing models, sedentism and mobility are viewed as being structured by the subsistence economy and by environmental variables. The following conclusions can be drawn from a review of these models: (1) there is no deterministic relationship between particular subsistence and mobility strategies; (2) there is a strong relationship between sedentism, mobility, and the *intensification* of a *variety* of subsistence strategies; and (3) there is a need to develop models of sedentism and mobility that integrate both ecological and social factors. Traditional models that were developed through examination of hunter-gatherer subsistence economies are inadequate for a full understanding of population movement, but they do provide an important foundation for developing a more satisfactory understanding of sedentism and mobility. The approach taken here is to extract what is useful from these models and specify how it applies to the Mesa Verde region.

SEDENTISM AND MOBILITY AS RESEARCH
ISSUES IN ANTHROPOLOGY

Since the beginnings of their discipline, anthropologists have recognized that sedentism and mobility are important characteristics of human societies (Morgan [1877] 1985). Whether or not groups were sedentary was considered both in unilineal models of social evolution from the late 1800s and early 1900s and in later multilineal models. These models were correct that increasing sedentism is correlated with increasing political complexity, but they viewed sedentism and mobility only as attributes useful in classifying societies and not as features worthy of study in their own right.

When mobility itself began to be studied, it was approached using a paradigm that stressed classification and typology. This approach recognized greater variation in mobility strategies, but the variation was accommodated by creating more categories: nomadic, seminomadic, semisedentary, and fully sedentary; or free wandering, restricted wandering, center-based wandering, and semipermanent sedentary (Beardsley et al. 1956).

The study of mobility strategies since about 1960 has been one of the great achievements of processual archaeology. This research documents and attempts to explain the considerable variability that characterizes the organization of mobility patterns. These studies have improved our understanding of human economic life and demonstrated how the organization of mobility patterns affects the formation of the archaeological record. Sedentism and mobility are seen as the result of economic and social decision making, and this decision making is typically modeled in terms of inputs versus returns in a cost-benefit analysis that incorporates the concepts of risk and uncertainty.

Risk taking and risk avoidance are usually defined as recognizing the probabilities of loss, where these probabilities are known or can be estimated (Cashdan 1985; Hegmon 1989; Wiessner 1982; Winterhalder 1986). For example, farmers do not know whether it will rain, but they do recognize the probability of loss if it does not rain. Loss is a somewhat clumsy concept when applied to human decision making, but it is typically defined as the probability of falling below a particular threshold (Hegmon 1989; Winterhalder 1990). When Hegmon simulated sharing behaviors among agriculturalists, she defined loss as occurring when productivity fell below the threshold of producing enough food to eat and meet social obligations (Hegmon 1989:90). In modeling risk-sensitive decision making, researchers have tried to identify the conditions that result in people's choosing risky behaviors, as opposed to the conditions that lead people to choose behaviors that minimize risk (Kohler and Van West 1996; Smith 1988; Winterhalder 1990). Uncertainty, as opposed to risk, is the condition of imperfect knowledge or insufficient information (Smith 1988). People never seek to increase uncertainty; instead, they typically respond to uncertainty by trying to reduce it (Smith 1988).

Inherently risky and uncertain conditions are produced by variation in the temporal availability and spatial distribution of resources and by environmental fluctuations that affect the availability and distribution of resources. Studies that employ the concepts of risk and uncertainty to model human decision making typically focus on actors operating in stochastic environments (Hegmon 1989). Nichols (1987) follows Sanders and Webster (1978:253) in defining environmental risk as present when any environmental parameter essential to the production of energy exhibits wide, relatively frequent, and unpredictable variation.

Mobility is seen as one means by which people cope with the risk and uncertainty produced by variation in the distribution of resources and by changing environmental conditions (Smith 1988). Individuals move to gain improved access to both productive and social resources, thereby reducing the risk of loss. Mobility also allows individuals to acquire knowledge about the distribution of resources, thereby reducing uncertainty. When mobility is restricted and groups become more sedentary, practices such as storage and exchange become more important in mitigating the effects of risk and uncertainty (Braun and Plog 1982). The consequence of this perspective is that practices such as exchange and storage have received considerable study for groups with limited residential mobility, but the low-frequency residential movement of these groups has been all but ignored.

Sedentism, too, has been viewed in evolutionary and comparative terms. Synchronic studies see one society as either more or less sedentary than another, while diachronic studies evaluate changes in the sedentariness of a specific group (Kelly 1992:49). Evolutionary theories that seek to explain the emergence of sedentism have been categorized as either push or pull theories (Kelly 1992:51). Pull models, sometimes termed the "Garden of Eden" hypothesis, argue that groups reduced their mobility and adopted sedentism to exploit abundant, concentrated resources. Push models see population-resource imbalances as stimulating intensification, which in turn results in sedentism. Push models can be divided into materialist and nonmaterialist theories; the former see the impetus for increasing sedentism as being external to the society (e.g., environmental change), and the latter argue that social factors within societies (e.g., competition for social power) stimulate increasing sedentism (Bender 1979, 1985, 1990; Kelly 1992; Lourandos 1985, 1988). These are important issues—a theoretical understanding of sedentism and mobility is critical to understanding human evolutionary change (Kelly 1992).

MOBILITY, SEDENTISM, AND THE
SUBSISTENCE ECONOMY

Sedentism and mobility are most often linked to the subsistence economy, which is seen as being structured by the environment. To examine how the subsistence economy might have conditioned sedentism and mobility, I place subsistence economies into four general categories: (1) hunting and gathering economies without food production, (2) extensive-mixed economies with food production but with an emphasis on wild food resources, (3) extensive agricultural economies, and (4) intensive agricultural economies. These are not discrete categories, and they are not offered as a typology of subsistence economies. Instead, they are heuristic categories that facilitate a discussion of the relationship between the subsistence economy and sedentism and mobility.

The following discussion demonstrates that there are correlations between the environment, the subsistence economy, and sedentism and mobility, but the relationship among these variables is not deterministic. Points that are specifically applicable to the Mesa Verde region are emphasized. Further, it is worth considering hunter-gatherer research because wild resources were always an important part of the subsistence mix in the Mesa Verde region.

Hunting and Gathering Economies

Binford's (1980) distinction between residential and logistical mobility is the key to distinguishing foragers from collectors. Binford (1980, 1990) examined how these mobility strategies were conditioned by the environment. He found that foragers commonly rely on residential mobility in tropical equatorial regions with high-biomass environments and arctic

regions with low biomass (Binford 1980:14). Conversely, collectors emphasize logistical mobility in temperate environments and boreal forests (Binford 1980:14). Kelly (1983) looked at how the general structure of the
environment affected accessibility to and monitoring of resources. He found
that hunter-gatherers in high-biomass environments (except those dependent on aquatic resources) move frequently because most resources are
relatively inaccessible, and resources that are accessible are quickly depleted.
In temperate environments, there is increased resource accessibility and
therefore reduced residential mobility. There is little need to monitor
resources in equatorial zones, with their year-long growing seasons, but
monitoring is critical in colder, seasonal environments. In those environments, logistical mobility is used to monitor resources and acquire information for future residential and logistical moves (Kelly 1983:298–299).

Kelly further demonstrates how the environment affects the distance
between residential moves. Moves are short in tropical, high-biomass environments where resources are evenly distributed. Conversely, residential
moves are longer in colder, lower-biomass environments where some
resources occur in particular, widely separated ecological zones. Binford
and Kelly both demonstrate an increasing reliance on storage in seasonal
environments, with storage being critical for surviving the winter. Storage
results in reduced residential mobility, shorter-distance moves, and
increased reliance on logistical mobility. Keeley's (1988) cross-cultural analysis of hunter-gatherers demonstrates a strong positive correlation between
storage dependence, increased sedentism, and higher population density
in these societies.

Less attention has been paid to the long-term movement of hunter-
gatherers, largely because ethnographic fieldwork cannot observe long-
term land use practices of hunter-gatherers. Binford's (1983) description
of long-term movement by the Nunamiut is one of the most frequently
cited discussions of long-term mobility. By interviewing Nunamiut elders,
Binford reconstructed a model of long-term land use in which Nunamiut
make long-distance residential moves every six to ten years as localities are
depleted of resources. In this way the Nunamiut circulate through a series
of adjacent localities. Depleted resources in previously utilized localities
are eventually replenished, and the Nunamiut return after several decades
to the locality where they were born to begin another cycle of long-term

land use. Kelly (1992:45) terms this "territorial" or "long-term" mobility. The Nunamiut model has been adopted by some researchers to characterize the long-term movement of groups in the Mesa Verde region (Kohler and Matthews 1988).

Finally, both Binford (1980:12) and Kelly (1983:296, 302, 1992:45) stress that foragers and collectors, and residential and logistical mobility, should not be made into types. Instead, these are sets of strategies that can be mixed by a single group, and this mix can change over time. Binford was concerned not just with reconstructing hunter-gatherer economies but with understanding how these general sets of strategies differentially affected the formation of the archaeological record (Binford 1982). The relationship between long-term mobility and site structure is particularly important in this regard; long-term changes in mobility strategies result in the changing use of a locality and in the deposition of functionally different assemblages at sites.

The research of Binford and Kelly suggests that the Mesa Verde region favors a collector strategy because of its seasonal environment and patchy distribution of wild foods. Residential moves should be relatively infrequent and cover relatively long distances. Storage would be needed to survive lengthy winters. The intensification of storage and the difficulty in obtaining wild foods in winter would promote residential stability for all groups living in the Mesa Verde region. Thus, all prehispanic settlement systems in the Mesa Verde region should be characterized by relatively few residential locations and numerous special-purpose resource extraction sites. Among groups who did practice seasonal movement of residential sites, it probably involved movement from lower elevations in the winter to higher elevations in the summer.

Extensive-Mixed Economies

The term *extensive-mixed economies* is used to refer to groups who depend on wild foods for the bulk of their subsistence but who also cultivate domesticated foods. Environmental archaeology provides a rich database on these subsistence economies in the ancient Southwest. By at least 1000 B.C. the subsistence base of these groups was a mix of wild and domestic resources (Matson 1991; Wills 1988a). Researchers have vigorously debated the importance of cultigens in these economies (Matson 1991; Smiley 1993, 1994; Wills 1988a, 1988b, 1990, 1992, 1995).

Matson (1991:222, 240) has argued that reliance solely on wild foods limited the degree of intensification that could occur on the Colorado Plateau and that the low environmental diversity and irregular spatial and temporal distribution of wild food resources could support only very low population densities. Matson and his colleagues have conducted a number of analyses that suggest that residents of the Mesa Verde region were heavily dependent on maize agriculture by 2,000 years ago (Matson and Chisholm 1991), and Matson (1991:243) sees the adoption of maize agriculture as the critical change that allowed larger populations to inhabit the plateau. Agricultural production, no matter how casually it was practiced, required that crops be harvested and stored for a period of time. Bulk storage restricts residential mobility and favors an increasingly logistically organized system of movement. In addition, agriculture requires increased monitoring—at least at some points in the cycle of plant growth—which also reduces residential mobility (Kelly 1983:301).

The Amazonian Machiguenga of southeastern Peru are an interesting example of a group with a mixed economy that includes hunting, gathering, and horticulture (Keegan 1986). When the Machiguenga forage for wild plant foods, a response to decreasing marginal returns is to move to a new patch. A garden can be thought of as another patch, and repeated maize cultivation in Machiguenga gardens results in decreasing yields owing to factors such as soil depletion. But the cultivation of gardens offers an alternative to abandonment and mobility: Machiguenga gardens can be intensified through practices such as weeding and the selecting of specific strains of plants. Keegan (1986:97) argues that the Machiguenga choose to intensify maize gardens because maize is an important and accessible source of protein and because gardening can be readily intensified. Because of its potential for intensification, cultivation—even when it forms only a small percentage of the subsistence base— can promote increased sedentism.

Extensive Agricultural Economies

"Extensive" refers to societies where agriculture is the preeminent food resource but where agricultural methods are simple, not labor-intensive, and characterized by long periods when fields are left fallow. Swidden systems are examples of extensive agricultural economies; as defined by Conklin (1961:27), these are systems in which the fallow period is longer than the cropped period. From a microeconomic perspective, extensive agriculture is characterized by low labor investments in cultivation, high returns to labor, and abandonment when yields decline (Stone 1993:74). Almost all cultivation degrades agricultural resources unless there is some form of intensification, and thus resource depletion results in increased production costs and often decreased yields. Among extensive agriculturalists, mobility is therefore stimulated by the decreasing yields that accompany the resource depletion associated with extensive agricultural practices.

Many researchers argue that a form of shifting or swidden agriculture characterized groups in the Mesa Verde region of the Southwest (Kohler and Matthews 1988; Lekson 1996; Matson 1991; Matson, Lipe, and Haase 1988; Schlanger 1988; Stiger 1979). Wild foods are common in the botanical remains from Mesa Verde–region sites, but they are dominated by plants that grow in disturbed areas (Matthews 1986; Petersen et al. 1987) and animals that thrive in active and abandoned fields (Neusius 1987; Petersen et al. 1987). Thus, the types of wild foods present at Mesa Verde–region sites are seen by many as further evidence of an extensive agricultural economy.

Those who interpret Southwestern agriculture as a type of swidden farming usually see resource depletion as the stimulus to mobility. But extensive agriculture on the Colorado Plateau differed in important ways from the swidden agriculture practiced in the tropics (Conklin 1961; Harris 1973). In the tropics, rapid revegetation is critical to the regeneration of soil nutrients. In Southwestern environments, revegetation does not happen quickly. On the Colorado Plateau, it takes 350 years for a mature pinyon-juniper forest to regenerate (Erdman 1970:18; Stiger 1979:136). Researchers have suggested that burning the pinyon-juniper forest was a means of increasing soil fertility (Matson 1991). Given the slow regeneration of the pinyon-juniper forest, this type of swidden farming could have occurred only at extremely lengthy intervals in the Mesa Verde region.

Kohler and Matthews (1988) argue that shifting cultivation results in deforestation and depleted firewood supplies, and that scarcity of firewood, as much as the depletion of soil, drives mobility. Schlanger (1988, 1992) also views the Mesa Verde–region inhabitants as shifting cultivators, but she sees their mobility as conditioned by uncontrollable climatic fluctuations, primarily the chronic problems of low rainfall and short growing seasons. In sum, many researchers see Mesa Verde–region agriculture as an extensive system in which movement was conditioned by both climatic conditions and the depletion of critical resources, but these studies focus on the Pueblo I period and not on the later, more populated Pueblo III period.

The addition of cultivation to the subsistence mix promotes sedentism. But with increased reliance on cultivation, groups face a new set of decisions with regard to lower-frequency, supra-annual residential movement. As the yields from cultivated plots decrease because of resource depletion, people are faced with the choice of abandoning fields or intensifying production in those fields. Stone (1993:78) argues that the decision to abandon or intensify depends in part on the "social technology" of particular societies. Groups that Stone (1993:79) calls "extensifiers," such as the Tiv who farm in the West African nation of Nigeria, abandon their fields and move to a new locale. The Kofyar, who inhabit the same territory, are "intensifiers" who stay put and intensify agricultural production.

Intensive Agricultural Economies

Land, labor, and technology are the universal resources of consequence in agricultural intensification, resulting in the cross-cultural and cross-disciplinary applicability of the concept of intensification (Brush and Turner 1987:12; Stone 1993:74). Operational definitions for intensification have been provided by economists, geographers, and anthropologists (Boserup 1965; Brookfield 1972, 1984; Brown and Podolefsky 1976; Stone 1996; Turner and Doolittle 1978:297). In these studies, agricultural intensification has been defined in terms of both the frequency of cropping and the changing technology of production. Most theories measure agricultural intensification in macroeconomic terms—at the scale of entire subsistence economies. Chayanov (1966; Netting 1993:295–319), on the other hand, examines the microeconomic logic of agricultural intensification, arguing that agricultural households in peasant societies alternately intensify and extensify production in response to the fluctuating ratio of producers to consumers in the household. A point of consensus that emerges is that agricultural intensification should be viewed as a continuous variable and not as a dichotomy between extensive or intensive systems. Here, I define intensification simply as an increase in energy inputs per unit area of land.

Boserup's (1965) model of intensification focuses on the increased frequency of cropping and treats population pressure as stimulating this form of intensification. Her model has been widely used and widely criticized (Cowgill 1975; Grigg 1979; McGuire 1984). Criticism focuses on two elements of Boserup's model: (1) that factors other than population growth can cause intensification, and (2) that mobility and abandonment are not considered as options in her model (Stone 1996).

With regard to the first criticism, environmental and social conditions—in addition to population growth—can both limit and promote intensification (Bender 1979, 1985; Bronson 1972, 1977; Brookfield 1972; McGuire 1984). In the Mesa Verde region, flexibility in cropping frequency, an important variable in Boserup's model, would have been limited by the relatively short growing season. In arid lands, risk management strategies might also have influenced agricultural technology, creating a wide diversity of cultivation strategies (Fish and Fish 1984:1; Nichols 1987); these diverse strategies should be kept conceptually distinct from intensification resulting from population pressure or social relations of production. Social relations of production—for example, the production of surplus to finance social and political activities—can promote intensification regardless of population density. Several researchers have argued that intensification requires a managerial hierarchy (Lightfoot and Plog 1984; Upham 1984:295; Vivian 1974, 1984, 1990), but a worldwide survey of intensive agriculturalists indicates that intensification can occur without managerial hierarchies, and managerial hierarchies can in fact inhibit the efficiency of intensified agricultural systems (Netting 1990:55, 1993).

Despite the criticisms of Boserup's model, an important insight from her work should not be lost: higher population density and subsistence intensification are directly and regularly associated (Bronson 1977; Keeley 1988; Netting 1990:38). Correlation is not causality, but unpacking the relationship between these variables is critical to understanding Mesa Verde sedentism and mobility. The work of Boserup and Chayanov also suggests that understanding agricultural intensification and its effect on population movement requires knowledge of the conditions affecting production at both the macrolevel (at least at the scale of communities interacting within a region) and the microlevel (households as units of agricultural production).

Further, Boserup and Chayanov suggest that farmers intensify production only when they *have* to, and agricultural production will reextensify if the demands that stimulate intensification are eased. The principle of least effort that is at the heart of the Boserup and Chayanov models runs counter to *social* strategies that seek to promote intensification. Primary producers seek to limit labor inputs while ambitious leaders seek to promote intensified production. This contradiction has potential for transforming the organization of society and promoting the development of social inequality (Bender 1979, 1985, 1990).

Mesa Verde–region agriculture was intensified both by shortening the fallow period and by changing the technology of production (Kohler and Matthews 1988; Rohn 1963, 1972, 1992; Schlanger 1988). Shortening fallow and traveling farther to fields were the primary means of intensification between A.D. 600 and 900 (Kohler and Matthews 1988:545). Shortening fallow remained important after 900, but the technology of production was also intensified sometime after 1000 when water and soil control facilities (e.g., reservoirs, check dams, and contour terraces) became more common (Kohler and Matthews 1988:557; Schlanger 1988:773; Wilshusen, Churchill, and Potter 1997). The post-1000 period is a time when population density may have risen to the point that residential mobility was restricted (Dean et al. 1985:547–549).

In summary, subsistence intensification has important implications for the study of sedentism and mobility, regardless of its causes or the nature of the subsistence mix. There is a relationship between intensification, the relative scarcity of productive resources, and the development of resource access systems (Adler 1996b; Netting 1982, 1993:157–188). More extensive systems result in temporary landownership only so long as the land is being used (usufruct rights), while intensification increasingly results in permanent private ownership and heritable property rights (Netting 1993:157–188). Furthermore, intensification involves the construction of agricultural facilities as well as more substantial residences and storage structures, with the result that people are reluctant to relinquish these investments. Thus, agricultural intensification can result in increased sedentism and reduced residential mobility.

CRITIQUING THE GENERALIZING MODELS

Wiessner (1982) offered an early critique of Binford's (1980) research into hunter-gatherer mobility. She argued that mobility and settlement systems are not just organizational systems that relate people to resources but also systems that relate people to other people. By acknowledging the role of the social relations of production, one can bring new data to bear on the problem of understanding mobility and settlement system organization. Adopting a risk-reduction model as her framework for examining the social relations of production, Wiessner looked at how the social relations of production shape material remains through inter- and intragroup interaction. Particularly important in her analysis are the strategies of pooling resources and unrestricted sharing versus storage and restricted sharing.

Halperin (1989) thoroughly critiqued mobility research in a review that traced the development and separation of ecological and economic anthropology. She borrowed Polanyi's (1957) distinction between locational and appropriational movements to trace the split between these two subfields. Locational movement involves "changing place," and this became the focus of ecological anthropology. Appropriational movement involves "changing hands," the traditional focus of economic anthropology. Studies of locational movement investigate the physical movement of people and goods across the landscape through spatial analysis. Research into appropriational movement examines organizational changes and the transfers of rights, requiring an analysis of people and their institutions (Halperin 1989:18).

The separation of these two subfields results in ecological anthropology's focusing on issues related to production and economic anthropology's focusing on matters relating to distribution. Ecological approaches deal with subsistence economies but pay little attention to concepts important in economic anthropology. The concept of the mode of production, which incorporates both the social relations of production and the forces of production, is a notable example. Conversely, economic anthropology largely ignores how economic decisions affect environmental processes and how the socially modified environment affects economic decisions (Green 1980). Further, many economic approaches view institutions as organizing production, distribution, and consumption, so that institutions take on a life of their own, resulting in a complete overlap between society and the economy (Halperin 1989; Ortner 1984).

Halperin points out that Binford articulates a "nearly perfect" elaboration of locational movement among hunter-gatherers using an ecological paradigm, and Wiessner illustrates how appropriational movements can be analyzed (Halperin 1989:32). Binford examines the forces of production, whereas Wiessner stresses the social relations of production (Halperin 1989:35). But all economies consist of locational *and* appropriational movements, and production and distribution each contain elements of both locational and appropriational movement. Defining the economy as an adaptive strategy for food procurement fails to distinguish between the physical movement of people and goods, on the one hand, and organizational changes and the transfer of rights, on the other. The adaptationist perspective sees appropriational movement as the outcome of the locational movement; the appropriational movements are assumed and not studied. This perspective also results in a materialist bias with almost no attention given to ideological factors. Halperin (1989:21–22) argues that this masks the Marxist implications inherent in ecological research by failing to acknowledge the appropriative, or exploitative, aspects of production.

Both locational and appropriational aspects of movement need to be studied while kept analytically distinct. This is particularly important for agricultural economies where land and labor must be mobilized for successful production. In the Southwest, ritual should be added to this primary list of resources, because so much ritual in historic Pueblo society is devoted to ensuring successful harvests.

Recent analyses of agricultural systems therefore see those systems as inextricably linked to social, political, economic, and environmental contexts (Brush and Turner 1987; Green 1980; Stone 1991a, 1996). Stone (1993) has documented that Tiv farmers choose to abandon fields as marginal yields decrease, but Kofyar farmers utilizing the same land (in some cases abandoned Tiv farms) choose to stay and intensify agricultural production. The differential sedentism and mobility of Kofyar and Tiv farmers can be understood only by considering a suite of cultural factors including a society's agricultural practices, social organization, ideology, and residential mobility (Stone 1993:78–79). The choice to abandon a farm or intensify production can be influenced by ecology—some Kofyar farms are located on soils so poor that intensification is not an option—but in many cases it is a close call, and the balance is tipped by these cultural factors (Stone 1993). The environment sets parameters, enabling and restricting choices, but in the end it is people who make the decision to move or stay—and this decision is influenced by their social technology.

The Rarámuri (Tarahumara), a group of agropastoralists in northern Mexico, are justly hailed as a case in which agriculture does not always result in increasing household sedentism (Graham 1993, 1994; Hard and Merrill 1992; Pennington 1963). But understanding the factors conditioning their mobility is far more interesting than debating whether or not agriculturalists move. They provide an example of the complexity of the decision-making process with regard to mobility and abandonment, and of how social factors—and the interplay of structure and agency—are critical in understanding human mobility.

One element of Rarámuri mobility, their winter moves into cliff dwellings, is largely conditioned by the pastoral component of their economy and the need to shelter livestock from the cold winter weather (Graham 1994:16; Hard and Merrill 1992:607–609). It is their agricultural, residential mobility that is of interest when considering the Rarámuri as a possible analog for Southwestern agriculturalists. One key to understanding this agricultural mobility is the recognition that only half of Rarámuri households practice residential mobility during the growing season. Hard and Merrill (1992:605) conclude that the primary stimulus for this movement is a pattern of dispersed fields that results from a land tenure system based on bilateral inheritance and marriage restrictions (Graham 1994:20–21; Hard and Merrill 1992:606). Rarámuri who have consolidated land holdings do *not* move, and some Rarámuri actively seek to consolidate land to avoid moving. Households that have inherited dispersed fields move between fields for periods ranging from a few days to many weeks, even though the distances between many of these fields would enable them to be reached with a round-trip walk from the main residence.

There are many proximate reasons why a Rarámuri household makes a residential move and eventually abandons a house. These include insect infestation, danger from the dead, access to particular resources, distance from neighbors, and perhaps local resource depletion (Hard and Merrill

1992:607; Pennington 1963). But the location and timing of these moves are dictated by social organization and land tenure systems. The residential movement occurs in a social context and is a socially negotiated activity. Rarámuri residential mobility therefore has aspects of both locational movement and appropriational movement.

It is clear that some Rarámuri households exhibit a high degree of residential mobility, but their communities are relatively fixed. The long-term mobility of the Rarámuri bears little resemblance to the long-term mobility described by Binford for the Nunamiut, and the Rarámuri case illustrates how the debate over whether a society is mobile or sedentary is ultimately unproductive. Rarámuri individuals and households are highly mobile, but Rarámuri communities are relatively fixed. It is the historical development of these communities and their social organization (and the place of these households and communities in the larger political economy of the Mexican state) that provide the structure within which Rarámuri individuals and households negotiate their residential mobility.

The Rarámuri case is an excellent example of mobility as a process that includes changing place and changing hands. Environmental and ecological variables are important in understanding the population movement of the Rarámuri, but this movement is fundamentally a social process. Understanding Rarámuri mobility, and the mobility of any society, requires integrating the environmental, ecological, and social factors that condition population movement. Were the inhabitants of the Mesa Verde region extensifiers, intensifiers, or both? Did their social technology change over time? These are questions that must be answered in order to fully understand sedentism and mobility in the region.

SEDENTISM

AND

MOBILITY

IN

THE

MESA

VERDE

REGION

Three widely disparate views of sedentism and mobility exist for the South-
west and the Mesa Verde region. Existing models range from (1) settlement
systems characterized by seasonal residential mobility to (2) those characterized by short-term sedentism and supra-annual residential mobility for
both households and communities and (3) those characterized by the long-
term sedentism of households and communities. I propose a fourth model
in which there is a relatively high frequency of household residential movement within and among communities but lower-frequency movement of
the communities themselves.

In what follows, I group existing models into three categories based on
which causal variable they emphasize as the prime reason for mobility—
environmental change, resource depletion, or social factors. It is likely,
however, that each of these variables contributed to the residential movement of households and communities. Not all of these models can be
correct, and the analyses presented in subsequent chapters attempt to
determine which, if any, most accurately characterizes the frequency of

population movement in the Mesa Verde region between A.D. 950 and 1300.

ENVIRONMENTAL CHANGE

The theory that links environmental change to mobility is relatively straight-forward and similar to the theory that underlies hunter-gatherer mobility models: mobility is a response to spatial and temporal variation in the distribution of productive resources, which results from spatial and tempo-ral variation in the environment. Groups can relocate from areas of lower productivity to empty areas of higher productivity. Alternatively, groups in low productivity areas can tap alliances and exchange relationships they have formed with groups living in areas of higher productivity and temporarily move into these areas.

In the Southwest, environmental change is often seen as a factor resulting in abandonment and hence mobility (Dean et al. 1985; Euler et al. 1979; Schlanger 1988; Schoenwetter and Dittert 1968). Research into the relation-ship between environmental change and population movement has focused on broad spatial and temporal scales, correlating migrations across regions with several dimensions of long-term environmental change (Berry 1982; Euler et al. 1979; Dean et al. 1985). Dean and others (1985) argue that mobility is the least costly solution to stress resulting from environmental change when groups have no heavy investment in residential and agricul-tural facilities and when mobility is not restricted by population density.

Environmental change includes climatic change—primarily fluctuations in precipitation and temperature—and nonclimatic change—primarily changes in hydrologic conditions. A brief review of paleoclimatic recon-structions for the Mesa Verde region shows how these climatic changes might have affected population movement. Next, a review of changing hydrologic conditions examines their effect on mobility.

Climatic Change

Petersen's (1986, 1987a, 1987b, 1988) Dolores Archaeological Program work developed the concept of a "farm belt" in the Mesa Verde region; the farm belt is the area where rainfall and growing season together are adequate for cultivation. Petersen examined changing ratios of spruce to pine pollen from Beef Pasture in the La Plata Mountains to identify changes in winter versus summer precipitation. Declining spruce pollen relative to pinyon pollen was interpreted as indicating a decrease in winter precipitation, whereas increasing pinyon pollen indicated an increase in summer rains. Because the intensity of summer rains correlates with elevation, these data indicate periods when the farm belt expanded or contracted along an elevational gradient. During periods of low summer rains the farm belt would contract, so the higher elevations where rainfall was greatest would be the favored area for occupation.

Petersen also examined high-frequency climatic change by reconstructing periods of drought. He used tree-ring indices from the Dolores River valley for the period until A.D. 1136 and tree-ring indices from Mesa Verde National Park for the years 1136 to 1280. The periods of drought identified by these analyses are shaded in figure 3.1.[1]

Van West (1994) recently finished the most thorough modeling of climate change and agricultural productivity done for the Mesa Verde region by focusing on an 1,816-square-kilometer study area in the central part of the region. Drawing inspiration from Burns's (1983) study of production shortfalls, she used GIS technology to integrate the following data sets: Palmer Drought Severity Index (PDSI) values based on tree-ring analyses; the distribution of different soil types; historic crop yields; and natural plant productivity for specific soil types. Using these data, she retrodicted annual bean and maize yields for each four-hectare cell within the study area for the period between A.D. 901 and 1970. Kohler and Van West (1996) used Van West's data to identify periods of high and low agricultural productivity; the periods of low productivity are shaded in figure 3.1.

Population Movement and Climate Change

Schlanger (1988) synthesized a number of paleoclimatic reconstructions for the Mesa Verde region and developed expectations for how patterns of population movement might have responded to climatic change. She argued that stable and favorable conditions over the long term should result in maintenance or growth of population levels, whereas unfavorable conditions would stimulate population movement. In response to high-frequency climatic variation such as droughts, people would be expected to move from lower and drier areas to higher, wetter areas. People would

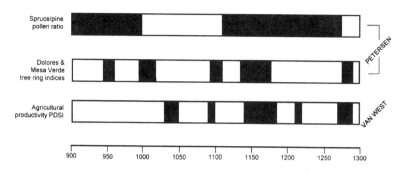

Figure 3.1 Climatic stress in the Mesa Verde region, A.D. 900–1300. Periods of drought (top two bars) and low agricultural productivity (bottom bar) appear in black.

be expected to move back into lower areas during periods of greater moisture to take advantage of the longer growing seasons at these lower elevations. Schlanger inferred population movement from survey data in three areas and found that population movement corresponded fairly well to expectations during the A.D. 720 to 880 period, but not during the 880 to 1250 period (Schlanger 1988:785).

Schlanger and Wilshusen (1993) analyzed mobility between A.D. 600 and 910 in the Dolores River valley at an even finer scale. They used tree-ring data to identify four periods when beam procurement took place, and they interpreted the intervals between these periods as times of abandonment (Schlanger and Wilshusen 1993:88). Climatic change was interpreted as the cause of each abandonment because each was associated with a drought.

They carried their analysis of mobility further by modeling four abandonment strategies that varied the distance of the residential move and whether return to the abandoned sites was anticipated. Schlanger and Wilshusen used floor artifact assemblages and roof treatment at abandonment to determine which abandonment strategy characterized each of the four abandonments, concluding that the first three abandonments were short term and reoccupation of the locality was anticipated. The last abandonment, in late 800s, appeared to be a regional abandonment with no anticipated return (Schlanger and Wilshusen 1993:95).

It is important to recognize that drought might have caused the periodic migration of *communities* out of localities and regions, but drought did not cause the more frequent abandonment of all residential sites by *house-holds;* many residences were abandoned during well-watered episodes (Schlanger and Wilshusen 1993:94). Thus, environmental change does not explain all household residential mobility in the Dolores River valley.

Turning to the A.D. 880 to 1300 period, Schlanger (1988) developed an argument for why population movement conformed so poorly to periods of drought. She argued that droughts after 920 favored population movement into the higher elevations, but short growing seasons made these higher elevations unsuitable for agriculture (Schlanger 1988:788). In effect, the area suitable for agriculture was environmentally confined to the lower elevations. This environmental circumscription stimulated changes in the technology of agricultural production to ensure successful farming in drier conditions (Schlanger 1988:789). These technological changes included the construction of water storage features and features for managing rainfall-runoff irrigation.

Schlanger (1988) chose survey areas that allowed her to examine population movement from lower to higher elevations, but they were not particularly well suited for examining conditions *within* the lower-elevation farm belt. Van West's (1994) modeling of agricultural potential did address variation in the conditions in this portion of the farm belt. First, Van West estimated the carrying capacity of the study area as a whole. Next, she evaluated the relationship between population and carrying capacity in two intensively surveyed localities in the study area: the Sand Canyon locality and Mockingbird Mesa. Finally, she examined the catchments around eight individual sites located throughout the study area.

A number of general conclusions can be drawn from Van West's study. First, she found that there was enough productive land in the study area as a whole to support a large population even during the driest times. Thus, drought and its effects on agricultural production did not present a sufficient cause for the complete depopulation of the Mesa Verde region (Van West and Lipe 1992:115).

Van West's study also demonstrated that the distribution of the most productive land varied from year to year throughout the study area, but particular localities were consistently more productive than others. Agricultural productivity in the Sand Canyon locality, for example, would have supported approximately twice the long-term population density of the Mockingbird Mesa locality; however, the agricultural potential of Mockingbird Mesa was generally representative of average conditions in the entire study area (Van West and Lipe 1992:115). Van West's analysis of individual site catchments, which included four small residential sites and four large community centers, suggested that farmers were aware that the productive potential of different places varied and that they selected those places with high potential (Van West 1994:185). She concluded that mobility, open access to productive resources, and extensive intercommunity food sharing would have been needed to buffer local shortfalls (Van West and Lipe 1992:118). Thus, environmental change and its effects on agricultural productivity might have stimulated population movement in many, but not all, parts of the Mesa Verde region.

Kohler and Van West (1996) examined the ways in which temporal and spatial variation in agricultural productivity affected the pooling and sharing of agricultural produce. Using microeconomic theory and utility functions to model behavior, they assumed that periods of high productivity favored pooling and sharing—behaviors they saw as being facilitated by the formation of strong regional systems and by aggregated settlement—and that households would avoid these behaviors during periods of low productivity. They further assumed that households avoided the obligation to pool and share resources through increased mobility and dispersed settlement patterns.

This study is important because it measures the relationship between climatic change and agricultural production and recognizes that *both* production shortfalls and surpluses could stimulate residential mobility. Using Van West's reconstruction of agricultural productivity, they argue that their model is generally supported by the data. The buildup of the Chacoan system between A.D. 1050 and 1130 and the formation of aggregated villages in the 1200s occurred during periods of high productivity, and the formation of both Chacoan communities and aggregated villages is interpreted as indicating times when households pooled and shared their food with larger social groups. Periods of low productivity are likewise identified, including the 1130–1179 and 1272–1288 periods, and these are seen as times of defection when mobility and dispersed settlement were strategies that households employed to restrict the networks with which they shared food. Thus, it is important to recognize that the residential mobility that Kohler and Van West describe is not necessarily the abandonment of entire localities and regions by communities but the movement between dispersed and aggregated settlement patterns.

In the reconstruction of settlement patterns that follows, I take issue with some of Kohler and Van West's conclusions. In particular, I argue that communities persist during periods when they predict defection. I also view aggregation more as a continuous process in which settlement became gradually more aggregated between A.D. 950 and 1300 than as an oscillation between dispersed and aggregated settlement. In this regard, Chacoan communities have a dispersed settlement pattern compared with that of the subsequent period. Thus, I see the maintenance of increasingly aggregated communities in much of the Mesa Verde region between 1130 and 1179, whereas Kohler and Van West (1996:183) see mobility, dispersal, and the breakup of communities. Finally, it is interesting to note that their assumptions are the opposite of what occurs in the Kayenta region, where aggregation occurs in bad times and dispersal during favorable periods. This calls into question the general assumption that links productivity, and the assumed sharing patterns that accompany fluctuating productivity, with specific settlement patterns.

A period of climatic unpredictability reported by Dean (1996) may have contributed to the eventual abandonment of the Mesa Verde region as an area of permanent residential settlement. Precipitation in the Mesa Verde region and elsewhere in the Four Corners area is typically characterized by a bimodal regime in which the majority of annual precipitation occurs in summer and winter. A sinuous transition zone that runs through Arizona and New Mexico separates this northern pattern from a southern pattern in which the majority of annual precipitation falls in the summer. Dean argues this has been the persistent pattern for most of the past millennium but that it was disrupted for 200 years between A.D. 1250 and 1450. During these centuries, the predictable bimodal precipitation pattern in the northwestern Southwest broke down into a chaotic absence of pattern. This breakdown may have contributed to the migration of people from the Mesa Verde region and other areas in the northern Southwest (Ahlstrom, Van West, and Dean 1995).

Nonclimatic Environmental Change

Changing hydrological conditions are the primary form of nonclimatic environmental change considered here. Force and Howell (1997) recently reported on the depositional history of McElmo Creek, which defines the southern boundary of the Sand Canyon locality. The Holocene stratigraphy there is exposed by historic-period arroyo cutting, and archaeological remains found throughout the stratigraphic sequence were used to date changes in the depositional regime. Force and Howell documented an aggrading hydrological system between A.D. 550 and 700, an erosional unconformity, or entrenchment, between 700 and 930, and a return to aggrading conditions and a braided main channel between 930 and 1300.[2]

The authors were able to examine the relationship between hydrological processes and ancient settlement in some detail. They show that both erosional and depositional events were diachronic processes and not abrupt, synchronic events. For the erosional cycle between 700 and 930, they estimate that stream entrenchment migrated upstream at a rate of about 20 meters per year, and they believe that settlement relocation moved upstream ahead of this entrenchment. They conclude that entrenchment might have resulted in local abandonments, but it was unlikely to have caused the rapid, sudden abandonment of the entire valley, much less entire regions.[3] In a recent geoarchaeological study of the southern piedmont of Ute Mountain, Huckleberry and Billman (n.d.) similarly conclude that stream entrenchment did not result in abandonment.

Force and Howell conclude by commenting on Schlanger's model of population movement, arguing that canyon systems in the low-elevation portion of the farm belt offered the best opportunity for people to pursue mixed agricultural strategies, combining dryland mesa-top agriculture with canyon-oriented floodwater farming. The high-elevation portion of the study area may have had a more favorable moisture regime, but it did not offer the same potential for a diversified and intensified agricultural system. They argue that it was not a constricted farm belt that circumscribed settlement into the low-elevation zone but, rather, opportunities for a diversified and intensified agricultural system that *attracted* people to the lower elevations.

Summary: Environmental Change and Mobility

The paleoenvironmental reconstruction for the Mesa Verde region is one of the most detailed reconstructions developed anywhere in the world. It indicates that the past climate was highly variable over space and through time. Using different methods, a number of reconstructions from the Mesa Verde region and elsewhere on the Colorado Plateau show a remarkable synchroneity in climatic and nonclimatic change (Dean et al. 1985; Euler et al. 1979; Force and Howell 1997; Petersen 1986:315; Schoenwetter 1966, 1967, 1970). Many researchers employ this environmental change as the primary causal variable in explanations of culture change, as if the environment set absolute limits on human occupation. Such deterministic interpretations are unwarranted. For example, in virtually every period sites can be found outside the farm belt as reconstructed by Petersen. Van West's study, which indicates that portions of the region had some potential for agricultural production even in the worst of times, is additional evidence that climatic deterioration did not make agricultural production impossible.

Still, the patterns identified by these studies are important: they measure climatic variation in time and space, they quantify how climatic change affected agricultural production, and they show how production varied across the region through time. Farmers in this region, who cultivated crops without the benefit of canal irrigation from permanent streams, had to feel the effects of environmental change and concomitant changes in agricultural production. Population movement is generally viewed by Southwestern researchers as having been stimulated by climatic change that negatively affected agricultural production, but people could also move in response to knowledge of better opportunities elsewhere, even when production was adequate where they lived. In particular, climatic change that resulted in increased productivity, including the production of surpluses in some areas, could stimulate residential movement.

The environmental changes identified by these studies are, therefore, best interpreted as both enabling and constraining behavior. One of these behaviors was mobility. The periods of environmental stress identified in figure 3.1 might have stimulated population movement, especially in areas where agricultural production was most difficult. Analyses presented in the chapters that follow look for evidence of mobility during these periods.

Many scholars see resource depletion as the primary cause of mobility in the American Southwest (e.g., Stiger 1979), but it has been addressed most explicitly by Kohler and Matthews (1988), Lekson (1996), and Nelson and Anyon (1996). As Lekson (1996:83–84) expressed it: "The firewood, game, soils, and other resources of one locale could be depleted; settlement would shift to the next valley and the process repeated; and after several generations of shifting sedentism, the cycle could begin again at 'Go'—without going to jail, because 'Go' had regenerated its resources. The sustaining hinterland for each settlement would be small; for the whole adaptive cycle, the area required would be enormous."

Lekson proposes a high degree of population movement as an adaptation to the entire Colorado Plateau. Whole communities were highly mobile, living in localities for only one or two decades until resources were depleted, at which time they moved to a new, unoccupied locality (Lekson 1993:8). A similar model, termed the "fallow-valley strategy," has been proposed for agricultural mobility in southwestern New Mexico (Nelson and Anyon 1996). These authors argue that from A.D. 1150 to 1450, Mimbres communities lived in relatively large, aggregated sites surrounded by large areas of empty territory. These aggregated communities are believed to have moved at regular intervals (perhaps as short as 20 years) as the resources of a local valley became depleted. Using this fallow valley strategy, relatively few communities circulated through a large, open territory, sequentially using the near-pristine resources of a number of valleys located throughout southwestern New Mexico.[4]

Kohler and Matthews (1988) and Kohler (1992a, 1992b) have argued that depletion of resources, especially fuelwood, stimulated population movement in the Mesa Verde region. They draw on Binford's (1983) model of long-term Nunamiut mobility to describe mobility patterns on a local and regional scale. They view residences as having moved around in relatively small areas of the landscape every one or two generations while maintaining affiliation with a specific community. Over a longer period, communities relocated to new areas as local resources became depleted. At the largest scale, resource depletion would have resulted in groups of communities abandoning regions over a period of two or three centuries.

This model is similar to the model I propose, in which households and communities move at different frequencies. The difference is that the Kohler and Matthews model assumes abundant open territory for community movement between A.D. 600 and 900, and it assumes that abandoned localities and regions were reoccupied only after depleted resources were restored. For the A.D. 950 to 1300 period, I argue that the landscape filled to the extent that abundant empty land was not available and that *if* localities were repeatedly occupied and abandoned, this occurred too frequently to allow for the regeneration of resources.

More research is needed on the rate at which specific resources were depleted and regenerated. As discussed in chapter 2, pinyon-juniper woodland takes almost 350 years to regenerate fully. Some proponents of resource depletion models have argued that it was important to burn the pinyon-juniper woodland to increase soil fertility and boost agricultural yields (Matson 1991) and that the depletion of fuelwood was a stimulus for mobility (Kohler and Matthews 1988; Kohler 1992a). The time it would have taken to deplete the timber resources of an area is unknown, but if areas were abandoned because of timber depletion they could have been reoccupied only after lengthy periods of abandonment.

Almost no information is available on the rate of soil nutrient depletion and how it affected agricultural productivity; however, Decker and Petersen (1987:141–142) examined what data were available and concluded that the Mesa Verde loess, which is the deepest and most productive soil, would not have become deficient in major nutrient elements under the type of cropping systems used by ancient farmers of the Mesa Verde region. The importance of soil depletion may be dependent in part on the quality of soils being farmed; soil depletion almost certainly affected people farming more marginal soils.

Without more empirical data on the rate at which resources were depleted, we can only assume that habitation in an area did deplete the resource base to some degree and that continuous occupation required greater energy inputs to obtain these resources.

Resource depletion models see Mesa Verde–region societies as having had a relatively extensive subsistence economy. These models propose that societies move, rather than intensify, as local resources are depleted. The theoretical underpinnings of these models are not too different from those of optimal foraging theory and evolutionary ecology. Groups are seen as monitoring the return on their labor; when the return falls below a certain level, groups move to a fresh patch where they can obtain a higher return. An implicit assumption made by these models is that there was abundant empty and unspoiled land into which communities could move. In addition, localities would have been reoccupied only after the regeneration of critical resources.

Following the model proposed by Kohler and Matthews (1988), resource depletion would have stimulated mobility at a number of social, spatial, and temporal scales. Households would have relocated relatively frequently over short distances within the locality. Communities would have relocated to new localities over longer time scales, and groups of communities would have moved between regions at even greater time intervals. Kohler and Matthews (1988:559) acknowledge intensification as an option but clearly believe that the early Puebloan societies they were considering favored mobility over intensification. To understand why groups move in response to resource depletion, or why they stay put and intensify production, mobility must be viewed as a social process.

SOCIAL FACTORS

Ecosystemic and adaptationist perspectives have not escaped criticism (Brumfiel 1992; Friedman 1974; McGuire 1992; Saitta 1983, 1990). Ironically, the detailed environmental reconstructions from the Southwest, coupled with fine-tuned chronologies, may themselves be the best evidence that mobility involved social processes and was not a simple response to environmental change or resource depletion. S. Plog (1986), for example, combined chronological and environmental data to argue that changing settlement patterns on Black Mesa were not merely responses to environmental change, as had been suggested previously (cf. Euler et al. 1979). Similarly, Kintigh (1985) questioned the interpretation that settlement shifts in the Zuni region were linked exclusively to climatic change. Van West (1994; Van West and Lipe 1992:115–118) found that climatically induced variation in soil moisture and its effects on agricultural production did not present a sufficient cause for the final migration from the Mesa Verde region. These studies highlight the need for models that include the social determinants of mobility (Lipe 1995).

Social Factors That Cause Mobility

There are two dimensions to consider when incorporating social factors into models of ancient mobility strategies. First, some social factors can directly cause or stimulate population movement. Second, regardless of the stimulus, all population movement takes place in a social context, and therefore social factors need to be considered in *any* model of sedentism and mobility. They cannot be explored simply as residuals when environmental change or resource depletion fails to explain population movement.

Among social factors that can directly cause or stimulate population movement, the generational domestic cycle (e.g., Goody 1958, 1972) may be related to household mobility. Construction of new residences may occur as households form at marriage. These households grow as children are added, and they decline as children leave to form their own households. Eventually residences are abandoned when the inhabitants become elderly and either die or move to be cared for in another household. The formation of new households should occur at relatively regular intervals equal to the length of a generation (approximately 20 years). To produce household mobility, the domestic cycle must result in the construction of the new residence at some distance from the founding settlement. Alternatively, the domestic cycle could reflect greater sedentism when new households are added to existing sites. Marriage and residence rules would provide the structure that influences decisions about residence, but individual agency would cause these rules to be followed only some of the time (Goodenough 1956).

A recent simulation suggests that there may be demographic limits on the length of time that small social groups can sustain the occupation of a residence, and this is another form of domestic cycling. Gaines and

Gaines (1997) examined the population dynamics of a hypothetical three-household settlement by simulating the biological, cultural, and behavioral characteristics of the group and tracking what happened to individuals living in the settlement on a year-by-year basis over a period of 70 years. They found that the longevity of such a settlement was extremely sensitive to the survival schedule and the marriage and residence rules employed. Small shifts in the ages and genders of surviving members of the group dramatically affected both the population growth in and the collapse of the settlement. In the Gaineses' simulation, only 47 percent of the runs survived for 70 years, and for 90 percent of the runs there was little or no growth over the last 40 years of the simulation.

Thus, there appear to be limits on the length of settlement occupation set by the demographic composition of small sites. Small residences that were occupied for two or perhaps three generations might eventually have been abandoned because they were no longer demographically viable. The mobility of small residential sites that were abandoned after having been occupied for 40 to 60 years might relate to this form of domestic cycling.

Social factors also affect the sedentism and mobility of communities. Kintigh (1985) documented community mobility in the Zuni region, arguing that this movement was the result of factionalism. There may have been social constraints on the sizes of households and communities that led to fissioning and recombination of social groups. Personal and factional disputes are therefore another social factor that could stimulate the residential mobility of individuals, households, and larger groups (Whiteley 1988).

Warfare and the need for defense were also social factors that stimulated mobility in the Southwest (Haas 1990; Haas and Creamer 1993, 1996; Kintigh 1985:109, LeBlanc 1978; Lightfoot and Kuckelman n.d.; Lipe 1995:156–158; Wilcox and Haas 1994). Warfare potentially resulted in (1) the movement of dispersed households and small communities into larger communities between A.D. 1150 and 1300, and (2) the movement of communities from mesa tops to more defensible canyon-oriented locations (Haas and Creamer 1996). This shift from mesa tops to canyon-oriented locations was accompanied by defensive architectural features at Mesa Verde–region sites (Fairchild-Parks and Dean 1993:5; Haas and Creamer 1996; Kenzle 1997; Lightfoot and Kuckelman n.d.; Nordenskiöld [1893] 1979:66; Wilcox and Haas 1994). Many canyon-oriented settlements were also at or near water sources, both natural springs and constructed reservoirs (Fetterman and Honeycutt 1987:127; Haase 1985:25; Neily 1983:122; Wilshusen, Churchill, and Potter 1997). The move to the canyon-oriented locations may have been an attempt to defend and control water (Haase 1985:25; Neily 1983:231–232), and proximity to a water source might have enhanced the defensibility of a settlement (Kintigh 1985:109).

Other social factors can promote mobility at a wide variety of social scales. Kelly (1992:48) notes that residential moves occur as people seek access to spouses or shamans or as they respond to death, sorcery, or political forces. For example, charismatic leaders could attract people into their communities, and particularly important communities could attract immigrants (Lightfoot 1984). Kent (1989; Kent and Vierich 1989) reports that 57 percent of the moves of Basarwa and Bakgalagadi groups in Africa are motivated by social or political factors (see also Kelly 1992:48). Finally, Kelly (1992:48) notes that residential mobility may itself be culturally valued. Naranjo (1995) argues that this is in fact the case in Puebloan society.

Mobility and the Social Context

These examples of social factors that serve as proximate causes of mobility also illustrate how the social context conditions all decisions concerning mobility and sedentism. Rohn (1965, 1977), who was one of the first to study Mesa Verde–region communities, discussed how social context affected mobility. He argued that the social context of the community provided stability; communities on Mesa Verde and in the Lowry area were established in the late seventh century and then grew steadily in size until they reached their peak population during the 1200s (Rohn 1977, 1984, 1992). Rohn saw limited evidence for mobility and interpreted many individual sites as having been continuously occupied for centuries, especially between A.D. 1100 and 1300. He saw people during this period as having been anchored to their sites and localities by water management systems (Rohn 1963, 1972, 1977). Rohn's model therefore emphasized the long-term sedentism of both households and communities.

Adler and Varien (1994) and Varien and others (1996) share Rohn's perspective on the stability of communities but argue that household movement and community movement occurred at different frequencies. Their research draws heavily on Adler's (1990) cross-cultural study of land tenure systems, which shows that community political organization structures local access to social and natural resources. Adler's is a density-dependent model in which increasing population density provides a context for intensification of the subsistence economy and the accompanying development of increasingly formalized land tenure systems.

Adler and Varien (1994) applied this perspective to communities in the Sand Canyon locality, where the spatial clustering of residential sites and public architecture were used to define the boundary between two communities, Sand Canyon and Goodman Point. Although individual structures and residential sites were abandoned frequently, public architecture and the largest residential site clusters maintained their same general locations within these two communities between A.D. 1000 and 1300. The spatial stability of the public architecture and major settlement clusters was interpreted as evidence that the Sand Canyon and Goodman Point communities remained intact during these three centuries (Adler 1992, 1994; Adler and Varien 1994).

In summary, the social determinants of mobility include residence decisions associated with the domestic cycle and establishment of new households. Mobility related to the domestic cycle in the Mesa Verde region would have occurred at the social scale of individuals, households, and perhaps small groups of households. Their residential movements would have occurred at regular intervals corresponding roughly to a generation. Personal and factional disputes, along with warfare, would also have resulted in the movement of social segments ranging in size from the subhousehold level to groups of several households. The temporal scale of population movement related to factional disputes and warfare would have been erratic and is difficult to predict. Finally, economic intensification and the development of more formal land tenure systems, part of what Stone (1993:78) terms the "social technology" of a group, would have promoted sedentism for both households and communities.

SUMMARY

Environmental change, resource depletion, and social factors affect the social, spatial, and temporal scales of population movement. With regard to the social scale of movement, all three variables can potentially affect both household and community mobility. Environmental change has the greatest potential for affecting larger social scales, stimulating the movement of an entire community or even groups of communities. Social factors tend to affect groups smaller than communities. Resource depletion would cause relatively small social groups to move over the short term but could potentially cause community movement over the long term.

In terms of the spatial scale, environmental change has the greatest potential for producing long-distance movement. With resource depletion, groups would move over shorter distances to the nearest available area with an adequate resource base, but again this could produce long-distance moves over the long term. Social factors would cause movement at a variety of spatial scales, and movement would likely be keyed to existing social ties. In most cases, movement caused by social factors would be over shorter distances because people have more social connections in the area close to where they live. But people also tap long-distance relationships to set up migration streams.

The temporal scale of movement caused by environmental change would be linked to identified periods of such change. Different social factors would affect the temporal scale of movement in a variety of ways. Residential mobility linked to the domestic cycle would be regular, and moves would occur at intervals of approximately one human generation. Movement related to factional disputes, warfare, or the other social factors noted previously would be sporadic and variable. There may have been a limit to the length of time small residential sites remained occupied, with abandonment after 40 to 60 years because they were no longer demographically viable.

Resource depletion would affect the temporal scale of movement in a variety of ways, depending on population density and the productive potential of local areas. With low population density and abundant open land, the slightest resource depletion might trigger population movement. But higher population density and competition for resources would provide a context promoting intensification and sedentism rather than abandonment and mobility. The productive potential of local areas plays a role as well—people living in relatively productive areas are more likely to stay put and intensify, whereas those living in more marginal areas may have no choice but to abandon their homes and move.

In the rest of this book, using archaeological data, I examine how these interrelated factors conspired to affect the movement of small-scale agriculturalists in the Mesa Verde region. In order to conduct the analysis, these factors had to be kept conceptually distinct, but in practice they probably were highly correlated. Further, decisions to move or stay put are historically situated, so responses to a specific factor—for example, environmental change—presumably varied at different times. The archaeological record for the Mesa Verde region is exceptional, and it provides an excellent case study with which to begin to unravel the complex relationships between these variables and their effects on residential mobility.

4

MEASURING

HOUSEHOLD

RESIDENTIAL

MOBILITY

Understanding residential mobility in any ancient society requires a method for measuring the length of site occupation and the frequency of residential movement. Establishing the frequency of such movement is essential for understanding how residential mobility operates within a specific group and for studying it comparatively. In the method developed here, I use the accumulation of cooking-pot sherds to estimate the occupation spans of 13 residential sites in the Sand Canyon locality. I calculate annual accumulation rates from strong archaeological cases, relying for the most part on the Duckfoot site. The Duckfoot cooking-pot sherd accumulation rate is found to be quite similar to pottery accumulation rates developed elsewhere in the Mesa Verde region, supporting the use of cooking-pot sherd accumulations for estimating the length of site occupation.

Accumulations studies seek to determine why, how, and at what rates artifacts accumulate in the archaeological record (Varien and Mills 1997). Accumulations research began in the early 1900s and continues to the present. Interest in it has been sustained because it examines the relationships among variables fundamental to the archaeological record: population size, time, and the use and discard of artifacts on sites.

Nels Nelson (1909) presented one of the earliest applications of this type of research when he tried to determine how long California shell mounds had been used. The premise behind Nelson's work was straightforward and similar to the assumption that underlies subsequent accumulations research: there is a direct relationship between the size of the site population, the length of time that material was discarded, and the amount of material discarded.

Nelson used the volume of a shell mound to estimate the total amount of accumulated shell (S), the number of house pits to estimate the number of households (H), and what he believed was a reasonable estimate of the daily deposition rate of mussel shells per household (R). To calculate the length of site occupation (T), Nelson multiplied his estimate of the number of mussel shells discarded per household per day by the total number of households and then divided this into the estimated total accumulation of shells ($T = S \div [R \times H]$).

Elsewhere I have reviewed the history of accumulations research and documented the methodological improvements that followed Nelson's pioneering approach (Varien 1997; Varien and Mills 1997). That review places the research on cooking pot accumulations in its larger context, emphasizing the substantial body of middle-range research upon which this study is based. The work of Sherburne Cook stands out, for it demonstrated the importance of understanding formation processes and provided some of the first sophisticated discussions of sampling in the archaeological literature.[1]

The trajectory of accumulations research was changed by archaeologists who questioned the basis for archaeological inference (see Ascher 1961; Binford 1962) and who began to examine living communities in an attempt to understand the formation of the archaeological record (see Ascher 1968).[2] Experimental archaeology and ethnoarchaeology have contributed to the middle-range theory of artifact accumulation and site formation.[3] While most research in the 1960s and 1970s focused on building this middle-range theory, the research of Cook (1972a, 1972b), McMichael (1960), Schiffer (1976), and Kohler (1978) continued to pursue accumulations research similar to that developed by Nelson.

Research during the 1980s and 1990s used computer simulations to examine how artifact frequencies were affected by the relationship between artifact use-life and site occupation span,[4] one dimension of which has become known as the "Clarke Effect" (Clarke 1972; Schiffer 1975, 1987:54–55). These studies demonstrated that variation in artifact use-life and accumulation rates could (1) produce variation in assemblage composition that might be interpreted erroneously as the result of different activities, (2) affect seriations, and (3) cause frequencies in the archaeological record to differ from systemic frequencies, that is, the actual number of artifacts in use at a given moment in a living household. Recently, simulations and mathematical models have returned to the original focus of accumulations studies: conducting empirical studies that attempt to answer specific questions about what happened in the past (Kohler 1978).[5]

The interplay of method and theory described by Clarke (1972:239) has come full circle. Methodological research in the first half of the twentieth century triggered the theoretical statements of the 1960s and 1970s, which in turn initiated a series of empirical studies that included ethnoarchaeological, archaeological, and experimental research along with computer simulations. Together these studies comprise a growing corpus of middle-range theory devoted to understanding how artifacts accumulate in the archaeological record. With the more secure footing provided by this middle-range theory, archaeologists have begun to use accumulations research to address questions of more general anthropological interest.

POTTERY ACCUMULATIONS AND
OCCUPATION SPAN

Inspired by Krieger's (Newell and Krieger 1949) painstaking refitting study, Baumhoff and Heizer (1959) conducted one of the earliest studies of pottery accumulations. They recognized that "pottery analysis here becomes more than a mere chronological device. For example, in a one-period site where the number of houses was known and where the number of pots could be calculated, one could easily determine the amount of pottery used per household. Additionally, if the length of time of occupation were known, the number of pots used per capita per year could be computed" (1959:308). They further demonstrated how weight could be used to estimate the number of discarded vessels (1959:312). In the analyses that follow, I use the total weights of sherd assemblages rather than vessel counts.

Foster (1960) followed with one of the first ethnoarchaeological studies of pottery use in four villages near Tzintzuntzan, Michoacan, Mexico. He presented data on vessel use-life and the size of household inventories and discussed factors affecting the breakage and replacement of pottery vessels, including basic strength, the type of use, breakage due to factors other than use, and pottery costs. Ethnoarchaeological studies on the production, use, exchange, and discard of pottery became increasingly common after Foster's study and continue to the present.[6]

A particularly important study contributing to middle-range theory about how pottery assemblages are formed is David's work on Fulani pottery (David 1972; David and Hennig 1972). He examined the factors that affect vessel breakage and concluded that frequency of use is a critical variable. David also documented that different vessel types have different use-lives. He then explored the effect that variation in vessel use-life has on the formation of pottery assemblages, arguing that the cumulative frequency of each vessel type in the discard assemblage does not accurately reflect the number of each type of pot in use at any one moment (see Mills 1989a, 1989b for a reassessment of the issues raised by David). DeBoer (1985) and Shott (1996) examined the physical properties of pottery that correlate with its use-life and concluded that vessel weight and size are key determinants of vessel use-life.

Ethnoarchaeological data have also been used to estimate the use-lives of pottery vessels and the size of the systemic number (the number of vessels in use at a specific point in time) in an assemblage. These variables have then been used in combination with archaeological data to address behavioral questions. For example, Pauketat (1989) used ethnoarchaeological and archaeological data to measure the occupation spans of Mississippian farmsteads. The use-lives of pottery vessels were derived from a cross-cultural sample. Assemblage data from a well-preserved site were used to estimate the household systemic number. Finally, an intensively excavated site was used to estimate the total accumulation of pottery. With these variables Pauketat calculated site occupation span and then based inferences about the political integration of Mississippian communities on his new understanding of how long sites were occupied. The analysis of cooking pot discard presented in this chapter builds on Pauketat's work, but I use different methods that I believe produce more accurate accumulation rates and better estimates of site occupation span.

COOKING POTS AS DATA FOR
ACCUMULATIONS RESEARCH

I view the accumulation rate of cooking-pot sherds as a general constant related to population and the length of site occupation. I use cooking-pot sherds to estimate the duration of site occupation for a number of reasons: their ubiquity among archaeologically studied groups; their relatively short use-lives, which result in the deposition of large numbers of sherds (and thus lower error in estimates); and their general survival in the archaeological record. In addition, experimental, archaeological, and ethnoarchaeological studies have clarified the relationship among the production, use, and discard of this vessel class.

Experimental Studies

David (1972) provided a key insight when he recognized that use frequency was a major determinant of vessel use-life, a point reinforced by subsequent research (Blinman 1988a:194, 1993; Nelson 1991; Pierce 1998; Tani 1994). Cooking pots are subject to both mechanical and thermal stress, but thermal stress is a more important factor in determining cooking pot use-life (Pierce 1998). Thermal stress in cooking pots is caused by repeated heating and cooling, which produces thermal fatigue that ultimately results in breakage (Rice 1987:105, 226–231, 363–368).

A large body of experimental research examines how thermal stress affects pottery (Bronitsky 1986; Bronitsky and Hamer 1986; Pierce 1998; Rye 1976; Schiffer et al. 1994; Steponaitis 1983, 1984; West 1992). These studies make two points relevant to the use of cooking pots in accumulations research. First, repeated use depletes cooking pots of their strength, ultimately resulting in breakage and discard. Second, ancient potters designed cooking pots that were resistant to thermal stress at the expense of resistance to mechanical stress. This last point indicates that failure due to depletion of vessel strength through use is a more important determinant of cooking pot use-life than are stochastic processes (e.g., accidentally dropping a pot). It follows that cooking pots should accumulate in the archaeological record at relatively regular rates, so long as food preparation techniques, raw materials, and techniques of ceramic manufacture remain relatively constant.

Thermal stress, or cracking, occurs when pottery is heated and cooled during cooking. Thermal stress produces micro-cracking that gradually depletes the strength of the vessel (thermal fatigue), and it potentially produces macro-cracking that can result in catastrophic failure of the vessel. Thermal stress is produced in two ways: by an extreme temperature gradient that exists between the heated and unheated surfaces of the vessel,[7] and by the differential thermal expansion coefficients of clays and aplastic inclusions (Bronitsky 1986:250; Schiffer et al. 1994; Skibo 1992).

Studies of thermal stress on low-fired pottery agree on several points. First, crack initiation and micro-cracking due to thermal stress are inevitable. Second, thermal stress resistance in pottery can be increased by minimizing the *extent* of crack propagation (Bronitsky 1986:253; Rice 1987:368; Rye 1976, 1981:27; Steponaitis 1983:36–45; West 1992:10–17). Finally, vessel properties that reduce crack propagation and promote thermal stress resistance include rounded forms, thin vessel walls, high elasticity, moderate strength, and irregularities produced by pores and temper (Pierce 1998; Rice 1987:368; West 1992:13).[8]

Experiments also indicate that surface texturing (Schiffer et al. 1994) and corrugated exteriors (Pierce 1998) promote thermal stress resistance. Cooking pot design may also address issues related to cooking control (e.g., boiling over), ease of handling, and manufacturing costs (Pierce 1998). Together these experiments identify a number of design trade-offs involved in the manufacture of cooking pottery; conflicting design choices mean that an optimal design for cooking pottery is unlikely (Pierce 1998).

Archaeological Studies

Steponaitis (1983:36–45) conducted strength tests on pottery from Moundville in Alabama. He found that fine-tempered vessels had the highest initial strength and would have been the most effective pots for resisting mechanical stress, or cracking due to impact. This fine-tempered pottery, however, lost a large proportion of its strength when subjected to thermal shock. The forms of these fine-tempered vessels suggested that they were used for serving and storage, and resistance to mechanical stress would have given them longer use-lives. Coarse-tempered pottery, on the other hand, had less initial strength but retained more strength after severe thermal shock than did the initially stronger, fine-tempered pottery. Coarse-tempered pottery was therefore interpreted as the most resilient and longest lasting choice for cooking pots (Steponaitis 1983:45).

Studies from other regions also show that potters manipulated the paste of cooking vessels to promote thermal stress resistance (e.g., Braun 1983, 1987). In the late 1800s Frank Cushing (1979:246) described how Zuni potters used a particular clay and temper in the manufacture of cooking vessels so that the pots would be "tougher and better able to withstand the effects of fire."

There is ample evidence that Mesa Verde–region potters produced cooking pots designed to be thermally stress resistant. Mesa Verde gray wares and white wares correspond to broad functional categories, with gray wares used primarily as cooking vessels and to a lesser degree for storage, and white wares used for serving and storage. The production technology of these two wares diverged soon after the inception of pottery in the Mesa Verde region (Blinman 1986b, 1993). By the A.D. 800s, most gray wares were made with coarse, angular rock and sand temper, and this was coupled with low firing temperatures to promote resistance to thermal stress. White wares contained fine temper, with sherd temper becoming dominant by 1000, and they were fired at higher temperatures. The latter is indicated by increased sintering, which is detected in sherds dating as early as the eighth century (Blinman 1988b:458, 1993:18). After 1100, the strength of white wares and their resistance to mechanical stress was increased by the use of even higher firing temperatures—a change that correlated with the widespread adoption of trench kilns—and by increasing vessel wall thickness (Blinman 1993:18).

The differences in the manufacture and use of gray wares and white wares are evident in the proportions of counts and weights of sherds from the 13 sites excavated as a part of the Sand Canyon Testing Program. The abundance of gray wares relative to white wares at these sites is consistently higher when using counts and lower when using weights, a pattern that derives from the consistent difference in the average size of gray and white ware sherds (Pierce et al. 1998). Gray wares consistently break into more and smaller sherds because their manufacture compromises their mechanical strength in order to promote resistance to thermal shock, and because their repeated exposure to thermal stress makes the vessels weaker until they eventually break. In other words, a gray ware pot breaks into smaller sherds because the walls of the vessels are relatively weak. White ware sherds, on the other hand, are larger on average because their manufacture promotes mechanical strength, and this strength is not depleted through use.

Ethnoarchaeological Studies

Mills (Varien and Mills 1997) has recently summarized ethnoarchaeological research on cooking pots. Her cross-cultural research attempts to determine (1) whether cooking pots accumulate faster than other pottery types; (2) whether cooking pots have low standard deviations for vessel use-life; (3) whether there are cross-cultural regularities in cooking pot use-lives; and (4) whether there are cross-cultural regularities in the number of cooking pots used by households. She concludes that there are strong patterns in cooking pot use-lives and that cooking pots are an appropriate vessel class for accumulations research.

Ethnoarchaeological studies are particularly helpful in examining cross-cultural variation in two variables critical for measuring cooking pot accumulations: vessel use-life and the size of the systemic number. With regard to vessel use-life, Mills finds that cooking pots have one of the shortest use-lives of any vessel category, with a median of 1.7 years (Varien and Mills 1997). The distribution of vessel use-lives is skewed by a few vessels with use-lives greater than five years; these vessels are used for special, often ceremonial, occasions. When these cases are removed, 85 percent (n = 48 cases) of all central tendencies for cooking pot use-life are less than four years (Varien and Mills 1997).

With regard to the size of the household systemic inventory, cooking pots exhibit the widest range of values of any pottery vessel category. A number of factors account for this variation, including household wealth, vessel stockpiling, whether or not a potter is present in the household, variation in cooking techniques, and the differing ages of villages (Nelson 1991:168–169; Tani 1994:56–57). This variation makes it difficult to estimate the number of cooking pots in a household inventory using cross-cultural data.

THE DISCARD EQUATION, ACCUMULATION
RATES, AND OCCUPATION SPAN

Total accumulation needs to be distinguished from total discard. Total accumulation refers to the total amount of material still present in the archaeological record, whereas total discard refers to everything discarded in the past, whether or not it survives in the archaeological record. Total discard is altered by a range of processes, including cultural processes such as recycling and natural processes such as erosion and decay.

Accumulations modeling is based on a discard equation. This equation was implicit in early-twentieth-century accumulations research, but more recently it has been stated as a formula (David 1972:142; de Barros 1982:310; Schiffer 1975:840, 1976:59; 1987:53). Mills (1989a, 1989b) compared several of the published discard equations and concluded that Schiffer's (1987:53–54) was the most parsimonious. It is commonly cited as follows:

$$T_D = \frac{S \times t}{L}$$

where T_D = total discard, S = the systemic number, t = the length of time over which the discard takes place, and L = the use-life of the item.

Archaeologists who use the discard equation to estimate occupation span typically use ethnoarchaeological data to obtain values for the systemic number and artifact use-life (Kohler 1978; Pauketat 1989). Both variables are characterized by variability within and among societies, and variation is especially great when one compares vessels with different functions (Varien and Mills 1997). For this reason, accumulation studies should isolate functionally specific classes of vessels rather than model the accumulation of entire pottery assemblages. Cooking pots are the ideal vessel category for initiating a new generation of accumulations research.

Even with cooking pots, problems remain when the discard equation is used in conjunction with ethnographic values. The most fundamental problem is that the accuracy of the discard equation is entirely dependent on the accuracy of the ethnographic estimates. Although values for cooking pot use-life exhibit a fairly narrow distribution, the size of the systemic number varies considerably. Nelson (1991) notes that despite the high degree of cross-cultural variation, variation within cultural or geographic boundaries is more constrained. Two conclusions can be drawn from this observation. First, it is difficult to choose an ethnographic case study that accurately duplicates an ancient case. Second, accumulation rates drawn from a strong archaeological case should be reasonably representative of the ancient society of which they are a part.

Yet another problem is the dynamic relationship between the size of the systemic number and an individual vessel's use-life. This relationship hinges on the assumption that use-life is largely determined by type of use, duration of use, and use frequency, which is similar to what has been termed the "use number" (Hildebrand 1978:274; Schiffer 1987:51). Clearly there are other factors that condition vessel use-life (see Shott 1996 for a recent review), but frequency of use is believed to be the most important factor—especially with regard to cooking pots (Varien and Potter 1997). Thus, the size of the systemic number influences vessel use-life such that the smaller the systemic number, the greater the frequency of use, which produces a shorter vessel use-life.

The relationship between vessel use-life and the size of the systemic number is illustrated by the case of Mayan households in San Mateo Ixtatan, Guatemala (Nelson 1991). San Mateo household pottery assemblages include large numbers of cooking pots that have especially short use-lives. San Mateo households stockpile vessels to ensure that pottery will always be available because of these short use-lives and because some vessels are difficult to replace (Nelson 1991:177–178; see also Tani 1994). Thus, San Mateo households have many vessels in their household assemblages that are not in use at a given time. Grossly inaccurate estimates of total discard are produced by using the discard equation in conjunction with the known values for the size of the systemic number and the vessel use-life of San Mateo pottery.[9]

The San Mateo case may be an extreme example, but it serves as a valuable warning to archaeologists: the systemic number reported by ethnoarchaeologists may not be the number of pots actually in use. The discard equation is accurate only so long as the systemic number refers to the number of vessels actually in use, but ethnographic estimates of the systemic number (and for that matter, estimates from well-preserved archaeological assemblages) often include stockpiled vessels.

Varien and Potter (1997) used a simulation to examine the relationship between the size of the systemic number and artifact use-life and to evaluate the accuracy with which the discard equation alone quantifies accumulations. Using data from the Duckfoot site, we simulated breakage and discard by programming an exponential function that increased the probability of vessel breakage with each use. We found that the number of accumulated cooking-pot sherds predicted by the simulation most closely tracked the number predicted by the discard equation when it was assumed that site occupation began with new pots and that only a single pot from among the household inventory was used at any one time, until it broke. When a site occupation began with used instead of new vessels, the discard equation *underestimated* the amount of accumulated cooking pottery during the initial years of occupation. When pot use was rotated among all vessels in the systemic number (as opposed to using only a single pot until it broke) breakage was delayed, and the discard equation *overestimated* the amount of accumulated cooking pottery during the initial years of occupation. If site occupation began with used pots, and use of the pots was rotated among all vessels in the use assemblage, these two factors canceled each other out, and results of the simulation and the discard equation were similar.

Variation in the size of the systemic number also created a discrepancy between the results of the simulation and the prediction of the discard equation. This discrepancy, however, was present only for the initial years of site occupation; after approximately five years, varying the size of the systemic number became irrelevant so long as there were enough pots in the inventory to make it through an annual cycle. In all versions of the simulation, differences between the simulation's predicted accumulation and that predicted by the discard equation was greatest for small (one-household) sites of short duration (less than 50 years). Increasing the number of households and/or the occupation span minimized the discrepancies between the results of the simulation and those of the discard equation (Varien and Potter 1997).

SUMMARY OF ACCUMULATIONS METHODS

The experimental, archaeological, and ethnoarchaeological information on cooking pots indicates that as a class, cooking pots are ideal artifacts for accumulation studies aimed at estimating site occupation span. However, the great variation in the size of the household systemic inventory indicates that using the discard equation and ethnographic data to model accumulation rates is a problem. The simulation just discussed (Varien and Potter 1997) illustrates that there is an inverse relationship between the number of vessels in use and vessel use-life. But these variables eventually cancel each other out, because the overall number of use events leading to failure for an individual pot is similar for all pots in the assemblage, regardless of the size of the systemic number. Thus, individual cooking pots in smaller assemblages have shorter use-lives than cooking pots in larger assemblages, but more pots are wearing out simultaneously in the larger assemblages. This means that after the initial years of site occupation the relationship between the size of the systemic number and cooking pot use-life ceases to be a factor in modeling accumulation rates. Developing annual accumulation rates at sites with sufficiently long occupation spans thereby avoids many of the problems that plague the use of the discard equation. Strong archaeological cases (*sensu* Montgomery and Reid 1990) are needed to estimate these accumulation rates. Well-controlled excavations at the Duckfoot site provide data with which to develop the accumulation rate of cooking-pot sherds in the Mesa Verde region.

THE DUCKFOOT SITE: ESTABLISHING ACCUMULATION RATES

The Duckfoot site is a Mesa Verde–region residential site occupied between A.D. 850 and 880 and located approximately 5.5 kilometers (3.4 miles) west of Cortez, Colorado (fig. 4.1). Duckfoot is an exceptionally strong case study because of the completeness of the excavation sample and the chronological precision provided by a wealth of tree-ring dates. There is a detailed site report (Lightfoot and Etzkorn 1993), as well as several detailed analyses of architectural patterns, artifact assemblages, and social organization at the site (Lightfoot 1992a, 1992b, 1993, 1994; Varien and Lightfoot 1989).

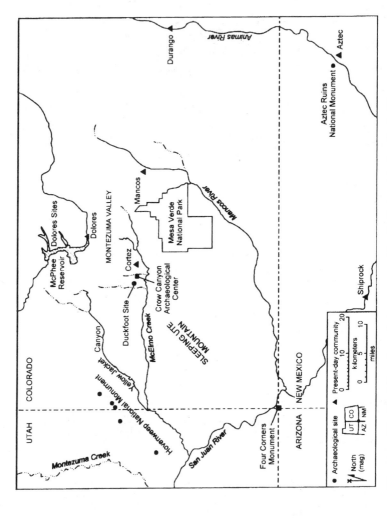

Figure 4.1 The Duckfoot site and sites excavated by the Dolores Archaeological Program.

Investigations at the site included the complete excavation of a 19-room pueblo and four associated pit structures—all of the architectural features at the site. In addition, extramural areas, the midden, and much of the site periphery were excavated. Most of the structures burned at abandonment, and 375 tree-ring dates were recovered from a variety of contexts, including 13 rooms, four pit structures, courtyard features, and midden deposits. Fifty-two percent (194) of these dates are cutting dates (Lightfoot 1994:26).[10] Lightfoot (1994:18–36) has provided a detailed interpretation of architectural data to reconstruct the sequence of room and pit structure construction. Tree-ring data are used to date these construction events and the site abandonment. He argues that initial construction occurred in the late A.D. 850s and that abandonment took place between 876 and 880 (Lightfoot 1994:34–36). Based on these interpretations, Duckfoot was occupied for 20 to 25 years.[11]

Lightfoot (1992a, 1994) analyzed architectural patterns to group pit structures and rooms into architectural suites. Floor artifact assemblages and floor features were analyzed to reconstruct activity areas and interpret the ways in which structures were used (Lightfoot 1994; Varien and Lightfoot 1989). Finally, artifact refitting was conducted to examine the interconnectivity of structures (Lightfoot 1994). Based on these analyses, Lightfoot concluded that the site was occupied contemporaneously by three households, probably equivalent to extended family groups, for the full duration of site occupation. Remodeling included the addition of a small, shallow pit structure in A.D. 873, late in the occupation of the site (Lightfoot 1994:32). This fourth pit structure was not associated with the addition of any new surface rooms, and it is interpreted as part of a larger remodeling of the pueblo by the three households that lived there and *not* as the addition of a fourth household.[12]

That the site was almost completely excavated permits reasonably accurate estimates of the total artifact accumulation. Together, the known occupation span, the contemporaneity of households, and the nearly complete excavation and screening make Duckfoot an excellent case study for examining the rate at which discarded cooking pots accumulated. These rates can be calculated as the average weight in grams of cooking-pot sherds discarded per household per year.[13]

Lightfoot (1994:78) reported the total weight of gray ware sherds as

581,647 grams (97,622 sherds). He added 10 percent to this figure to account for sherds missing as "a result of postabandonment processes and our failure to recover every last sherd from the site" (1994:78), producing a total of 639,812 grams. To estimate the number of cooking pots present in the gray ware pottery assemblage, Lightfoot conducted a rim-arc study of gray ware sherds from the midden (1994:74–78).[14] The rim-arc analysis produced three important results: (1) the frequency of large, medium, and small gray ware cooking jars was determined; (2) small cooking jars were separated from a differently shaped storage jar, the olla, which had orifices similar in size to those of small cooking jars; and (3) the frequencies of other gray ware forms were documented (Lightfoot 1994:74–79).

Lightfoot checked the accuracy of his rim-arc study by comparing the expected weight for the estimated number of gray ware vessels based on the rim-arc analysis with the actual weight of gray ware sherds from the midden excavation units.[15] The difference in weight between these two values was less than the weight of one average medium-sized gray ware jar—that is, Lightfoot found a difference of less than 1 percent between estimated discard and actual discard as measured by gray ware sherd weight (Lightfoot 1994:78). Given the accuracy of the rim-arc analysis, Lightfoot used its results along with his estimate of the total quantity of gray ware sherds at Duckfoot to estimate the number of vessels in the gray ware assemblage from the entire site (table 4.1).

Duckfoot data indicate how vessel size affects sherd assemblages, an issue addressed by several authors who have debated whether sherds or vessels are the appropriate measure for quantifying pottery (Egloff 1973; Orton 1993). Feathers (1990) argues that the relationship between vessel size and the quantity of pottery in a sherd assemblage is a problem only if vessels make up the unit of comparison, and not when sherd assemblages are compared with each other. Pierce demonstrates that the relationship between sherd abundance and vessel count and size is not a bias but a potential source of meaningful variation among assemblages (Pierce et al. 1998). Sherd assemblages are used in the analyses that follow, but sherd weights are translated into vessel counts in order to compare the Duckfoot data with the larger cross-cultural sample.

Lightfoot's estimates indicate that by weight, cooking-pot sherds comprise 62.4 percent of the Duckfoot gray ware sherd assemblage. Given his

Table 4.1 The Duckfoot Site Gray Ware Pottery Sherd Assemblage

VESSEL FORM	ESTIMATED NO. OF VESSELS	% OF VESSEL ASSEMBLAGE	MEAN VESSEL WEIGHT (G)	TOTAL SHERD WEIGHT (G)	% OF SHERD ASSEMBLAGE
Small cooking jar	134.3	34.3	583	78,297	12.4
Medium cooking jar	122.5	31.3	1,635	200,288	31.6
Large cooking jar	48.8	12.5	2,551	116,836	18.4
Olla	49.0	12.5	4,083	200,067	31.6
Miniature jar	14.4	3.7	126	1,814	0.3
Seed jar	3.0	0.8	1,655	2,043	0.3
Bowl	19.0	4.9	681	34,542	5.4
Total	391.0	100.0	1,616	633,887[a]	100.0

[a]This estimate of total discard differs from Lightfoot's reported actual discard (639,812) because, for ease of calculation, Lightfoot estimated that vessels from the midden represented 50 percent of those from the total site, whereas the midden vessels actually make up 55 percent of the total sherd assemblage (Lightfoot 1994:78–79).

estimate of 639,812 grams for the total gray ware sherd assemblage, the total accumulation of cooking-pot sherds at the site is then 399,243 grams. Turning this estimate into an annual rate per household is a simple matter of dividing by the momentary number of households, three, and the 20- to 25-year length of site occupation.[16] The result is that for 20 years of site occupation, the cooking-pot sherd accumulation rate is 6,654 grams per household per year, and for 25 years of occupation, the rate is 5,323 grams per household per year.

Approximate use-life estimates for Duckfoot cooking pots can be generated using data provided by Lightfoot (1994:79) on the composition of Duckfoot cooking pot assemblages. Duckfoot cooking pots included small, medium, and large vessels. The use-life estimate for small vessels ranges between 0.4 and 0.6 years, for medium pots, between 0.5 and 0.6 years, and for large cooking pots, between 1.2 and 1.5 years.[17] Thus, each year, each Duckfoot household broke approximately two small and two medium-sized cooking pots, and each broke a large cooking pot approximately every 1.5 years.

The use-life estimate for the large cooking pots at Duckfoot is close to the cross-cultural median for cooking vessels as reported earlier in this chapter (Varien and Mills 1997). The use-life estimates for small and medium vessels are within the range of the cross-cultural variation but on the low end of it; they are most similar to the use-life values reported by Deal (1983) and Nelson (1981) for the Maya area. That Duckfoot vessels are on the low end of the cross-cultural distribution may be related to the fact that most of the ethnographically known societies have incorporated at least a few metal or plastic pots into their vessel assemblages, which serves to extend the use-life of their pottery vessels.

COMPARING THE DUCKFOOT RATE WITH OTHER ESTIMATES OF POTTERY ACCUMULATION

A number of studies have quantified pottery accumulation. Cook (1972b) developed annual rates of pottery accumulation to estimate population at four sites, but his methods were too coarse-grained to enable direct comparison with the Duckfoot rates. More applicable are the pottery accumulation rates developed by Kohler and Blinman (1987) and by Nelson, Kohler, and Kintigh (1994) for sites in the Dolores River valley, located approximately 20 kilometers west-northwest of the Duckfoot site (fig. 4.1). Kohler and Blinman (1987) estimated annual accumulation rates for the *total* pottery assemblage at Grass Mesa Village, arguing that rates were variable between A.D. 730 and 910. Between 850 and 880, the annual accumulation was estimated at 1,425 sherds per pit structure.[18] Kohler and Blinman (1987:8) estimated an average sherd weight of 6.5 grams, producing an annual accumulation of 9,265 grams per pit structure. In Duckfoot pottery assemblages, cooking-pot sherds comprised 57.5 percent of the *total* pottery sherd assemblage (including gray, white, and red ware). Reducing Kohler and Blinman's accumulation rate for the *total* sherd assemblage by this amount produces an annual accumulation rate for cooking-pot sherds of 5,327 grams, a rate similar to that calculated for the Duckfoot site.

Nelson, Kohler, and Kintigh (1994:132) developed accumulation rates for the *total* pottery sherd assemblages at nine Dolores sites, producing a slight revision of the Kohler and Blinman figures.[19] They reported an estimate of 750 (± 255) sherds per household per year and an average sherd weight of 5.35 grams, producing an annual rate of 4,013 grams (± 1,364 grams) per household (Nelson, Kohler, and Kintigh 1994:132–134). They also calculated an annual household accumulation rate of all pottery sherds of 3,000 grams using the discard equation and ethnographically derived values for systemic inventory and vessel use-life. Combining these two approaches, they concluded that an annual rate of between 500 and 1,000 pottery sherds (2,675 and 5,350 grams) per household was reasonable. Dolores researchers argue that there were 2.6 households per pit structure during the A.D. 850 to 880 period, so these rates translate into 6,955 to 13,910 grams per pit structure per year. To convert this *total* sherd accumulation rate to a rate for cooking-pot sherds, this estimate is again reduced to 57.5 percent—the percentage of the total Duckfoot sherd assemblage that were cooking-pot sherds—producing an annual household accumulation rate of cooking-pot sherds of between 3,900 and 7,998 grams per year. This relatively large range encompasses the Duckfoot rate presented earlier.

Calculating an annual accumulation rate using the median cross-cultural values for cooking pot use-life (1.7 years; n = 48 cases) and the size of the systemic number (1.6 vessels; n = 39 cases) reported by Mills (Varien and Mills 1997) illustrates the problems of using the discard equation and ethnographic values. Using these values in the discard equation produces an estimate of 0.94 vessels discarded per year. If all the vessels were large Duckfoot cooking pots, then the accumulation rate would be 2,551 grams per year; if all were medium-sized vessels, the rate would be 1,635 grams; and if all were small vessels, it would be 583 grams. Each of these estimates is far below the Duckfoot rate.

The results of these various accumulations studies, standardized to look only at the accumulation of cooking-pot sherds, are summarized in table 4.2. The similarity in these accumulation rates, except for those calculated with the discard equation, supports the proposition that cooking-pot sherds accumulated at a relatively regular rate in the Mesa Verde region. Given the high quality of the Duckfoot data, I use the Duckfoot rate as a baseline for annual household accumulation rates of cooking-pot sherds, at least for Mesa Verde–region sites dating to the A.D. 800s. Applying the Duckfoot accumulation rate to the Sand Canyon locality sites, however, means assessing the difference between the plain gray cooking vessels used at

Table 4.2 Cooking-Pot Sherd Accumulation Rates from Various Studies

STUDY	COOKING-POT SHERD ACCUMULATION (GRAMS/HOUSEHOLD/YEAR)
Duckfoot: Varien, this volume	5,323 to 6,654
Dolores: Kohler and Blinman (1987)	5,327
Dolores and cross-cultural data: Nelson, Kohler, and Kintigh (1994)	3,900 to 7,998
Discard equation and ethnographic values	2,551

Duckfoot and the corrugated cooking vessels used at the later Sand Canyon locality sites.

APPLICATION OF THE DUCKFOOT ACCUMULATION RATE

The application of pottery accumulation rates is invariably met with a seemingly endless list of "what ifs"—hypothetical behaviors or formation processes that would undermine the applicability of a single accumulation rate to a wide range of sites. What if some households had easier access to cooking pots while for others cooking pots were in short supply? What if there were ritual deposition of cooking pots? What if different types of cooking pots were used in different ways, producing different breakage rates?

To begin examining variability in cooking pot accumulations, I consider the general characteristics of assemblage formation in the Pueblo I and III periods. The similarity of these assemblages supports the idea that cooking pots accumulated at relatively regular rates and that no matter how many of these "what ifs" occurred in the past, they produced relatively limited variation in the rate of cooking pot accumulation, particularly in sites with occupations that lasted for more than a few years.

The proportions of artifact types at sites are the result of the rates at which those artifacts accumulated and of the post-depositional processes that affected the artifacts after discard. Therefore, examining the variation in artifact frequencies is one means of assessing the variability in artifact accumulation rates.

Nelson, Kohler, and Kintigh (1994:128–133) used data from 14 Dolores Archaeological Program (DAP) sites to examine the relationship between statistical point estimates for all pottery sherds and for the following artifact categories: chipped-stone debris, flaked stone tools, and nonflaked stone tools. They presented a scatterplot matrix and correlation coefficients that showed a strong linear relationship between pottery and the other artifact categories. The authors concluded that it was person-years of occupation, which combines the length of occupation with the average momentary population, that was responsible for the strong relationships among categories (Nelson, Kohler, and Kintigh 1994:130). In other words, these artifact categories *must* have accumulated at relatively regular rates in order to occur in such similar proportions at the sites examined.

To illustrate this point, the relationship between cooking-pot sherds and chipped-stone debris is examined here in three scatterplots and regression equations. The first (fig. 4.2) combines Duckfoot data with data from eight Dolores sites interpreted as year-round habitations occupied during the Pueblo I period.[20] The next plot (fig. 4.3) shows the following Pueblo III sites: the 13 sites that were tested in the Sand Canyon locality; Green Lizard Hamlet—an intensively excavated unit pueblo in the Sand Canyon locality (Huber 1993); and two contexts from Sand Canyon Pueblo itself—a midden in an abandoned structure and the probability sample from the nonarchitectural areas of the site. The final scatterplot (fig. 4.4) combines the data from the Pueblo I and Pueblo III sites.

A linear relationship between cooking-pot sherd and chipped-stone debris accumulation is demonstrated by all three scatterplots. When the Pueblo I sites alone are considered, Duckfoot is the site farthest from the regression line. Most of the Dolores sites have more chipped-stone debris than cooking-pot sherds, but Duckfoot has greater amounts of cooking-pot sherds. As discussed previously, Duckfoot and Dolores cooking-pot sherds accumulated at similar rates. Therefore, the slight difference between Duckfoot and the Dolores sites in the proportions of cooking-pot sherds and chipped-stone debris is probably due in part to variation in the rate at which the chipped-stone debris accumulated at these sites.

When the Pueblo III sites are examined, the relationship is still strong,

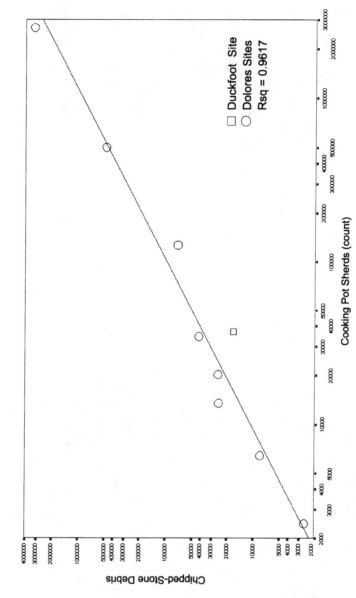

Figure 4.2 Scatterplot showing the relationship between cooking-pot sherds and chipped-stone debris at Duckfoot and several Dolores Archaeological Program sites, all of which date to the Pueblo I period. Axes are logged and the regression analysis is on the logged data.

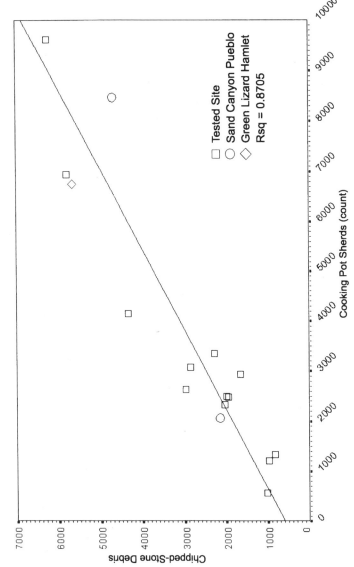

Figure 4.3 Scatterplot showing the relationship between cooking-pot sherds and chipped-stone debris at the Sand Canyon locality tested sites, at Green Lizard Hamlet, and at two contexts from Sand Canyon Pueblo, all of which date to the Pueblo III period.

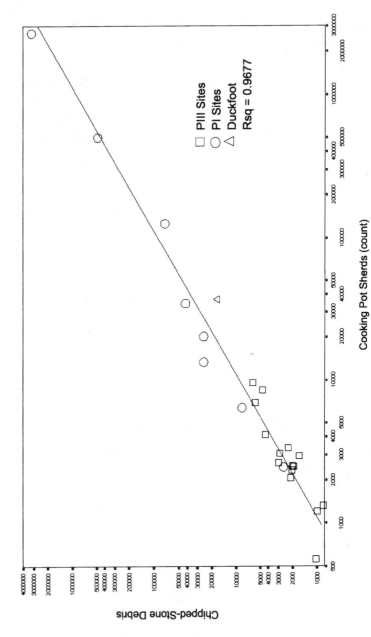

Figure 4.4 Scatterplot showing the relationship between cooking-pot sherds and chipped-stone debris at Pueblo I and Pueblo III sites. Axes are logged and the regression analysis is on the logged data.

although not quite so strong as in the Pueblo I sites. Combining the Pueblo I and Pueblo III data, however, produces the strongest relationship of all three plots. Again, there is a slight tendency for the Pueblo I sites to have higher amounts of chipped-stone debris relative to cooking-pot sherds, although there is overlap with the Pueblo III sites in this regard.

These data do not mean that none of the what-ifs mentioned earlier occurred. These and many more probably did occur. But the strong relationship between the accumulations of functionally distinct artifact categories indicates that either these what-ifs affected most sites in roughly the same manner or their effect on accumulations over the long term was not large. With regard to cooking-pot sherds, this suggests that daily cooking activities, which occurred year after year at sites, produced the majority of cooking-pot sherd accumulation. Other activities, such as cooking pot deposition associated with rituals, probably contributed a relatively small amount to the overall accumulation. Therefore, the accumulation rates developed here hold great promise for estimating the length of site occupation.

APPLYING ACCUMULATION RATES TO SAND CANYON LOCALITY SITES

A number of analyses refine the Duckfoot accumulation rate. These analyses are described in detail elsewhere (Varien 1997: Appendix A) and are only summarized here.

Duckfoot cooking pots were plain gray vessels, but the cooking pots used by Pueblo II and III households in the Mesa Verde region were corrugated gray ware. Three characteristics of plain and corrugated cooking pots were examined to determine whether they accumulated at different rates: the intensiveness of their use, their size, and their performance. There were clear differences between plain and corrugated cooking pots that probably affected their accumulation rate, but they did so in opposite ways.

First, the presence of sooting on a higher percentage of corrugated jars than of plain gray cooking pots (Blinman 1988a:127; Mills 1989b:154; Rohn 1971:143; Varien 1997:298) led to the interpretation that corrugated vessels were more specialized for cooking and were used more intensively as cooking vessels than were plain gray vessels (Blinman 1988b:454; Mills

1989b:136–147). More intensive use of corrugated cooking pots would have subjected these vessels to greater thermal stress, resulting in shorter vessel use-life and greater accumulation rates.

Second, corrugated cooking pots were also larger than plain gray cooking pots (Blinman 1988b:457; Mills 1989b:147–150; Rohn 1971:142; Varien 1997:299–302). Assuming that the size of the household cooking pot inventory was similar for corrugated and plain vessels, the larger size of the corrugated cooking pots would also have resulted in corrugated vessels accumulating at a faster rate than plain gray vessels.

Third, in terms of performance, corrugated vessels have greater thermal stress resistance than plain gray vessels (Pierce 1998). Greater thermal stress resistance would have resulted in corrugated pots lasting longer and accumulating slower than plain gray vessels.

In short, there are important differences between plain and corrugated cooking pots that have the potential to affect their accumulation rates. The absolute change in the accumulation rate of plain versus corrugated cooking pots was, therefore, an empirical problem that needed to be solved.

This problem was addressed with three analyses. The first examined the changing proportions of vessel forms between the late A.D. 800s and 1300, focusing on changes in the proportions of cooking pots to bowls and cooking pots to ollas (storage jars with long necks and restricted orifices). A heuristic assumption—that the changing proportions of these vessel types were due entirely to changes in the accumulation rate of cooking-pot sherds—was used to evaluate the *maximum potential* difference between plain and corrugated cooking-pot sherd accumulations. Using this assumption and the changing proportions of vessel types, the *maximum possible range* for the annual household accumulation rate of corrugated cooking-pot sherds was calculated to be 2,012 to 9,788 grams.

Second, the maximum range was evaluated by comparing it with a strong archaeological case in which reasonable estimates existed for population size, total accumulation, and the length of time during which the accumulation occurred. The strong case was a midden inside an abandoned structure at Sand Canyon Pueblo. This produced a refined accumulation rate for corrugated vessels—3,810 to 6,654 grams—termed the *core range*.

Third, the three ranges—the maximum range, the core range, and the Duckfoot range—were used to estimate the occupation spans at 13 sites in the Sand Canyon locality. These occupation span estimates were compared with independent evidence for the maximum occupation span at each site. This evidence included the following: when available, tree-ring dating to determine site construction dates; pottery and archaeomagnetic dating to bracket the period of occupation; and the known date for the abandonment of the Mesa Verde region to establish the latest possible site abandonment date. Possible accumulation rates were rejected when they produced occupation span estimates that exceeded the maximum occupation span as indicated by the independent evidence.

These analyses indicate that the best estimate for the accumulation rate for corrugated cooking pots is similar to the Duckfoot rate for plain gray cooking pots. The low end of the Duckfoot rate—5,323 grams—is the lowest possible annual household accumulation rate for corrugated cooking-pot sherds. Using this rate, the occupation span estimates for the Pueblo III sites are just below the maximum occupation spans suggested by independent evidence. The high end of the Duckfoot rate produces estimates that are always less than the independently derived maximum occupation spans, indicating that this rate is possible for each of the sites. The upper end of the Duckfoot rate—6,654 grams—is therefore considered the best available estimate for the annual household accumulation of corrugated cooking-pot sherds.

The interpretation that the accumulation rates of plain and corrugated cooking-pot sherds were similar is supported by the scatterplot presented previously (fig. 4.4). The similarity of these rates suggests that the differences between these plain gray and corrugated cooking vessels tend to counteract one another. Increased specialization and increased average vessel size would have increased accumulation rates for corrugated cooking pots, but this appears to have been offset by the enhanced performance of corrugated vessels.

These conclusions rest on two assumptions: (1) that the rate of accumulation of cooking-pot sherds is uniform, and (2) that the point estimates of the total accumulations are reasonably accurate. There is undoubtedly some interhousehold variation in the accumulation rate of cooking-pot sherds, but the analyses presented earlier indicate that this variation is limited. The point estimates for total accumulation were generated using sound sampling procedures, so they should be reasonably accurate. Further, these point estimates can be used in conjunction with confidence intervals to provide a statistically valid range for the total accumulation. These data— the accumulation rate and the estimates for the total accumulation of corrugated cooking-pot sherds—are used in the following chapter to generate occupation span estimates for the Sand Canyon locality sites. These occupation span estimates are the basis for measuring the frequency of household residential mobility in the Sand Canyon locality.

5

HOUSEHOLD

RESIDENTIAL

MOVEMENT

IN

THE

SAND

CANYON

LOCALITY

In the next step of the analysis, I use the best estimate for the annual household accumulation rate of corrugated cooking-pot sherds—6,654 grams—to estimate site occupation span and frequency of household residential movement at 13 tested sites in the Sand Canyon locality (fig. 5.1). This rate is used in conjunction with statistical estimates of the total weight of corrugated cooking-pot sherds at the 13 sites. First, the total weight estimates are divided by the annual household accumulation rate. Next, this figure is divided by the number of kivas or pit structures at each site to control for differences in site size. This produces a range for the average length of occupation per household.

Next, dating, architecture, and stratigraphy are examined for each site to determine whether multiple households were present and whether those households were occupied simultaneously or sequentially. This contextual information from each site is used in conjunction with the average length of occupation per household to determine the total occupation span at each site. The resulting occupation span range provides the best estimate

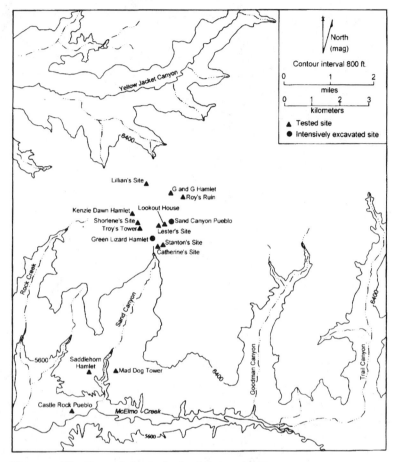

Figure 5.1 The 13 tested sites in the Sand Canyon locality.

for the frequency of household residential movement in the Sand Canyon locality.

A *minimum* occupation span estimate is also calculated by using the high end of the maximum possible annual accumulation rate—9,788 grams—and the low end of the 95-percent confidence interval for the total estimated cooking pot accumulation. This minimum estimate is extremely conservative because the true value for the total accumulation is almost certainly higher than the low end of the 95-percent confidence interval, and the true accumulation rate is almost certainly lower than the high end of the maximum range. This minimum estimate is nonetheless useful as a baseline for the shortest possible occupation span, but it is worth remembering that the true occupation span is almost certainly higher.

Site occupation span and the frequency of household movement are found to vary considerably among the Sand Canyon locality residential sites, and accumulations research allows this variation to be quantified for the first time. This variation suggests that social factors, and not only resource depletion or environmental change, are important in determining the frequency of residential moves. Pueblo II habitations were typically occupied for one generation or less, but many of the Pueblo III residential sites were occupied for two and perhaps three generations.

SAND CANYON LOCALITY RESIDENTIAL SITES

Detailed descriptions of the 13 Sand Canyon locality sites used in the analyses that follow appear elsewhere (Varien 1998), and only brief descriptions are included here (table 5.1).

Eleven sites are interpreted as year-round habitations dating between A.D. 1180 and 1280. Five of these 11 sites had earlier occupations dating sometime between 1050 and 1150. Of the five earlier occupations, two were year-round habitations; the remaining earlier components represent limited use of the sites. Thus, the 11 sites comprise 15 components dating to either the Pueblo II or III period. (Basketmaker III and Pueblo I components were also identified at several sites, but they are not considered here because they did not result in the deposition of corrugated potsherds.)

Two additional tested sites, Troy's Tower and Mad Dog Tower, had architectural features and artifact assemblages distinct from those of the other 11 sites. These two sites might have been habitations occupied by households of atypical composition (e.g., small households or unmarried individuals) or they might have had some specialized, nonhabitational use (Varien 1998). These sites are included in the analysis, but the accumulation rates developed in chapter 4 are probably less accurate when applied to them.

Table 5.1 Summary Information on Tested Sites in the Sand Canyon Locality

SITE/SITE NUMBER	LOCATION	ROOMS/KIVAS	TOWER	MAX. MIDDEN DEPTH (CM)	COMPONENT[a]
Lillian's Site (5MT3936)	Mesa top	7–10/1	1	57	Late PIII, late PII
Roy's Ruin (5MT3930)	Mesa top	5–7/1	1	42	Late PIII, late PII
Shorlene's Site (5MT3918)	Mesa top	5–7/1	1	50	Late PIII, late PII, BMIII
Troy's Tower (5MT3951)	Mesa top	0/1	1	29	Late PIII
G and G Hamlet (5MT11338)	Mesa top	3–5/1	0	48, 45	Early PIII, late PII
Kenzie Dawn Hamlet (5MT5152)	Mesa top	6–10/2	0	50	Early PIII, late PII, BMII
Lester's Site (5MT10246)	Talus slope	3–5/2	0	60	Late PIII
Lookout House (5MT10459)	Talus slope	5–10/2	1	40[b]	Late PIII
Stanton's Site (5MT10508)	Talus slope	3–5/1	1	125	Late PIII
Catherine's Site (5MT3967)	Talus bench	5–7/2	1[c]	95	Late PIII
Mad Dog Tower (5MT181)	Lower Sand Canyon	1/1	1	25	Late PIII
Saddlehorn Hamlet (5MT262)	Lower Sand Canyon	3–5/1	1[c]	90	Late PIII
Castle Rock Pueblo (5MT1825)	Lower Sand Canyon	50–75/16	1	120	Late PIII

[a]BMIII = 550–700; Late PII = 1050–1150; Early PIII = A.D. 1150–1225; Late PIII = 1225–1300.
[b]This is the depth of the talus slope midden; another midden on the site, found in an abandoned kiva, was 70 to 80 cm thick.
[c]Probable tower, but evidence is not conclusive.

Estimating Total Cooking-Pot Sherd Accumulation

Stratified random samples were excavated at each of the 13 sites. The number of sampling strata at each site varied, but all sites were stratified into the same general depositional contexts. These sampling strata included surface architecture, subterranean architecture, courtyard, midden, inner periphery (the area adjacent to the architecture and midden), and outer periphery (the area extending to the limit of the surface artifact scatter).

Both Pueblo II and Pueblo III components were present at five sites. Corrugated cooking pots were the only vessels used for cooking in both Pueblo II and III. It is impossible to distinguish Pueblo II from Pueblo III corrugated body sherds, so a method was devised to estimate how much of the corrugated pottery was associated with each component.[1]

The formulas for calculating point estimates for weights of the total populations of corrugated cooking-pot sherds at each site and for calculating confidence intervals are those presented by Kohler (1988:55–56). The point estimates were obtained by multiplying the total number of corrugated sherds from each sampling stratum by the inverse of the sampling proportion in each stratum and then cumulating this product over all strata. Confidence intervals were calculated by first computing the variance of the point estimate and then multiplying its square root by the appropriate value of *t*, which was obtained from table D in Blalock (1979:603). Point estimates and 66-percent, 80-percent, and 95-percent confidence intervals were calculated for the corrugated pottery at each site (table 5.2).

Estimating Site Occupation Span

The point estimates and confidence intervals are used in conjunction with the accumulation rates to calculate site occupation span. The initial step is obtaining the estimate for the total household years of site occupation, which is accomplished by dividing the point estimate and confidence interval by the accumulation rate range. At sites with one household, this estimate for the total household years of occupation is also the occupation span estimate for the site. At sites with more than one household, the total household years of occupation must be divided by the number of

Table 5.2 Point Estimates and Confidence Intervals for Corrugated Pottery from the Sand Canyon Locality Tested Sites, in Grams

SITE/COMPONENT	PT. EST.	66% CONF. INTERVAL	80% CONF. INTERVAL	95% CONF. INTERVAL
G and G Hamlet, PII	106,886	94,571–119,201	90,876–122,896	82,256–131,516
G and G Hamlet, PIII	123,950	109,749–138,151	105,489–142,411	95,548–152,352
Lillian's Site, PIII	327,465	277,986–376,944	263,142–391,788	227,518–427,412
Roy's Ruin, PIII	414,297	354,244–474,350	336,228–492,366	294,190–534,404
Shorlene's Site, PIII	430,440	373,571–487,309	356,510–504,370	315,564–545,316
Kenzie Dawn, PII	170,176	139,575–200,777	130,395–209,957	108,975–231,377
Kenzie Dawn, PIII	792,646	616,784–968,508	564,026–1,021,266	440,923–1,144,369
Troy's Tower, PIII	86,110	59,257–112,963	50,664–121,556	29,987–142,233
Lester's Site, PIII	417,191	339,464–494,918	316,146–518,236	261,736–572,646
Lookout House, PIII	508,965	355,034–662,896	308,854–709,076	198,024–819,906
Stanton's Site, PIII	498,753	337,159–660,347	285,449–712,057	165,869–831,637
Catherine's Site, PIII	443,512	395,953–491,071	381,686–505,338	347,444–539,580
Saddlehorn Hamlet, PIII	154,039	108,060–200,018	93,347–214,731	54,943–250,135
Mad Dog Tower, PIII	61,088	50,236–71,940	46,871–75,305	38,841–83,335
Castle Rock, PIII	2,818,742	2,274,744–3,362,740	2,116,985–3,520,499	1,741,626–3,895,858

households on the site to obtain occupation span estimates. In addition, it must be determined whether the occupations of multiple households were simultaneous or sequential.

The total household years of occupation are divided by the number of kiva suites at sites with more than one household. Kiva suites (Bradley 1992:80)—a kiva and its associated surface rooms—are interpreted as the architectural features typically used by a household. A kiva suite is analogous to what Prudden (1903) termed a "unit type pueblo." The kiva suite is also analogous to the pit structure suite at the Duckfoot site (Lightfoot 1994), which Lightfoot interprets as the architectural correlate of a Duckfoot household.[2]

Not all researchers will agree that a kiva suite was used by a single household; many would interpret kivas as integrating a larger group, such as a minimal lineage. Lipe's (1989) discussion of the social scale of small Mesa Verde–region kivas, however, supports the interpretation that a kiva suite is the architectural correlate of a large household, as does Ortman's (n.d.) analysis of the distribution of mealing bins (see chapter 1 for a more detailed discussion of household organization). Further, the Duckfoot accumulation rate should apply because the pit structure suite used to determine the Duckfoot rate is the architectural predecessor of the kiva suite. Regardless of how one interprets the social scale represented by a kiva, dividing the point estimate for the total weight of corrugated sherds by the number of kivas is a viable means of standardizing the accumulation rate at sites of differing sizes.

Dividing the total household years of occupation by the number of kivas provides the average length of occupation per kiva suite. This does not provide a precise measure of the length of occupation of each kiva suite because the point estimates of corrugated sherds are for the entire site and not for individual kiva suites. This issue is discussed in greater detail in the sections that describe each site.

Three variables are used to calculate occupation span estimates: (1) the number of kivas at the site, (2) the point estimates and the 80-percent confidence interval for the total accumulation of corrugated cooking-pot sherds, and (3) the upper end of the Duckfoot accumulation rate (6,654 grams). The point estimate and 80-percent confidence interval for the total accumulation of cooking-pot sherds are divided by the upper end of the

Table 5.3 Estimates for Length of Occupation per Kiva Suite, Rounded to Nearest Year

SITE/COMPONENT	MINIMUM ESTIMATE	80% CONF. INTERVAL	POINT ESTIMATE
Troy's Tower, PIII	3	8–18	13
Mad Dog Tower, PIII	4	7–11	9
G and G Hamlet, PII	8	14–18	16
G and G Hamlet, PIII	10	16–21	19
Lillian's Site, PIII	23	40–59	49
Roy's Ruin, PIII	30	51–74	62
Shorlene's Site, PIII	32	54–76	65
Kenzie Dawn, PII	11	20–32	26
Kenzie Dawn, PIII	15	28–51	40
Lester's Site, PIII	13	24–39	31
Lookout House, PIII	7	15–36	25
Stanton's Site, PIII	17	46–107	75
Catherine's Site, PIII	18	29–38	33
Saddlehorn Hamlet, PIII	6	14–32	23
Castle Rock Pueblo, PIII	14	24–41	33

Duckfoot accumulation rate, and the result is then divided by the number of kivas. This produces a point estimate and range for the length of occupation per kiva suite that can be accepted with a relatively high degree of confidence. A minimum occupation span is also calculated; we can be confident that the minimum range is the lowest possible occupation span and that the true length of site occupation was higher (table 5.3).

DETERMINING THE LENGTH OF SITE OCCUPATION

Having worked through the application of the accumulation rates to estimating the length of occupation per kiva suite, there is still the problem of determining the best estimate for the total length of occupation for each of the Sand Canyon locality residential sites. In the sections that follow, each habitation component at each site is evaluated to interpret the frequency of household residential movement in the Sand Canyon locality. If kiva suite occupations were fully contemporaneous, then the total occupation duration would be the same as the estimated length of occupation per kiva suite. If, however, kiva suite occupation was either partly contemporaneous or sequential, then the occupation span would exceed the estimated length of occupation per kiva suite. If kiva suite occupation was fully sequential, the total length of site occupation would be the estimate per kiva suite times the number of kiva suites.

To determine whether kiva suite occupation was contemporaneous, partially contemporaneous, or sequential, the following data are evaluated: tree-ring, pottery, and archaeomagnetic dates; architectural style; and stratigraphy (Varien 1998). The two sites with the smallest quantity of corrugated cooking-pot sherds by weight are examined first.

Troy's Tower

Troy's Tower consists of a masonry tower, a masonry kiva, two large pit features, and a small but well-defined trash area. The kiva and tower are linked by a tunnel, as is common in the Mesa Verde region after A.D. 1150 (Varien 1998). Tree-ring dates from a large bell-shaped roasting pit document site use in the 1270s, while an archaeomagnetic date from the kiva hearth provided a dating range between 1225 and 1325. Pottery dating suggests occupation in the middle to late 1200s.

Troy's Tower lacks the surface roomblock that characterizes sites interpreted as year-round habitations. In addition, its assemblage composition contrasts with those of the other sites, particularly with regard to macrobotanical remains. Troy's Tower has twice the diversity of reproductive plant parts when compared with the other sites (Adams 1998). In addition, the site has fewer artifacts than all other sites except Mad Dog Tower. This is reflected in the relatively short point estimate—13 years—for its length of site occupation.

The site was interpreted as being either a habitation with an atypical household composition or a nonhabitational site with more specialized function (Varien 1998). Examples of atypical household composition include a single adult or a married couple with no children. An example of a site with a specialized function would be one used periodically for ritual activity. In either case, the cooking-pot sherd accumulation rate may have been affected. A smaller-than-typical household would probably use and break fewer cooking pots, and the same would be true for a site used periodically for some special activity. The use-life estimates for Troy's Tower should therefore be considered low.

Mad Dog Tower

Like Troy's Tower, this site might have been used for specialized, nonhabitational activities (Kleidon 1998b), or it might have been a year-round habitation occupied by an atypical household. Mad Dog Tower consists of a masonry tower, a partially masonry-lined kiva, a single surface room, and dispersed sheet trash. The Mad Dog artifact assemblage differs from those of the other sites, having high frequencies of chipped-stone debris, projectile points, and bifaces relative to the entire chipped-stone assemblage. The site also has relatively low frequencies of white ware jars. Given the possible differences in site use, the annual household corrugated cooking pot accumulation at Mad Dog Tower may have been less than at the other sites, and the accumulation rate may underestimate the true length of site occupation. The estimated length of occupation for Mad Dog Tower, ranging from 4 to 11 years (that is, from the minimum occupation estimate to the high end of the confidence interval range), should therefore be considered a minimum.

G and G Hamlet, Pueblo II Habitation

G and G Hamlet is a mesa-top unit pueblo with two distinct periods of occupation (Kuckelman 1998a). The Pueblo II habitation is interpreted as a year-round habitation for a single household. The major features at the site include a roomblock, pit structure, and well-defined midden (well-defined means a distinct mound with abrupt horizontal boundaries). The Pueblo II midden on this site was spatially discrete from the Pueblo III midden. The Pueblo II architecture is earthen and includes a post-and-adobe roomblock and an earth-walled pit structure. Tree-ring dates place construction sometime between A.D. 1065 and 1070. As noted in the discussion of the Duckfoot site, there are use-life limits to earthen architecture; the maximum use-life for earthen structures is 25–30 years with extensive remodeling. We found no such evidence for remodeling, although our test excavations exposed only limited portions of the architectural features.

Given the earthen architecture and the lack of evidence for extensive remodeling, the point estimate of 16 years is reasonable, and the range provided by the minimum occupation estimate and the high end of the confidence interval range (8 to 18 years) is also possible. These estimates indicate that occupation of this site was limited to a single generation, and it probably occurred sometime in the 1065 to 1085 interval.

G and G Hamlet, Pueblo III Habitation

This component is interpreted as a year-round habitation occupied by a single household. Architectural features include a masonry roomblock, a masonry kiva, and a midden with well-defined boundaries (Kuckelman 1998a). The presence of masonry architecture means that the architectural limitations on site use-life were not as severe as with earthen buildings. Pottery dating indicates that the most likely period of occupation was between A.D. 1180 and 1220 (Varien 1998).

The point estimate of approximately 19 years is reasonable, but there is no reason to reject the low estimate of 10 years or the high estimate of 21 years. The dating evidence and the length-of-occupation estimates indicate that the Pueblo II and III occupations of G and G Hamlet could *not* have been continuous; the two occupations were probably separated by approximately 100 years. Further, the Pueblo III habitation probably lasted a little longer than the Pueblo II habitation. As with the earlier habitation of G and G Hamlet, the Pueblo III component was probably limited to a single generation.

Lillian's Site, Roy's Ruin, and Shorlene's Site

These sites are all mesa-top unit pueblos, each with a masonry roomblock containing fewer than 10 rooms, a single masonry kiva, and a well-defined trash area (Varien 1998). All are interpreted as year-round habitations for a single household. Evidence of architectural remodeling was found at all three sites. Tree-ring dates were obtained from Lillian's and Roy's; their context is somewhat ambiguous but they are interpreted as evidence for occupation in the early 1200s (Varien 1998). Pottery assemblages indicate that all three sites were contemporaneously occupied, that occupation began sometime after 1180, and that they were abandoned as habitations by the middle 1200s (Varien 1998). That roof timbers were salvaged from the kivas indicates that they were abandoned as habitations before the regional abandonment between 1280 and 1290.

The minimum possible occupations at these sites range between 23 and 32 years; therefore, they were almost certainly occupied longer than G and G Hamlet. The point estimates for length of site occupation range between 49 and 65 years, and the high ends of the confidence interval ranges are between 59 and 76 years. All of these estimates are possible, but the high end of the confidence interval range approaches the maximum possible occupation span when tree-ring and pottery dating are considered.

The point estimates for these sites indicate lengthy, multigenerational occupations.[3] This is true even for the minimum estimates of Roy's Ruin and Shorlene's Site. It is also possible that these sites continued to be used seasonally and that pottery continued to be discarded at the sites after they were abandoned as permanent habitations. This could have occurred if the people living at Sand Canyon Pueblo used these sites as field houses during the late 1200s, an interpretation that is discussed in greater detail in chapter 6.

Kenzie Dawn Hamlet, Pueblo II Habitation

Kenzie Dawn Hamlet is another mesa-top unit pueblo (Kuckelman 1998b). Like G and G Hamlet, it has both Pueblo II and Pueblo III habitation components, with the Pueblo II component consisting of a post-and-adobe roomblock and an earth-walled pit structure. Any discrete midden associated with this component was either covered by the later occupation or dispersed by plowing and the clearing of trees in areas surrounding the core of the site. Tree-ring dates indicate that construction of this habitation occurred sometime in the A.D. 1080s (Kuckelman 1998b).

The 26-year point estimate for the length of occupation for this habitation component is on the high end of what is possible for the earthen architecture present at the site. The true length of occupation is probably somewhere between the 11-year minimum estimate and the 32-year high end of the confidence interval range. The probable period of occupation of this component is between 1080 and 1110.

Kuckelman (1998b) argues, on the basis of absolute dates, pottery dating, and stratigraphy, that there was nearly continuous occupation at Kenzie Dawn Hamlet for over a century, beginning with the occupation in the late 1000s and continuing throughout most of the 1100s. This interpretation is examined in the discussion that follows on the Pueblo III length-of-occupation estimates.

Kenzie Dawn Hamlet, Pueblo III Habitation

The Pueblo III habitation of Kenzie Dawn Hamlet included several building episodes that resulted in spatially separate and stratigraphically distinct architectural facilities (Kuckelman 1998b). Extensive remodeling was evident in each architectural area. Tree-ring dates are few, and the beginning of the Pueblo III component cannot be dated with certainty, but the tree-ring dates do indicate that there was Pueblo III occupation as early as the A.D. 1140s. Pottery dating indicates that occupation extended into the early 1200s but that Kenzie Dawn, as a year-round residence, may have been abandoned slightly earlier than Lillian's, Roy's, and Shorlene's sites (Varien 1998).

The earlier of the Pueblo III architectural components consists of a masonry-lined kiva and a masonry roomblock; the midden associated with this component has been obscured by the later component and by historic land use. The later Pueblo III architectural component has two masonry-lined kivas and a masonry roomblock, several deep pit features or pit rooms, and a spatially discrete, well-defined midden. Stone appears to have been robbed from the earlier Pueblo III roomblock to construct the later roomblock, and the later roomblock exhibits extensive remodeling (Kuckelman 1998b).

The presence of multiple kivas, and the stratigraphic evidence for the sequential occupation of these kivas, makes the interpretation of the total length of site occupation more difficult. The length-of-occupation estimates per kiva suite presented in table 5.3 would equal the total length of site occupation only if all of the kiva suites were fully contemporaneous.

In the case of Kenzie Dawn Hamlet, the point estimate for the length of occupation for each of the Pueblo III kiva suites is 40 years. Stratigraphic and contextual evidence indicates that during the initial Pueblo III period there was a single household living in a kiva suite, and at some later point this kiva suite was dismantled and replaced by kiva suites for two additional households. There is no stratigraphic evidence for a hiatus in the site occupation between these two building episodes. If the early kiva suite was used for 40 years, and the later architectural component with two kivas suites was used for 40 years, then the total length of the Pueblo III habitation component would be 80 years. This estimate of 80 years would hold only if the two households in the later architectural component were fully contemporaneous, so this is a conservative estimate. The minimum per-household length of occupation estimate is 15 years, which, taking the sequential nature of the Pueblo III occupation into account, would produce a minimum estimate of 30 years for the total length of Pueblo III site occupation. Similarly, the maximum estimate of the confidence interval range would produce a maximum estimate of 102 years for the total length of the Pueblo III occupation.

In sum, architectural details suggest a long period of occupation for the Pueblo III component at Kenzie Dawn. An 80-year length of occupation, as suggested by the point estimate accumulation rate, is supported by the architectural, stratigraphic, and chronometric evidence. Together these data indicate that Kenzie Dawn Hamlet was occupied for more than one genera-tion and probably for several generations. The accumulation data could also be marshaled to support Kuckelman's interpretation that there was relatively continuous occupation of the site from construction of the Pueblo II habitation component beginning in the 1080s and lasting through most of the 1100s and perhaps into the early 1200s. Cumulatively, the Pueblo II and III occupations of Kenzie Dawn Hamlet might comprise a minimum occupation of approximately 40 years, with a substantial hiatus in occupa-tion between the Pueblo II and III occupations. A more likely interpretation is an occupation of 100 to 130 years with little or no break in the occupation between the Pueblo II and III period components.

Lester's Site

This site, located on the talus slope just outside the Sand Canyon Pueblo site enclosing wall, consists of two masonry-lined kivas, several masonry surface rooms, and a midden on the talus slope (Kuckelman 1998c). One of the kivas had burned. Despite the fact that 89 of 192 tree-ring specimens produced dates, only one cutting date was obtained—A.D. 1270. This may date kiva construction, but there is also a cluster of near-cutting ("v") dates from the early 1200s that could reflect the true construction date. All that can be stated with certainty is that the kiva was in use after 1271, which is the latest noncutting date (Kuckelman 1998c). An archaeomagnetic date from the hearth provided a dating range of 1275 to 1600, indicating that kiva abandonment postdates 1275. Thus, this kiva appears to have been used up to the time of the regional abandonment at approximately 1290. Pottery dating from the site indicates that Lester's was roughly contemporaneous with Sand Canyon Pueblo (Varien 1998), where the primary occupation dates between 1240 and 1290 (Bradley 1992).

Stratigraphic interpretation suggests that roof beams were salvaged from the unburned kiva at the time of its abandonment, indicating that the kiva was abandoned before the regional abandonment. Thus, the households using these two kivas do not appear to have been fully contemporaneous.

The point estimate for the length of a kiva suite occupation is 31 years. If the two kiva suites were entirely sequential, then the point estimate for the total length of site occupation would be 62 years. If, however, the two households were partially contemporaneous, then the total length of site occupation would be between 31 and 62 years, with a minimum estimate between 13 and 26 years and a maximum between 39 and 78 years. These estimates indicate that a multigenerational occupation of Lester's is likely; however, the minimum estimate indicates that occupation for a single generation is possible. If the total length of site occupation is estimated at 45 years (that is, if the point estimates are used and the two kiva suites are interpreted as having been largely but not entirely contemporaneous), and if abandonment occurred no later than 1290, then the period of site occupation would be approximately 1245 to 1290.

Lookout House

This site, located on the talus slope 150 meters southwest along the canyon rim from Lester's Site and Sand Canyon Pueblo, consists of three masonry-lined kivas, masonry surface rooms, and a midden on the talus slope (Kuckelman 1998d). One of the kivas was constructed early in the occupation of the site. It was abandoned, dismantled, and filled with trash while the rest of the site remained occupied. A tree-ring date from the midden in this abandoned kiva indicates that some of the midden was deposited after A.D. 1257. The timbers from the other kivas appear to have been salvaged at the time of their abandonment, indicating that the site was abandoned before the regional abandonment. The occurrence of burials in the naturally deposited fill of two abandoned structures also indicates that people remained in the area after Lookout House structures were abandoned. Therefore, the site was abandoned sometime after 1257 but before 1290. Pottery dating supports an interpretation that the site was occupied in the middle to late 1200s.

The point estimate for the length of occupation for each household is 25 years. Given the sequential occupation of the households, the total length of site occupation must have been somewhat greater. If the household using the earliest kiva was abandoned and replaced, without a hiatus in occupation, by two households that occupied the site contemporaneously, then the point estimate for the total length of site occupation would be 50 years. Again, this is a conservative estimate because it assumes both the full contemporaneity of the later households and that occupation was continuous. The minimum length of occupation would be 14 years (twice the minimum estimate), with a maximum estimate of 72 years (twice the upper end of the confidence interval range). Thus, stratigraphy and the point estimate for the total length of occupation indicate that Lookout House was probably occupied for more than one generation, but the minimum estimate indicates that a single-generation occupation is possible. All things considered, the best estimate for the period of occupation at Lookout House is sometime between 1230 and 1280.

Stanton's Site

This site is located on an upper talus slope in Sand Canyon, approximately 1.4 kilometers from Sand Canyon Pueblo (Varien 1998). Architectural features include a masonry-lined kiva, a masonry roomblock, and a free-standing masonry tower. A midden is located on the talus slope below the architectural features. With a depth as great as 1.25 meters, it is the deepest midden encountered during testing program excavations. There are no absolute dates from the site, but pottery dating indicates an occupation in the middle to late 1200s. Roof timbers appear to have been salvaged from the abandoned kiva, indicating that the site was abandoned sometime before 1290.

Stanton's Site is a single-component, single-kiva occupation. The point estimate of 75 years is the longest occupation span for any of the tested sites. A lengthy occupation is supported by the depth of the midden. The minimum estimate for the length of occupation at this site is 17 years. The low end of the 80-percent confidence interval range is much longer, 46 years. The large difference between the estimates at this site is due in part to the high variance in the quantity of material found in each sampling unit and the resulting large range in the 95-percent confidence interval for the estimate of total corrugated sherd accumulation. Greater variance is true for most of the sites located on talus slopes, where the presence or absence of large boulders creates differences in the depth of deposits among sampling units.

The point estimate, confidence interval range, and depth of the midden deposits indicate that Stanton's Site had a lengthy occupation. This is important because it indicates, first, that Stanton's Site was probably occupied for more than one generation, and second, that the shift in site location from the mesa tops to the canyons began in the early 1200s rather than the middle 1200s as had been argued previously (Adler and Varien 1994:90). It is possible that Stanton's Site was occupied for most of the 1200s. The lengthy occupation also calls into question the interpretation that the inhabitants of small sites in the canyon were economically marginal relative to the inhabitants of Sand Canyon Pueblo (Munro 1994; Varien 1998).

Catherine's Site

This site is located on a bench in Sand Canyon 100 meters downslope from Stanton's Site (Varien 1998). The site consists of two masonry-lined kivas, a small masonry roomblock, and a well-defined trash area. Timbers appear to have been salvaged from both kivas, indicating that the site was abandoned before A.D. 1290. Pottery dating suggests occupation in the middle to late 1200s.

The two kivas on the site have similar fill sequences, including distinctive water-deposited strata in the upper fill that appears to have been the result of a single storm. Therefore, the kivas appear to have been abandoned and filled at approximately the same time, indicating that they may have been occupied largely contemporaneously.

If the two households were fully contemporaneous, the point estimate of 33 years would also be the length of occupation. If the two households were only partially contemporaneous, the total site occupation point estimate would be somewhere between 33 and 66 years. The minimum estimate for the total length of site occupation is 18 years (if both kivas were fully contemporaneous). Thus, Catherine's Site was probably a multigenerational habitation with occupation in the middle 1200s, sometime between 1230 and 1270.

Saddlehorn Hamlet

Saddlehorn Hamlet is a year-round habitation occupied by a single household. Major features include a masonry-lined kiva, a roomblock (including two rooms constructed in a sandstone alcove), and a well-defined midden (Kleidon 1998a). Tree-ring dates indicate that the kiva was occupied sometime after A.D. 1256, and construction may have occurred near that date. That the kiva was burned with no timbers salvaged indicates that the site was probably occupied until the region was abandoned, sometime between 1280 and 1290. Pottery dating supports the interpretation that occupation was in the late 1200s (Varien 1998).

The point estimate for the length of site occupation, 23 years, is consistent with these archaeological data. The minimum possible occupation span, 6 years, almost certainly underestimates the true length of occupation. If site occupation began sometime around 1256 and Saddlehorn was occupied for 23 years, abandonment would have occurred at approximately A.D. 1280.

Castle Rock Pueblo

This is the largest site excavated during the Sand Canyon Project Testing Program (Kleidon 1998c). It contains approximately 16 kivas, 40–75 masonry rooms, and associated refuse deposits. Not all the kivas are residential, and an estimate of 13 residential kivas at the site is used here.

Tree-ring dates indicate that occupation began sometime between A.D. 1240 and 1250. Stratigraphy and structure abandonment indicate that the site was occupied up to the time of the regional abandonment and that site abandonment was accompanied by warfare (Lightfoot and Kuckelman n.d.). Pottery dating supports this chronological interpretation. Thus, a 40- or 45-year length of occupation seems likely given the evidence from tree-ring dating, pottery dating, and structure abandonment. This span fits fairly well with the point estimate of 33 years based on cooking-pot sherd accumulation.

Together, tree-ring dating and length-of-occupation estimates provide

Table 5.4 Occupation Span Estimates for Sand Canyon Locality Tested Sites

SITE/COMPONENT	RANGE (YEARS)	BEST ESTIMATE (YEARS)	NO. OF GENERATIONS
Troy's Tower, PIII	8–18	13	1?
Mad Dog Tower, PIII	7–11	9	1?
G and G Hamlet, PII	14–18	16	1
G and G Hamlet, PIII	16–21	19	1
Lillian's Site, PIII	40–60	49	2+
Roy's Ruin, PIII	51–74	62	3
Shorlene's Site, PIII	54–76	65	3
Kenzie Dawn, PII	20–32	26	1+
Kenzie Dawn, PIII	55–102	80	4
Lester's Site, PIII	36–60	46	2+
Lookout House, PIII	30–72	50	2+
Stanton's Site, PIII	46–107	75	3+
Catherine's Site, PIII	44–58	50	2+
Saddlehorn Hamlet, PIII	14–32	23	1+
Castle Rock Pueblo, PIII	24–41	33	1+

evidence that most of the residences at Castle Rock were occupied contemporaneously. This means the site must have been established by a relatively large group of households and that it did not grow by accretion. This observation is particularly important for interpreting the last decades of occupation of the Mesa Verde region, a topic discussed in chapter 8.

CONCLUSIONS: HOUSEHOLD RESIDENTIAL MOBILITY IN THE SAND CANYON LOCALITY

Table 5.4 gives the best estimate for the total length of occupation for each site, taking into account the architectural, stratigraphic, and chronometric data. A range is also calculated using the contextual information from each site and the 80-percent confidence interval. The best estimates for occupation span and the confidence intervals are illustrated in figure 5.2.

Perhaps the most striking feature of the length-of-occupation point estimates is their variability. It is unlikely that this variability is the result of sampling error; it would be present even if the annual accumulation rate were in error. There simply is significant variation in the amount of material that accumulated per household at the 13 tested sites. The accumulations research allows us for the first time to quantify that variability. These data indicate that occupation spans ranged between approximately one and three generations.

Year-round residential sites with single-generation occupations include the Pueblo II habitation components at G and G Hamlet and Kenzie Dawn Hamlet and the Pueblo III habitation components at G and G Hamlet, Saddlehorn Hamlet, and Castle Rock Pueblo. Single-generation occupation is also possible for many other sites if the low end of the range is correct. Residential mobility at sites occupied for a single generation may relate to the domestic cycle. These residential sites might have been established as new households formed at marriage, and they continued to be occupied until grown children left the household.

The best estimates for the remaining sites indicate that they were probably occupied for more than a single generation (table 5.4). Occupation for more than one generation is virtually certain at sites where multiple kiva suites were occupied sequentially—the Pueblo III habitations at Kenzie Dawn Hamlet and Lookout House. Partly sequential occupation of kiva suites at Lester's Site and Catherine's Site also indicates a high probability that occupation was longer than one generation. There may have been accretional growth at sites with more than one kiva suite; as new households were added, new residential facilities might have been constructed at these sites. Occupation longer than one generation is also likely at many of the residential sites with a single kiva suite (table 5.4). At these sites, the same residential facilities must have been used by multiple generations. In general, the mesa-top unit pueblos had the longest occupation spans, but all of the talus sites, especially Stanton's Site, were probably occupied for more than one generation.

The impact of environmental stress on residential mobility in the Sand Canyon locality can be addressed using the occupation span estimates and the relatively precise dating. Kohler and Van West (1996) identified a period of production shortfalls in the A.D. 1089 to 1099 interval, the result of a

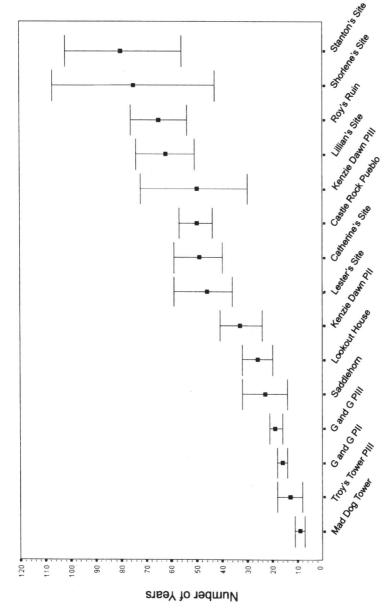

Figure 5.2 Best estimates for total occupation span and 80-percent confidence intervals for the Sand Canyon locality tested sites.

drought that occurred during that time. The abandonment of the Pueblo II habitation component at G and G Hamlet could conceivably relate to this drought; however, it appears more likely that the abandonment occurred before the period of environmental stress. The Pueblo II habitation component at Kenzie Dawn Hamlet was almost certainly occupied throughout this period of low productivity. In addition, the Pueblo III habitation component at Kenzie Dawn was probably occupied through the droughts that occurred repeatedly between approximately 1130 and 1180—the longest period of environmental stress recorded for the four centuries between 900 and 1300. The dating at Roy's Ruin and Lillian's Site indicates that these habitations were occupied during the 1212 to 1221 period of low productivity identified by Kohler and Van West (1996).

It is important to remember that Kohler and Van West's (1996) model does not predict the abandonment of small hamlets during periods of climatic deterioration and reduced agricultural productivity. Instead, they argue that aggregated settlements would not have formed during these periods, because aggregated settlements require extended food sharing networks that could not be sustained during times of low agricultural productivity. That the small Sand Canyon locality sites continued to be occupied through periods of low productivity could be seen as supporting their model.

What is important to the immediate discussion, however, is that climatic change severe enough to affect agricultural productivity did not result in the complete abandonment of the Sand Canyon locality. Van West's (1994) research indicates that the agricultural potential of the Sand Canyon locality was greater than most of the rest of the Mesa Verde region. Given its high agricultural potential, it is possible that the Sand Canyon locality *received* immigrants from less productive areas within the region during periods of environmental stress. Further research is needed to resolve this issue.

Resource depletion is difficult to evaluate with these data because catchment analyses for each site are not available and the rate of resource depletion is unknown. However, these sites are located relatively close to one another, and in general they were using the same local resources for basic raw materials. If resource depletion stimulated household mobility in the manner suggested by Kohler and Matthews (1988), Nelson and Anyon (1996), and Lekson (1996), the following is expected: (1) frequent residential movement, (2) residential movement at relatively regular intervals, and (3) little evidence for the multigenerational occupation of sites. The variation in the occupation span estimates and the occupation of sites for multiple generations suggest that resource depletion was not the sole cause of household residential movement in the Sand Canyon locality during the Pueblo III period, at least not at the frequency suggested by other researchers. This does not mean that resource depletion was not the cause of household residential mobility at other times and in other places in the Southwest, or that it was not a contributing factor in the residential movement of Sand Canyon locality households.

The variation in the occupation span estimates suggests that no single factor determined the frequency of household residential movement. The variation does suggest that social factors affected the frequency of residential movement and that residential mobility was sensitive to contextual information specific to a particular time and place. Also, the demographic viability of small sites may set upper limits to their occupation span. To unravel how these factors interact, future research needs to examine the occupation span for individual sites in conjunction with a detailed analyses of their local catchments, the degree to which those catchments were depleted over time, the evidence for climatic change and its effect on agricultural productivity, and the social context of the larger community. In the next chapter I attempt to advance our understanding of the social factors that influenced household residential mobility by considering the larger social context of the communities of which the households were a part.

COMMUNITY

PERSISTENCE

IN

THE

SAND

CANYON

LOCALITY

The analyses that follow compare the frequency of household movement, as determined in the previous chapter, with the frequency of community movement. Community sedentism and mobility are examined in three ways. First, stratigraphic evidence from pit structures and kivas is examined to determine whether the roofs were removed from the structures, providing a means of inferring whether localities remained occupied after structures were abandoned. Second, artifact density in the fill of pit structures and kivas is quantified to determine whether sites continued to be used after individual structures were abandoned. Third, tree-ring dates are analyzed in order to determine how continuously trees were harvested within individual communities and within the Sand Canyon locality as a whole. Each of these analyses is interpreted in light of a growing body of middle-range research on abandonment processes.

ABANDONMENT PROCESSES

Recently developed middle-range theory examines how abandonment processes affect the formation of the archaeological record (Ascher 1968; Binford 1978a, 1978b; Cameron and Tomka 1993; Schiffer 1987; Stevenson 1982, 1991). This theory specifies the ways in which the behaviors that accompany abandonment affect site formation. Important aspects of abandonment that condition site formation include: (1) whether abandonment was gradual or rapid and planned or unplanned; (2) whether return was anticipated; and (3) whether the distance to the next site was short or long.

These factors affect several behaviors crucial to the interpretation of abandonment (Bonnichsen 1973; Cameron 1991, 1993; Lightfoot 1993; Schiffer 1972, 1976, 1987; Stevenson 1982). The first is whether de facto refuse—usable materials that become refuse as a result of their being abandoned—is present or absent (Cameron 1993:3; Schiffer 1972:160, 1976:33–34, 1987:89). The second is whether there is evidence of artifact curation—the removal of usable items at the time of abandonment for use elsewhere (Cameron 1993:3; Schiffer 1987:89–91). Related to artifact curation is salvaging—the removal of items from de facto refuse by people still living in the site or in the region (Schiffer 1987:104). By examining these behaviors, middle-range research has helped us recognize that abandonment is typically a process that occurs over time, rather than an instantaneous "Pompeii-type" event (Ascher 1961:324; Binford 1981a; Schiffer 1985:18).

The mode of abandonment results in a number of general patterns. Curation and salvaging leave little in the way of de facto refuse; these behaviors occur when abandonment is gradual and planned, when the distance to the next occupied site is short, and when there is no anticipated return to the abandoned site. Conversely, curation and salvaging are limited, and large quantities of de facto refuse are produced, when abandonment is rapid and/or unplanned and when the distance to the next occupied site is great. If return to an abandoned site is anticipated, de facto refuse may be cached to protect it for future use (Stevenson 1982).

In the analyses presented in this chapter, the treatment of pit structure and kiva roofs is examined to determine whether roof timbers were abandoned as de facto refuse or salvaged at the time of structure abandonment. The distance of the move to the next occupied site is the most important variable conditioning whether timbers will be abandoned in place or salvaged; however, the distance over which salvaging occurs will also be affected by the supply of timber in the new locality.

Like all other behavior, abandonment behavior is historically contingent;

it is conditioned by prior events. Examples of historically contingent abandonment behavior include culturally specific rituals that accompany the
abandonment of a structure or site (Cameron 1993). The historical factors
that condition abandonment behavior do not invalidate the general principles identified by middle-range theory. Rather, understanding the historically contingent aspects of abandonment behavior is a challenge that must
be addressed when applying the middle-range generalizations.

One aspect of the historical nature of abandonment works in favor of
the analyses described here. As discussed by Cameron (1993), abandonment
processes operate at increasingly inclusive scales: activity areas, structures,
sites of all kinds, and larger settlement systems. Abandonment at a smaller
scale—for example, the abandonment of activity areas and structures—is
partly contingent on circumstances at the larger, more inclusive scales—
individual sites and regional settlement systems. Therefore, the abandonment of activity areas, pit structures, sites, and the many settlements that
compose communities occurs in the context of the long-term occupation
of particular places. The middle-range theory of abandonment helps us
understand the behaviors associated with the abandonment of specific
places and the larger context in which the abandonment occurred.

PIT STRUCTURE AND KIVA ABANDONMENT

Typically, kiva roofs in the Mesa Verde region were massive constructions.
Examination of intact kiva roofs at cliff dwellings in Mesa Verde National
Park indicates that Mesa Verde kiva roofs contained between 96 and 192
beams each (Hovezak 1992). In addition, pit structures and kivas constructed between A.D. 950 and 1300 were either entirely subterranean or
were built within enclosed spaces that made them appear subterranean; in
both cases the roof timbers were completely within the structure and below
the level of the courtyard. This means that post-abandonment natural
processes could not ordinarily disperse roof timbers outside the subterranean chamber. In sum, it is unlikely that unburned pit structure and kiva
roofs would simply have disappeared without a trace, because (1) they
contained so many timbers, (2) the timbers would typically have remained
within the structure unless they were deliberately removed, (3) the dry

conditions in the Mesa Verde region would typically have preserved roof timbers, and (4) the rare cases in which all timbers did entirely decay would be evident in stratigraphic profiles as dislocation structures or as strata with high organic content.

In this section I examine the abandonment of 57 pit structures, 51 of which are masonry-lined kivas. Two structures date between A.D. 1060 and 1090, and the remainder date between 1140 and 1290. Complete excavation occurred in eight kivas, seven at Sand Canyon Pueblo and one at Green Lizard Hamlet. Forty-nine structures from 14 sites were tested, permitting a thorough evaluation of the post-abandonment stratigraphy.

Stratigraphic analysis indicates that the 57 kiva and pit structure roofs were treated in one of four ways upon abandonment: (1) the entire roof was burned, resulting in the deposition of many large, burned beams; (2) large roof timbers were salvaged and small timbers were subsequently burned, resulting in the deposition of small pieces of charcoal mixed with roof construction sediments; (3) all roof timbers were left in place unburned, resulting in the deposition of rotted, unburned wood and a poorly defined stratum of roof construction sediments; and (4) all roof timbers were salvaged unburned, resulting in the deposition of roof construction sediments with no trace of the roof timbers. In addition, there were three cases in which roof treatment could not be determined.

Structures from which no timbers were salvaged imply (1) a long-distance move to the site occupied next and (2) no residents remaining in the vicinity of the abandoned structure. A long-distance move is defined as one beyond the immediate sustaining area of the abandoned site, or what has been termed a locality. Long-distance moves are implied by both burned and unburned structures in which all of the roof timbers were abandoned as de facto refuse. Burning may have been an abandonment ritual in the structures where it occurred.

Salvaging timbers implies a short-distance move, and a short-distance move implies that the locality remained occupied. Sometimes all timbers in a structure were salvaged, and sometimes only the large timbers were salvaged and then the small timbers were burned. This burning might also have been an abandonment ritual.

Sand Canyon Locality Roof Treatment

There are 15 cases of completely burned roofs in the site sample (26 percent of 57 roofs), all but three of them at Sand Canyon Pueblo. All 15 structures have kiva-style architecture. In Cameron's analysis of Basketmaker III and Pueblo I pit structure abandonment in the Four Corners region, half of the pit structures had burned (Cameron 1990:32). In Structure 501 at Sand Canyon Pueblo and in the burned kivas at Lester's Site, Saddlehorn Hamlet, and Castle Rock Pueblo, the burned roof fall lies directly on the structure floor, indicating that burning occurred at or near the time of abandonment. In five kivas at Sand Canyon Pueblo, there was a thin (less than 15 centimeter) layer of naturally deposited sediment between the roof fall and the floor, indicating that these structures were unused for a short time before the roof burned.

Next are structures that appear to have burned after their large roof timbers were salvaged. Cameron (1990:33) reports only three cases of this type of roof treatment (3 percent of her sample) in her survey of pit structure abandonment in the Four Corners region. Burning after salvaging is the most difficult treatment to recognize and interpret archaeologically, but there appear to be 11 cases (19 percent) in the Sandy Canyon locality sample. These cases are similar to unburned structures in that large roof timbers are clearly absent and a cultural deposit that includes roof construction sediments covers the floor.[1] They differ from other roof treatments in the abundance of small pieces of charcoal (2–7 centimeters) in the stratum above the floor. The walls of these structures are also burned, and patches of ash are present on the floors and benches, indicating that fire was associated with their abandonment. The interpretation of this context is that the main roof timbers were salvaged but the smaller closing material was burned when the structures were abandoned (Varien 1998).

It is unclear why this type of abandonment occurs in such a large percentage of the Sand Canyon Project structures and why the percentage is so small in other samples (e.g., Cameron 1990). This could be the result of a real difference—that is, Sand Canyon Project structures were treated differently at the time of their abandonment—or it could be that Sand Canyon Project researchers focused on the question of roof treatment in greater detail as a part of a larger interest in abandonment processes (Lipe 1992).

Salvaging of timbers from Sand Canyon Project structures was the most common treatment of roofs at abandonment, occurring in 21 cases (37 percent of the excavated structures). This is not simply a catch-all category for all unburned pit structures and kivas; instead, specific stratigraphic evidence supports the interpretation that timbers were salvaged (Kilby 1998; Varien 1998). In her survey of pit structure abandonment, Cameron (1990:33) interpreted 28 pit structures in her sample (32 percent) as having dismantled roofs. She noted that the dismantling of roofs was sometimes inferred from the *absence* of a clearly defined roof fall layer (Cameron 1990:29). Examination of the stratigraphy of Sand Canyon locality structures produces the reverse observation: there is a stratum of unburned roof sediment covering the floor of every pit structure or kiva interpreted as having a dismantled roof (see note 1 for a description of these strata).

The next category is that in which roof timbers were neither burned nor salvaged at abandonment but were left behind as de facto refuse. This occurs in seven structures at two sites: Kenzie Dawn and Sand Canyon Pueblo. At Kenzie Dawn, two of the structures are small, earth-walled pit structures that were deliberately filled at abandonment, after which a roomblock was constructed on top of them. The structures at Sand Canyon Pueblo were abandoned near the time of the regional abandonment, and it appears that the roofs were left to collapse naturally with no further use of the structures.

Changes in Roof Treatment over Time

To examine the distribution of different roof treatments through time, structures were assigned to one of four time periods. These assignments were made on the basis of tree-ring dates when they were available; otherwise, the dating was inferred from stratigraphy, pottery, and archaeomagnetic samples. The earliest structures date to the A.D. 1060 to 1090 period, or Period I. Period II falls between 1140 and 1240 and includes structures interpreted as having been built before 1225 and abandoned by 1240. Period III structures are interpreted as having been constructed after 1225 and abandoned by 1260. Period IV includes structures built after 1250.

The changing frequency of four types of roof treatments is illustrated in figure 6.1. Period I includes one unburned pit structure with salvaged roof timbers and one in which roof treatment could not be inferred. In Period II, salvaging of timbers was the most common roof treatment, with five cases in which timbers were salvaged from unburned structures and two cases of salvaged timbers in subsequently burned structures. In Period II, there also were three cases of unburned structures where timbers were abandoned as de facto refuse.

In Period III, all pit structures and kivas are unburned structures from which timbers were salvaged (n = 6). Period IV displays a wide variety of structure abandonments. There were 18 cases in which timbers were abandoned as de facto refuse, including 15 cases in which entire roofs were burned and three in which unburned timbers were left behind. This period also has the largest number of burned structures with salvaged timbers (n = 9) and unburned structures from which timbers were salvaged (n = 9), for a total of 18 cases in which timbers were salvaged.

Interpreting Roof Treatment

The treatment of pit structure and kiva roofs can be evaluated in terms of the middle-range theory presented earlier. Timbers would be salvaged for future use when structures and the site were abandoned as part of a short-distance move to the next occupied site. Conversely, timbers would be left behind as de facto refuse when there was a long-distance move to the next occupied site.

In this model, the salvaging of timbers would occur in cases of gradual, planned abandonment with a short-distance move to the next site. Reuse of timbers from so many Sand Canyon locality structures strongly supports the inference that the locality continued to be occupied after these structures were abandoned. Salvaging of roof timbers was the most common roof treatment in all periods. This provides general evidence for relative continuity in the occupation of the Sand Canyon locality. The abandonment of timbers as de facto refuse occurred only three times in Periods I through III; each case was a small, earth-walled pit structure at Kenzie Dawn Hamlet. Perhaps these timbers were so small that they had little value for reuse.

The differing modes of abandonment suggest that timbers would likely be left behind as de facto refuse when abandonment was rapid and there was a long-distance move to the next occupied site. The Sand Canyon locality data conform to this model; timbers were left behind (that is, in

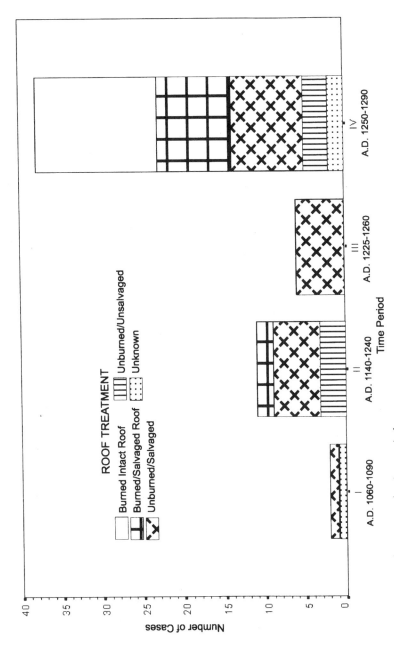

Figure 6.1 Roof treatments by time period.

structures with entirely burned roofs and in unburned structures where timbers were abandoned as de facto refuse) most often in structures occupied in the years just before the regional abandonment. There were three cases in which unburned timbers were abandoned in kivas at Sand Canyon Pueblo. Why were these timbers not salvaged? One possible interpretation is that these kivas were abandoned near the time of the regional abandonment, a time when many structures were being abandoned and few new ones were being built. Thus, there may have been a surplus of abandoned timber and relatively little demand for it. As a result, timbers may have been left in place.

The model helps us understand why timbers were salvaged or abandoned as de facto refuse, but it does not tell us why kiva roofs were burned. The traditional interpretation for entirely burned pit structure and kiva roofs is that an accidental event occurred—a spark from the hearth, for instance, accidentally caused the roof to burn. Wilshusen (1986) has demonstrated that the burning of pit structures was not random over time (that is, burned structures do not occur in similar proportions through time) or by type of structure (certain types of pit structures and kivas are more likely to have burned than others). He found a relationship between burned pit structures and interior features interpreted as having been used in ritual. Based on these associations, he argued that the burning of Pueblo I pit structures was intentional and that whether or not a structure was deliberately burned related in part to whether it had a ritual function.

Cameron's (1990) subsequent work questioned the interpretation that pit structure burning related to structure function, but her research supports the interpretation that burning was intentional and not an accidental event. Approximately half of the pit structures in her sample had burned roofs, a figure that may be inflated by a bias among archaeologists for the excavation of burned structures (Cameron 1990:33). She cites ethnographic examples in which intentional burning was associated with ritual abandonment.

Lightfoot (1994:43–48) interprets Duckfoot pit structures as having been intentionally burned during an abandonment ritual. The Duckfoot pit structures, along with most of the burned pit structures in the Dolores River valley (Schlanger and Wilshusen 1993; Wilshusen 1986), are cases in which the timing of the pit structure abandonment corresponded with an abandonment of the region and a long-distance move to the next occupied area. Thus, the burning of Sand Canyon locality kiva roofs may have been an abandonment ritual that occurred most often when structure abandonment coincided with abandonment of the region.

Abandonment ritual might also explain the cases in which pit structures and kivas were burned, but only after the large timbers had been salvaged for reuse. Salvaging of large timbers from these structures may have occurred because the locality remained occupied.[2]

The Period IV structures from which timbers were salvaged deserve discussion. The relatively large number of cases in which timbers were salvaged—from either burned or unburned structures—indicates that the decades before the regional abandonment were characterized by considerable household mobility. These may be structures that were built relatively late but were abandoned some years before the regional abandonment. The timbers from these structures might have been salvaged for use as firewood or for construction.

The abandoned kivas at Castle Rock Pueblo do not fit the pattern predicted by the general model of abandonment processes. The abandonment of this site is interpreted as having been associated with a battle in which almost 40 people died (Lightfoot and Kuckelman n.d.). The disarticulated remains of these individuals were found primarily in kiva fills. There are 16 kivas at the site, and 8 of these underwent testing sufficient to enable interpretation of the post-abandonment stratigraphy. Six of the tested kivas are interpreted as having been burned after their timbers were salvaged, another kiva had an unburned roof from which timbers were salvaged, and only one kiva had a completely burned roof. The dating of this site indicates that it was abandoned near the time of the regional abandonment. Given the timing of the site abandonment and the sudden conflict apparently associated with it, the question becomes, who salvaged the beams from these kivas and for what purpose?

SITE ABANDONMENT

To determine whether particular sites continued to be occupied after pit structures and kivas in them were abandoned, the density of artifacts in structure fills is examined next. This measure is similar to the Relative

Room Abandonment Measure (RRAM) used at Grasshopper and Chodistas Pueblos (Montgomery 1993; Reid 1973) to identify rooms that were abandoned relatively early in the pueblo's history versus rooms abandoned relatively late. The RRAM employs the distribution of pottery on floors and in fills and rests on the straightforward argument that rooms with few whole pots on their floors but large quantities of potsherds in the fill were abandoned early, and rooms with many whole pots on their floors and few potsherds in the fill were abandoned late.

This interpretation is in line with the general model of abandonment processes outlined earlier. The model predicts that usable pottery will be salvaged from rooms abandoned relatively early, when much of the site or surrounding area remains occupied. Conversely, usable pottery will be abandoned as de facto refuse in rooms abandoned late in the use of the site, when the distance traveled to the next occupied site is greater. With regard to artifact density in structure fills, rooms abandoned early in the occupation of a site are used for both formal middens and less formal, periodic trash deposition. On the other hand, there is little opportunity for trash deposition in rooms abandoned late.

The structures examined by the Sand Canyon Project Site Testing Program were not fully excavated, so it is impossible to evaluate the quantity of de facto refuse on floors. For the most part de facto refuse was absent in the excavated portions of the tested structures; the only complete vessels found were on a kiva floor at Castle Rock Pueblo. Although information on de facto refuse is limited, information about artifact density in structure fills remains a means of determining whether sites and communities continued to be occupied after those particular structures were abandoned.

The analysis that follows uses 28 pit structures and kivas sampled by the Sand Canyon Project Site Testing Program because excavation methods, particularly the use of screening, were consistent for all of them (Varien 1998). Artifact density was measured using pottery sherds and stone artifacts. Burned or unburned roof fall covered the floors of these structures; artifact density was calculated only for the fill above roof fall because roof fall might contain artifacts associated with the construction or use of the structures. Fill can be grouped into three general categories: cultural deposits, natural deposits, and mixed deposits. Culturally deposited strata include both household refuse (ash from hearths, artifacts, animal bones, botanical remains, etc.) and construction deposits (discarded construction materials from abandoned structures, mostly adobe and sandstone). Natural deposits include sediments transported by wind, water, or gravity. Mixed deposits are some combination of natural and cultural deposits.

Figure 6.2 shows box-and-whisker plots (Shennan 1988:45–46) summarizing the data for artifact density in cultural, natural, and mixed deposits. As expected, natural fill has the lowest artifact density, mixed fill has a higher artifact density, and three cases of cultural fill also exhibit high artifact densities.

The presence of cultural deposits in a particular structure fill is a clear indication that the site continued to be used after the structure was abandoned. Twenty-five percent of the pit structures examined in Cameron's (1990:32) study were trash filled, but trash was found in only three structures at two sites in the Sand Canyon locality. Both sites have more than one kiva, and the trash in the abandoned structures was probably deposited while the site continued to be occupied year-round by the inhabitants of the other kiva.[3]

Because culturally deposited strata were so rare, natural deposits and mixed deposits were examined in greater detail. The artifacts in both of these types of fills are too heavy to have been deposited by wind, so if they were deposited by natural processes, then water, gravity, or both must have been the agents. On all sites, pit structures and kivas are on nearly level ground located upslope from the middens, and in most cases they are on the highest portion of the site, so only the smallest artifacts could have been transported by water. The main source of naturally deposited artifacts in the pit structures and kivas would have been the roomblock to the north and the courtyard immediately surrounding the subterranean structure. Because the source area for naturally deposited artifacts is so limited, high artifact densities were not expected.

Natural deposits do have the lowest overall artifact densities, but there are two cases in the natural fill category that have artifact densities as high as those in cultural deposits. Both statistical outliers occur in kivas at Castle Rock Pueblo.[4] The higher artifact densities in these two structures indicate that they might have been deliberately filled, which might relate to unusual circumstances associated with the abandonment of Castle Rock Pueblo. When the two statistical outliers from Castle Rock Pueblo are removed,

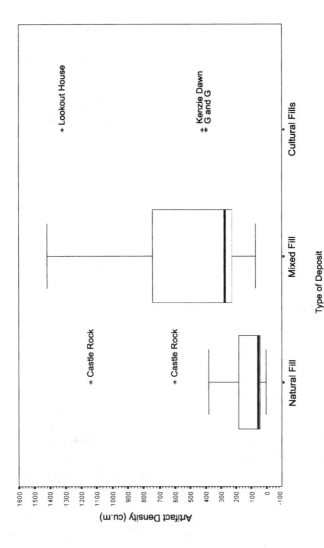

Figure 6.2 Box-and-whisker plots showing artifact density in fills of 28 pit structures and kivas sampled in the Sand Canyon locality. Each box shows upper and lower quartiles (the interquartile range, or the middle 50 percent of the distribution); the heavy bar represents the median. The lines emanating from each box—the "whiskers"—extend to the smallest and largest observations in a group that is less than one interquartile range from the end of the box. Asterisks mark outliers outside this range.

the mean artifact density from the remainder of the naturally deposited fills on all of the tested sites is 97 artifacts per cubic meter.

There are six additional cases of natural fill in which artifact density is well above the mean. Three cases are kivas at Castle Rock, and these may have been intentionally filled. The remaining three cases of high artifact density in natural fill are in the latest kivas occupied at two mesa-top sites: Kenzie Dawn Hamlet (Kuckelman 1998b) and Shorlene's Site (Varien 1998). These mesa-top sites are located on what are today some of the best agricultural soils in the locality, and because of their association with fertile soils these sites might have continued to be used as field houses after having been abandoned as permanent, year-round habitations.

This interpretation is supported by the five sites at which mixed fills occurred, in a total of 11 pit structures and kivas.[5] These structures have artifact densities ranging between 74 and 1,420 artifacts per cubic meter. It may be that the sediments in mixed deposits accumulated gradually, predominately by wind deposition, with the high artifact content due to the periodic discard of artifacts in abandoned structures (Kilby 1998). Four of the five sites with mixed fills are mesa-top habitations, and the mixed fill occurs in the latest kiva on each site. Again, the location of these sites on the fertile mesa-top soils suggests that they might have been used as field houses.

In sum, the examination of artifact density in abandoned pit structures and kivas identifies structures with unusually high artifact densities in strata that otherwise appear to be naturally deposited sediments. In the case of the kivas at Castle Rock, these may be structures that were deliberately filled after a warfare event that coincided with the end of occupation of that site. In other cases, higher artifact density occurs in kivas on mesa-top sites that were abandoned in the middle A.D. 1200s. The high artifact density is interpreted as the periodic deposition of refuse in these abandoned structures. The function of these sites in the larger settlement system probably changed, but their continued use argues for continuity in the occupation of the locality, indicating that community movement occurred at a frequency different from that of household movement.

COMMUNITY SEDENTISM AND MOBILITY IN
THE SAND CANYON LOCALITY

In the next step of the analysis, more than 1,500 tree-ring dates from 19 sites are examined to evaluate the length of time that three Sand Canyon locality communities occupied their sustaining locality. The total includes dates from the 13 tested sites and from the intensively excavated sites Sand Canyon Pueblo and Green Lizard. These sites provide the dates for the Sand Canyon and Castle Rock communities. In the Goodman Point community, dates come from the Mustoe Site and the Shields Complex (5MT3807), which were excavated by Gould (1982) and Colorado Mountain College (see Adler 1990:258–261 for a discussion of these excavations). Two additional sites in the Sand Canyon locality also have cutting dates: Gnatsville (5MT1786), located approximately 7 kilometers northwest of Sand Canyon Pueblo (Kent 1991b, 1992), and in Rock Canyon, approximately 4 kilometers northwest of Castle Rock, a small cliff dwelling where Deric O'Bryan collected a sample in the 1940s. For comparison, the exceptional tree-ring record for communities on Chapin and Wetherill Mesas in Mesa Verde National Park are also examined.

The analyses that follow use tree-ring dates differently from the way they are used in most traditional interpretations, in which the focus is on the dating of particular structures and individual sites. Instead, these data are used to determine how continuously trees were being harvested within the spatial confines of a number of particular communities and within the locality used by a few closely spaced communities (cf. Lipe 1995; Schlanger and Wilshusen 1993). Key to the interpretation is the idea that beams were salvaged from abandoned structures and reused in nearby, newly constructed buildings. Stratigraphic evidence from the Sand Canyon locality indicates that roof beams were often salvaged from abandoned structures in the Sand Canyon and Castle Rock communities, and there is ample tree-ring evidence that beam reuse was pervasive in both ancient and historic-period pueblos (Ahlstrom 1985:629; Ahlstrom, Dean, and Robinson 1991; Ferguson and Mills 1988; Robinson 1990). Thus, the dates from a particular building provide information not only on that structure but on earlier wood use as well, and examining all the dates from all sites in a particular community provides a means of evaluating the history of wood use in that community.

With regard to population movement, tree-ring dates are interpreted in the following manner. First, continuity in the occupation of the community is inferred when trees were harvested on a continual basis. Second, the abandonment of a locality and the relocation of a community to a new locality *may be* indicated by periods with no tree-ring dates. The second interpretation is tentative because it depends in part on having a representative sample of all tree-ring dates from a locality, something we do not yet have.

Interpreting Tree-Ring Data

Both cutting dates and noncutting dates are accurate and precise to the year (Ahlstrom 1985:30–37).[6] The precision and accuracy of tree-ring dating is not a problem, but the interpretation of both cutting and noncutting tree-ring dates is subject to error. Interpretations must link the "dated event," which in the case of cutting dates is the death of the tree, with the "target event," or the behavior that resulted in the wood's ending up in the archaeological context in which it was discovered (Dean 1978a). Typically the target event of interest to archaeologists is the construction of a particular structure. Archaeologists propose "bridging events," such as the cutting down of a tree, to link the dated event with the target event (Dean 1978a:226).

The target event in the analyses that follow is the harvesting of timber, or beam procurement. Bridging events for timber harvesting include cutting living trees and collecting dead wood, but most cutting dates probably reflect the harvesting of living trees rather than the collection of dead wood (Robinson 1967). Collecting dead wood probably does not significantly affect the sample of cutting dates because outside rings would erode from dead wood, producing noncutting dates (Ahlstrom 1985:57). In addition, Robinson (1967) argues that most trees harvested after about A.D. 600 were living, because the stone axes used to fell trees and shape logs are suitable for cutting living timber but not dead wood (see Haury 1935:103; Varien 1984). Thus the target event is usually the same as the dated event, the death of the tree (Ahlstrom 1985:43, 55).

Tree-ring dates are therefore an ideal means for examining the continuity of occupation of Sand Canyon locality communities, because of the precision and accuracy of tree-ring dating and the relatively straightforward bridging arguments that link the dated event and the target event. The following analyses focus only on cutting dates; I have examined the noncutting dates elsewhere (Varien 1997). Analysis of the noncutting dates suggests that communities continuously harvested timbers for even longer intervals than the periods documented by the analyses of cutting dates.[7]

The Sand Canyon Community

There are 1,022 dates from the Sand Canyon community, one of the three communities in the Sand Canyon locality. These include 296 cutting dates between A.D. 900 and 1300. Most of these dates come from Sand Canyon Pueblo (n = 274, 93 percent), with a smaller portion coming from eight other sites within 2 kilometers of Sand Canyon Pueblo. Figure 6.3 shows these cutting dates by 10-year intervals. These data indicate that trees were harvested continuously between 1190 and 1280, with a small earlier cluster between 1060 and 1090. The large, late cluster is a reflection of the fact that Sand Canyon Project excavations were biased toward sites dating to the 1180–1290 period (Lipe 1992). Therefore, this cluster of dates indicates that the *minimum* period of continuity for the Sand Canyon community was approximately 100 years, but it does not preclude the community's having had an even longer period of occupation. A longer history for the community is hinted at by a smaller cluster of dates in the late 1000s from the Pueblo II components at G and G Hamlet and Kenzie Dawn Hamlet, which were stratigraphically beneath the Pueblo III components at those two sites.

The Castle Rock Community

The next largest assemblage of dates comes from the three sites in the Castle Rock community, with 88 cutting dates present. There is a continuous distribution between A.D. 1200 and 1280, and a nearly continuous distribution between 1170 and 1280 (fig. 6.4). The similarity in dates between the Castle Rock and Sand Canyon communities indicates that the two were occupied contemporaneously rather than sequentially. Again, the minimum occupation span for the Castle Rock community is approximately 100 years.

Figure 6.3 Sand Canyon community tree-ring cutting dates between A.D. 900 and 1300.

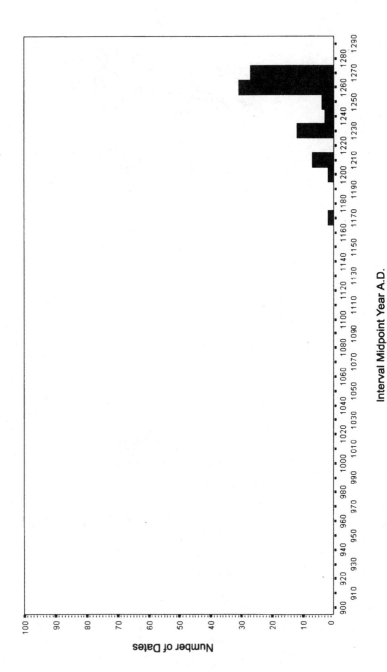

Interval Midpoint Year A.D.

Figure 6.4 Castle Rock community tree-ring cutting dates between A.D. 900 and 1300.

The Goodman Point Community

Two excavation projects in the Goodman Point community (Adler 1990:258–261; Gould 1982) produced 38 tree-ring dates, a sample too small to display in a histogram. There are 20 cutting dates, and they indicate that trees were harvested in the 1060s, in the 1129–1150 interval, in the 1170s, and in the 1212–1231 interval. While few in number, these dates suggest that the Goodman Point and Sand Canyon communities were occupied contemporaneously, at least during the 1060s and again in the early 1200s. These dates also hint at a centuries-long occupation history for the Goodman Point community.

SAND CANYON LOCALITY COMMUNITY
SEDENTISM

Figure 6.5 is a histogram of all Sand Canyon locality cutting dates (n = 408) between A.D. 900 and 1300. This histogram includes dates from Gnatsville and the cliff dwelling in Rock Canyon. The sample of cutting dates indicates that timber was harvested continuously within the locality throughout most of the 1200s and almost continuously between 1125 and 1275. There is a 30-year period with no cutting dates between 1095 and 1125, and then another cluster of dates between 1025 and 1095.

These cutting dates indicate relatively continuous harvesting of timber in the Sand Canyon locality beginning in the early 1000s and lasting through the late 1200s, when the region was abandoned. This is remarkable considering that the sample includes only 19 sites, that 67 percent of the cutting dates come from a single site, Sand Canyon Pueblo, and that this sample is biased toward late, Mesa Verde–phase sites.

CONTINUITY IN OCCUPATION ON CHAPIN
AND WETHERILL MESAS

To compare the Sand Canyon locality with other areas in the region, dates from Chapin and Wetherill Mesas in Mesa Verde National Park were analyzed. There are 566 cutting dates from 55 Chapin Mesa sites in an area of approximately 36 square kilometers extending from Far View House on

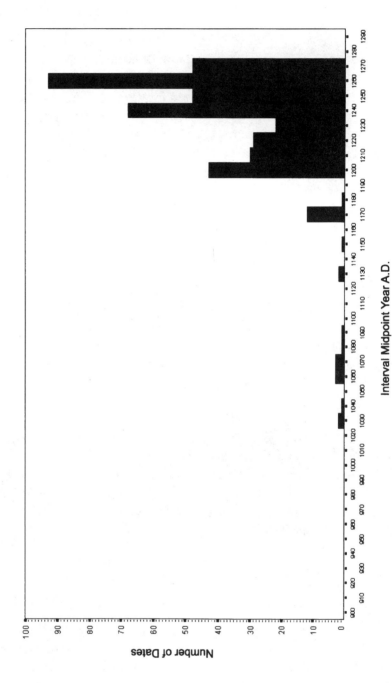

Figure 6.5 Sand Canyon locality tree-ring cutting dates between A.D. 900 and 1300.

the north to the head of Pool Canyon on the south. This area was probably used by several communities (Rohn 1977). Grouping these data into 20-year intervals shows a nearly continuous distribution of cutting dates from the late A.D. 500s to the 1280s (fig. 6.6). The majority of dates come from the late cliff dwellings—Spruce Tree House, Balcony House, Oak Tree House, and Square Tower House—which have recently been resampled, producing a strong peak in cutting dates in the 1180 to 1290 period. Looking at just the tree-ring dates from the 900 to 1300 period, there is a nearly continuous distribution of dates between 1010 and 1290, with almost no dates in the 900s, the late 1000s, and the early 1100s (fig. 6.7), which is similar to findings in the Sand Canyon locality.

For Wetherill Mesa, there are 184 cutting dates from 34 sites located within approximately 10 square kilometers. The distribution of these dates is similar to that of the Chapin Mesa dates, with a nearly continuous distribution except for the late A.D. 600s to early 700s and throughout most of the 900s (fig. 6.8). The period between 900 and 1300 shows a nearly continuous distribution from about 990 to 1290; however, as in the case of the Chapin Mesa dates, there are few Wetherill Mesa dates for the late 1000s to middle 1100s, and there is an additional prominent gap between 1155 and 1175.

SUMMARY: COMMUNITY SEDENTISM AND MOBILITY

These analyses support the interpretation that people in the Mesa Verde region occupied localities for extended periods of time and that communities moved less frequently than households. The analysis of roof treatments documents substantial salvaging of timber from abandoned pit structures and kivas in all periods, suggesting a general continuity in the occupation between the late A.D. 1000s and 1290. This analysis also shows how roof treatment changed during the period immediately before the regional abandonment—the occurrence of timbers as de facto refuse is largely limited to this period. Burned kivas probably indicate an abandonment ritual in some buildings.

The salvaging of timbers from pit structures and kivas before they were burned depended in part on the historical placement of the structures in

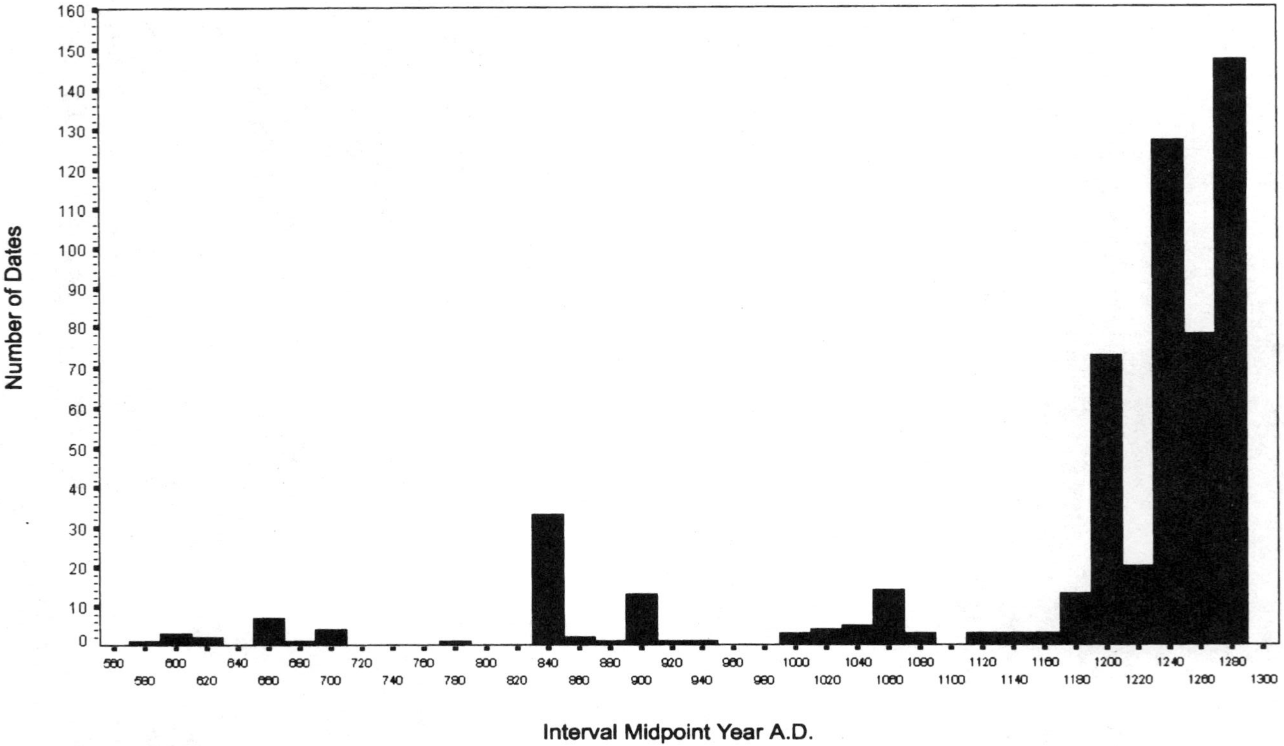

Figure 6.6 All Chapin Mesa tree-ring cutting dates.

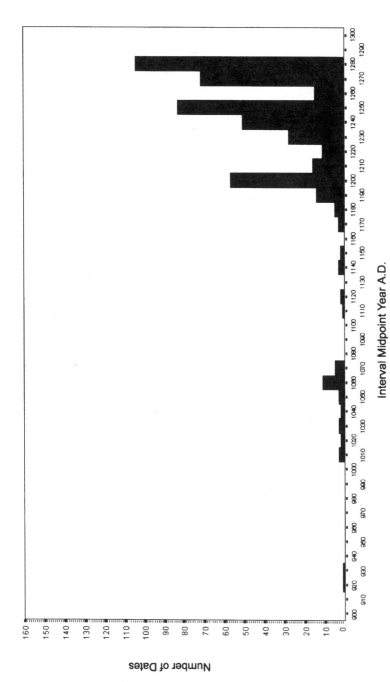

Figure 6.7 Chapin Mesa tree-ring cutting dates between A.D. 900 and 1300.

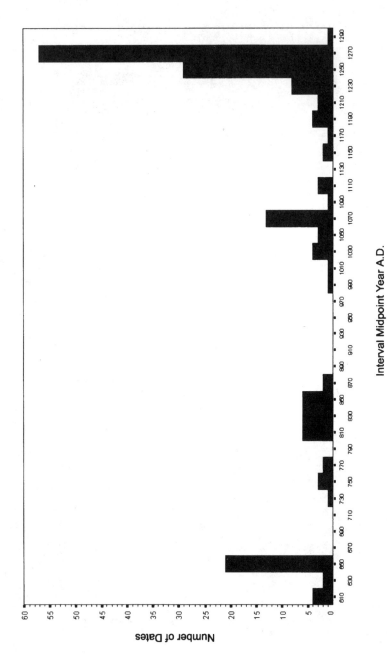

Figure 6.8 All Wetherill Mesa tree-ring cutting dates.

the larger settlement system: if a structure was abandoned before the regional abandonment, timbers were typically salvaged. Castle Rock Pueblo, however, does not conform well to this general model. It appears to have been abandoned because of a violent episode near the time of the regional abandonment, but the timbers from its kivas appear to have been salvaged, and some kivas may have been deliberately filled immediately following this episode.

Analysis of artifact density in pit structure and kiva fills indicates that many mesa-top habitations continued to be used after these particular structures were abandoned. It is possible that these sites continued to be used as field houses after they were abandoned as permanent habitations. Thus, artifact density in abandoned structures also supports the interpretation of continuity in occupation.

Finally, timber was harvested almost continuously throughout the A.D. 1200s in the Sand Canyon community, and similar patterns are present in the Castle Rock and Goodman Point communities. The tree-ring sample from the Sand Canyon locality is biased toward late sites, but there is evidence for periodic harvesting of timbers in the 1000s and 1100s as well. The tree-ring data indicate that these communities were fixed for at least a century, and they could have histories approaching 300 years. Comparative data from Chapin and Wetherill Mesas in Mesa Verde National Park support the interpretation of continuous or nearly continuous occupation of these localities for at least three centuries.

These data convincingly document the relative persistence of occupation in the Sand Canyon locality and on Chapin and Wetherill Mesas. But do they indicate continuity of occupation by a single community? The definition of community developed in this study emphasizes regular face-to-face interaction as determined by the copresence of individuals in time and space. The form and composition of the community cannot help changing over time (for example, with the deaths of particular individuals or with the relocation of particular households), but the continuous occupation of a particular space would produce interaction in the context of copresence that is consistent with what I term a community. The time span documented by the analyses indicates that these conditions were sustained for at least a century, between A.D. 1180 and 1280, and perhaps for as long as three centuries, between the late tenth century and the end of the thirteenth century.

It is possible to argue, given the current state of the data sets described earlier, that localities were repeatedly occupied, abandoned, and reoccupied between A.D. 950 and 1300 and that there was rotating use of localities by completely unrelated communities. I acknowledge this possibility but regard it as unlikely, at least for the Sand Canyon locality and those localities on Mesa Verde that I have examined. I believe the evidence indicates that localities had long and relatively continuous occupations.

Continuous interaction in the context of copresence results in systematized patterns of social relations, or, to use Giddens's (1984:17) terms, historically derived practices with the greatest time-space extension. These practices can be viewed as institutions. Evidence for the development of such institutions would support the inference that specific communities persisted over time. The next chapter examines sites interpreted as community centers, which provide evidence for the development of institutions and for the persistence of specific communities within the Mesa Verde region.

7

THE

SOCIAL

LANDSCAPE

IN

THE

MESA

VERDE

REGION

Up to this point I have reconstructed the frequency of household residential movement and community movement at the scale of the locality. I now turn to population movement at an even larger scale—the region (fig. 7.1)—in order to address a number of issues. First, I examine how the rugged terrain of the Mesa Verde region conditioned movement. Second, I describe the regional social landscape, as inferred from settlement patterns, and evaluate how competition for resources changed through time. Third, I assess the geographic scale of community movement within the region. Finally, I examine the frequency of movement between the Mesa Verde region and adjacent regions.

Three data sets are used in these analyses: (1) settlement pattern data that include every known community center in the Mesa Verde region dating between A.D. 950 and 1300; (2) the physiography of the Mesa Verde region, which displays dramatic ranges in terrain, from mountains and nearly level mesas to valleys and deeply incised canyons; and (3) every tree-ring date from the Mesa Verde region.

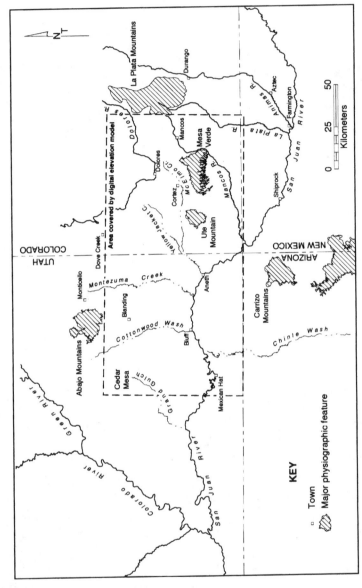

Figure 7.1 The greater Mesa Verde region showing the area analyzed in chapter 7. The area covered by the digital elevation model is shown in figure 7.2.

MESA VERDE–REGION COMMUNITY CENTERS

Community centers are dense concentrations of residential settlement, often accompanied by public architecture, that occur in the cores of the settlement clusters that compose communities. Data collection on community centers began with a conference at the Crow Canyon Archaeological Center in 1990.[1] The settlement data collected for this conference, or portions of these data, have been used in previous analyses of regional settlement (Adler 1990; Adler and Varien 1994; Kelley 1996; Lipe 1994, 1995; Neitzel 1994; Sherman 1995; Varien et al. 1996).

Crow Canyon researchers have continued data collection since the 1990 conference, in part through a community center survey program. This program produced aerial photographs and maps of several large sites, a chronological analysis of pottery, and interpretations of the large sites for nominations to the National Register of Historic Places. In addition to analyzing the sites included in the community center survey, Crow Canyon researchers have continued to visit and revisit the other community centers to verify their size and dating. In preparation for the analyses presented here, nine Mesa Verde–region archaeologists were given a copy of the database and asked to comment on sites in the portion of the Mesa Verde region where they work.[2] As a result, the database has grown since the initial inventory, and the documentation of each large site has been refined.

The database contains 134 large sites dating between A.D. 950 and 1300. The 50-room threshold established for the original database has been relaxed to include a few sites with fewer than 50 rooms if they have public architecture. Most community centers with fewer than 50 structures date before 1150 (n = 21); the only small community center that is later than this is Hovenweep Cajon Ruin, which dates to the late 1200s (Thompson 1993).

Two facets of the sites in the data set require some discussion: their dating and their size. The evidence indicates that the community centers had longer occupation spans than did the smaller sites examined in the previous chapters, and the community centers were therefore placed into longer time periods. Centers were assigned to one of four time periods: Period 1 is A.D. 950 to 1050, Period 2 is 1051 to 1150, Period 3 is 1151 to

1225, and Period 4 is 1226 to 1290. Temporal assignments were based on tree-ring dates when available (32 sites; 24 percent). When tree-ring dates were absent, pottery, architecture, and settlement patterns were used to date sites.

Tree-ring dated community centers were used as an independent control to establish the architectural, settlement pattern, and pottery attributes believed to be temporally sensitive. Period 2 community centers include great-house-like architecture (compact, multistoried buildings), typically situated on prominent locations on the mesa tops. The pottery assemblages at Period 2 centers include Mancos Black-on-white as the most common decorated white ware and Mancos Corrugated as the most common gray ware. Period 3 community centers are characterized by clusters of many roomblocks, again located on the mesa tops. McElmo and Mesa Verde Black-on-white are the most common decorated white wares, occurring in roughly equal proportions, and Dolores Corrugated is the most common gray ware. Finally, aggregated villages located in canyon settings characterize Period 4 community centers. At these Period 4 villages, Mesa Verde Black-on-white is the most common decorated white ware, and Mesa Verde Corrugated is the most common gray ware. Pottery analyses range from detailed studies at a few sites where attribute-based seriations were conducted (Ortman 1995) to assessments of which chronologically sensitive traditional types were most common in the surface assemblages.

Community centers were typically assigned to only one period. The only exceptions were sites at which there were spatially discrete buildings with more than 50 rooms that dated to multiple time periods. Only eight large sites met these criteria.[3] Treating most centers as single-component sites is considered a conservative approach because pottery, and sometimes tree-ring dating, indicates that most large sites were occupied in more than one period.[4] By focusing only on communities with large sites, and by assigning these large-site communities to only one period, the analyses that follow do not "overfill" the Mesa Verde–region social landscape.

The precision of the size estimates varies according to data collection methods and site preservation. Some large sites were mapped with surveying instruments, others were sketch-mapped, and still others have size estimates based on information available in archival records or on personal observations. Most large sites have relatively clear surface expressions, allowing us to estimate the area of rubble and the number of kiva depressions. There are probably few or no sites with more than 200 structures that remain unknown. There may, however, be several smaller community centers—especially those of between 50 and 100 rooms—that have yet to be included.

The community centers used in the analyses that follow are the largest and longest-lived sites in the Mesa Verde region. Surveys in southwestern Colorado and southeastern Utah have also recorded tens of thousands of small sites with shorter occupations that date between A.D. 900 and 1300. Surveys indicate that the large community centers are typically surrounded by clusters of smaller residential sites (Adler 1990; Fetterman and Honeycutt 1987; Neily 1983; Rohn 1977). Even in the final period of Mesa Verde–region occupation, when settlement patterns were most aggregated, there were a few small residential sites in the areas surrounding the large villages (Varien 1998).

The relationship between community centers and the surrounding smaller sites is evaluated by comparing the locations of the community centers in a particular time period with the location of every other site with a tree-ring cutting date from the same time period. In general, the small, tree-ring-dated sites are spatially associated with larger community centers. But there are some areas in which small sites are not associated with a larger center, indicating that there were probably some communities composed entirely of small sites. In addition, not all small sites occur in well-bounded clusters. Thus, the model that follows, in which a community consists of a community center and an associated cluster of small sites, is only one settlement configuration present in the Mesa Verde region.

The community centers examined in this analysis are associated with some of the most persistent communities in the Mesa Verde region, and as such may have been especially important nodes in the regional landscape. A detailed analysis of the use of individual centers is beyond the scope of this study, but previous research supports the interpretation that these sites were particularly important as ritual and economic centers (Adler 1990, 1994; Bradley 1988, 1993; Driver 1995; Martin 1936; Varien et al. 1996). Thus, the community centers analyzed here represent only one portion of the regional settlement system, but they were a crucial element of the Mesa Verde–region social landscape.

THE CHANGING FACE OF THE MESA
VERDE—REGION COMMUNITY

Crow Canyon researchers have summarized important changes in the settlement patterns of Mesa Verde–region communities between A.D. 950 and
1300, including data on the population size and spatial scale of these
communities (Adler 1990; Adler and Varien 1994; Lipe 1992; Varien et al.
1996). Their model, which builds on the work of many Mesa Verde–region
archaeologists (Eddy 1977; Eddy, Kane, and Nickens 1984; Fetterman and
Honeycutt 1987; Neily 1983; Rohn 1977), draws on a case study of community
organization in the Sand Canyon locality (Lipe 1992) and relies on cross-
cultural research on community organization (Adler 1990).

In discussing these settlement patterns, I emphasize modal tendencies.
These patterns have been documented by every intensive survey conducted
in the Mesa Verde region (Adler 1990; Fetterman and Honeycutt 1987;
Greubel 1991; Hayes 1964; Neily 1983; Rohn 1977), and similar patterns have
been reported elsewhere on the Colorado Plateau (e.g., Duff 1994; Fowler
and Stein 1992; Fowler, Stein, and Anyon 1987; Kintigh 1985, 1996; LeBlanc
1978). These robust patterns provide the context for the analysis of community centers that follows.

Settlement Organization

Previous studies of community organization in the Mesa Verde region
relied almost exclusively on the clustering of residential settlements to define
community boundaries. Following Linton (1936) and Murdock (1949),
communities were seen as local groups for whom the spatial proximity of
households allowed individual community members to have regular face-
to-face contact. These studies reveal an important aspect of Mesa Verde–region settlement patterns: residential sites are clustered at a number of levels,
and different researchers have used various levels of clustering to define
community boundaries (cf. Adler and Varien 1994; Dykeman and Langenfeld 1987; Eddy 1977; Fetterman and Honeycutt 1987; Neily 1983; Rohn 1977;
see also Lipe 1994 for a discussion of multicommunity clustering).

Which level of settlement clustering represents a community? Adler's
cross-cultural research helps answer this question. He found that the sizes

of communities in politically nonstratified societies are typically below 1,500 people (Adler and Varien 1994). Other research on this issue places the upper limit somewhat higher, between 2,000 and 2,500 inhabitants (Forge 1972; Kosse 1990, 1992; Lekson 1984, 1988). Adler (Adler 1989; Adler and Wilshusen 1990) also found that public architecture was used by groups larger than households for ritual and other types of activities, and that public buildings used by entire communities had the largest floor areas and the highest degree of specialized use of any buildings in nonstratified societies. Adler (1990, 1996b) also examined the role of communities in the context of larger regional systems, finding that communities were critical in the perpetuation of access to resources by community members. Finally, Adler's cross-cultural research documented that ethnographic communities exhibit a wide range of settlement patterns, from widely dispersed to tightly aggregated.

Drawing on this body of cross-cultural research, Adler and Varien (1994) combined the spatial clustering of residential sites and the presence of public architecture to identify community boundaries. On the basis of these criteria, they identified two communities in the upper Sand Canyon locality—the Sand Canyon and Goodman Point communities—which, despite changing settlement patterns, could be recognized throughout the A.D. 1000 to 1300 period. This model, in which communities consist of a community center and an associated cluster of residential settlement, is applied in the analyses that follow.

Period 1 Communities: A.D. 950 to 1050

The A.D. 900s remain the least understood century in the Puebloan culture history of the Mesa Verde region. There is a growing consensus, however, that there was a significant abandonment or depopulation of the central Mesa Verde region sometime between 880 and 1000 (Schlanger and Wilshusen 1993; Varien 1994, 1997; Wilshusen and Schlanger 1993). It also appears that Cedar Mesa in the western Mesa Verde region was largely abandoned during this period (Matson, Lipe, and Haase 1988:247). The timing of both the migration out of the Mesa Verde region and its subsequent resettlement is an important problem for future research, but currently it appears that migration out of the central Mesa Verde region began in the late 800s, with resettlement after 950. This migration did not result in the complete abandonment of the region, but a substantial depopulation did occur.[5]

In the Sand Canyon locality in Period 1 (A.D. 950–1050), population density was low, settlement was dispersed, and residential sites each consisted of a small roomblock with a single pit structure or kiva; the average size for habitation sites is six rooms (Adler 1990:232). The recurring association of a pit structure or kiva with a roomblock and a trash area is representative of Prudden's (1903) "unit type pueblo" (see also Lipe 1989:55), and each kiva unit is interpreted as the residence of a single household.

Settlement clusters that form both the Sand Canyon and Goodman Point communities can be recognized in this period (Adler and Varien 1994:89). Residential sites cluster within each community, and the density of habitations declines noticeably in the area between the two clusters (Adler 1990:244–252, 1992:18; Adler and Varien 1994:89). Using the area of sparser settlement as the boundary between these two communities, each settlement cluster has a radius of approximately 2 kilometers (Adler and Varien 1994:86). Period 1 residential architecture consisted of earthen buildings, and a reasonable estimate for the use-life of an earthen residential site is 20 years. Using this use-life estimate, the average momentary population in the entire upper Sand Canyon survey area was between 70 and 160 people (Adler 1990:232, 1992:13), with each community having been between 35 and 80 people.[6]

In the Sand Canyon community, the Period 1 small residential sites cluster around a great kiva (Adler 1990). There is no known public architecture in the Goodman Point community; however, public architecture in this period is extremely rare. As discussed in the analyses that follow, the only other Period 1 great kiva is associated with a settlement cluster along the Mancos River.

Period 2 Communities: A.D. 1051 to 1150

Communities remained dispersed and residential sites consistently small between A.D. 1051 and 1150. Sand Canyon locality habitation sites averaged eight rooms (Adler 1990:232). Dispersed settlement of small sites is documented throughout the Mesa Verde region, including Cedar Mesa, where occupation resumed in Period 2 (Matson, Lipe, and Haase 1988). Indeed, the pattern of dispersed settlement has been documented throughout the northern Southwest (Lipe 1978:370). But, as Lekson (1991:52) has pointed out, it is a misconception to think of Pueblo II settlement patterns as evenly dispersed. Instead, these small residences form larger clusters, with relatively empty areas between clusters.

Small residential sites in Period 2 typically cluster around a larger site. The settlement clusters represent a pattern that Lekson (1991) aptly described as many "small bumps" clustered around a "big bump," or great house. He argued that the small site–big site clusters represented communities, and he used the geographic distribution of these communities to map the extent of the Chacoan regional system.

A few Mesa Verde–region sites are consistently labeled Chacoan great houses (Judge 1991:17; Marshall et al. 1979; Powers, Gillespie, and Lekson 1983).[7] The large-site reconnaissance undertaken by Crow Canyon researchers has identified 36 community centers dating to Period 2; few of them, however, display all the attributes of Chacoan great houses. Lekson (1991:36) has commented on the wide variation present in great-house architecture, arguing that the only consistent attribute is that they are large relative to surrounding contemporaneous sites. Because there are no excavation data from most of these sites, the relative difference in size is the only attribute shared by all the Mesa Verde–region community centers in Period 2. Little is known about the relationship between these centers and the smaller sites, and less is known about the relationship between the Mesa Verde–region communities and Chaco Canyon. For the analyses that follow, it is enough to know that these centers are consistently associated with smaller residential sites.

The Sand Canyon and Goodman Point communities continue as distinct settlement clusters in Period 2. The Sand Canyon community contains a great house, Casa Negra. There may be a Period 2 great house and great kiva near the center of the Goodman Point community, but excavation is needed to determine whether this is the case. There is also an ancient road running between Casa Negra and the center of the Goodman Point community, where the possible great house and great kiva are located (Adler 1994:98). The geographic scale of these communities remains the same, but population grows to about 125 persons in each community (Adler 1990:232, 1992:13).

Period 3 Communities: A.D. 1151 to 1225

In the Sand Canyon locality, the main change in settlement pattern during Period 3 is an increase in settlement clustering (Adler 1990:264–270). Two types of clustering are present: (1) household clustering, in which increasing numbers of households aggregate into a single roomblock with an associated kiva or kivas; and (2) settlement clustering, in which several of these individual roomblock-kiva complexes are grouped together, often much less than 100 meters apart. Adler (1990:267) labeled these tightly clustered sites "multiroomblock settlements." This trend toward larger and more closely spaced residences holds true for only some sites; small, relatively isolated habitations are still present during this period. The average number of rooms at habitation sites in Period 3 increases to 13, but the standard deviation is 10 rooms as a result of the disparity in site size (Adler 1990:267; Adler and Varien 1994:85).[8]

Forty-four large sites are interpreted as community centers for Period 3. All are multiroomblock sites containing more than 50 rooms. Considerable variation exists among multiroomblock complexes; some contain one building that is larger than the other buildings in the complex.[9] The larger buildings may be analogous to what have been called post-Chacoan great houses in the Zuni region (Fowler and Stein 1992; Kintigh 1994, 1996; Kintigh, Howell, and Duff 1996). Size differentiation among the roomblocks is less pronounced at other multiroomblock centers. All multiroomblock centers are accompanied by a cluster of smaller residential sites. Thus, the small bump–big bump settlement pattern of Period 2 continues in a modified form in Period 3.

In the Sand Canyon locality, the geographic scale of the settlement clusters composing the core of the Sand Canyon and Goodman Point communities remains approximately the same. Population growth continues, and estimates for the size of each community range between 175 and 350 people (Adler 1990:232, 1992:13).

Period 4 Communities: A.D. 1226 to 1290

Two dramatic changes in settlement patterns took place during Period 4. First, the location of most residential sites changed. In previous periods, most residential sites were located on mesa tops where they were associated with deep, aeolian soils. In contrast, residential sites in Period 4 were predominantly in or near canyon environments. Second, large, tightly aggregated villages were common in this period, and the majority of the members of each community appear to have been living in these aggregated villages. These changes are documented through survey and testing in the Sand Canyon locality (Adler 1990, 1992; Varien 1998; Varien, Kuckelman, and Kleidon 1992) and by every other survey in the central Mesa Verde region.

In the upper Sand Canyon survey area, settlement aggregated into two large villages: Sand Canyon Pueblo and Goodman Point Pueblo. These two large sites exhibit features shared by many of the other large villages of this period: they are completely or partially surrounded by a low enclosing wall; they are bisected by a drainage; they surround or are adjacent to a spring; and they contain public architecture. Each village has more than 400 total structures, and each may have housed between 225 and 400 individuals.

The dramatic changes in settlement pattern that characterize this period make large sites particularly easy to identify. Fifty-nine Period 4 villages have been recorded throughout the Mesa Verde region. On Mesa Verde proper, the larger sites are the cliff dwellings for which Mesa Verde National Park is famous, although there are hundreds of smaller cliff dwellings on Mesa Verde as well. Beyond Mesa Verde, large sites occur in many locations; most common are villages in which some of the structures are on the canyon rim and the remainder are scattered on the talus slope below the rim. Architectural differentiation is present in most of these large sites, with some buildings being larger and more substantial than others. The big bump–small bump settlement pattern of previous periods is still present, albeit within a tightly aggregated site layout.

THE MESA VERDE–REGION SOCIAL LANDSCAPE

Describing the social landscape is critical to evaluating the factors that affected mobility strategies. If resource depletion stimulated mobility, there must have been an adequate amount of undepleted, unclaimed territory to which groups could move once they depleted their local resources. There must also have been adequate time for resources to regenerate in depleted localities before they were reoccupied. The geographic scale of community movement is particularly important in evaluating whether or not environmental deterioration stimulated population movement; groups would have needed to move far enough to encounter different environmental conditions if environmental change caused population movement. Finally, regional population density affects competition for resources and intensification of subsistence economies, which are important social factors conditioning mobility.

I begin by describing the procedures used in the geographic information systems (GIS) analyses. Next, cross-cultural research on population movement is summarized. Finally, the analyses of the Mesa Verde–region community centers are presented. Several use the physiography of the Mesa Verde region as data, which is important for three reasons. First, it takes into consideration how the rugged terrain of the Mesa Verde region shaped community interaction and boundaries. Second, it provides a realistic assessment of the sizes of community catchments and the distances between communities that were occupied during the same period. Finally, it permits a more realistic assessment of the scale of community movement between periods.

The GIS Analyses

Site distributions have traditionally been analyzed in two-dimensional space—for example, by constructing Thiessen polygons around sites. Thiessen polygons might be appropriate for relatively flat and featureless terrain, but the extremely rugged physiography of the Mesa Verde region renders two-dimensional analysis problematic. Physiography is incorporated into the analyses of the Mesa Verde–region social landscape by constructing cost-based polygons and cost-based catchment areas around each community center and by analyzing the geographic scale of population movement in cost-equivalent distance.

Each step of the GIS analysis has been detailed elsewhere (Varien 1997: Appendix B), and only a general outline is provided here. Calculating distance that incorporates the frictional effect of the rugged terrain was accomplished using a digital elevation model (DEM) of the Mesa Verde region. A DEM is an electronic, raster-based elevation map in which elevation data are recorded for each 30-by-30 meter pixel. The DEM for the study area measured approximately 167 kilometers east-west and 84 kilometers north-south (approximately 100 by 50 miles), or 14,022 square kilometers (5,000 square miles). Figure 7.2 illustrates this DEM using a gray-scale palette in which increasing lightness of shading indicates higher elevation.

The next step was the creation of a friction surface, which evaluates how variable terrain affects the cost of moving across that terrain on foot. The formula for calculating this friction surface was taken from Hill (1995, n.d.), and it measures the energy it takes to walk across variable terrain. The friction surface contains a value for the energy required to walk across each pixel of the study area.

The next step was creating cost surfaces for each period, obtained by overlaying community centers from Periods 1 through 4 on the friction surface. The cost surface for each period measures the energy required to walk out from each community center until a pixel that is closer to a neighboring center is reached. The cost surface for each period was used to construct the cost-based polygons and catchment areas associated with each community center and to document the geographic scale of community movement by identifying the "cost-equivalent distance" between a community center in one time period and its nearest neighbor in the subsequent time period.

The concept "cost-equivalent distance" accounts for the fact that crossing a deep, 1-kilometer-wide canyon, for example, consumes much more energy than does walking 1 kilometer across nearly level terrain. The friction surface was used to calculate cost-equivalent distance by taking into account the energy used in walking across the region's rugged terrain. A cost-equivalent kilometer was calculated on the basis of the energy required to travel 1 kilometer on a 2-percent grade; this energy value was used as the standard for 1 cost-equivalent kilometer. Thus, a cost-equivalent kilometer on terrain greater than a 2-percent grade is shorter than an actual kilometer. Incorporating cost-equivalent distance is important because the ease or difficulty of walking between centers would have had a direct effect on social interaction within and between centers and on the sizes of the catchment areas surrounding the centers.[10]

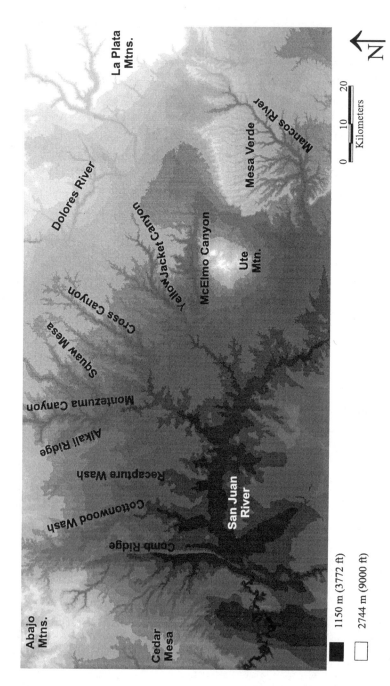

Figure 7.2 Digital elevation model of the study area.

Cross-Cultural Data on Population Movement

Many studies have examined the relationship between resource exploitation and the distance traveled to acquire those resources (Arnold 1985:32; Chisholm 1970:131; Roper 1979:120). A basic assumption of these studies is that energy expenditure is related to the distance to the resource. Cross-cultural analyses establish that the cost of travel is indeed an important consideration when people walk to either natural or social resources. The speed of foot travel has been measured to be between 3 and 5 kilometers per hour (Arnold 1985:34; Drennan 1984; Stone 1991b:347). Using these figures, the Sand Canyon and Goodman Point settlement clusters, each of which has a radius of roughly 2 kilometers, could have been traversed in less than an hour. A 2-kilometer radius therefore conforms to the assumption that communities are places where community members engage in regular, face-to-face interaction.

Cross-cultural studies of agricultural communities support the interpretation that a 2-kilometer radius is a reasonable estimate for the size of the area most regularly used and the area of most intensive cultivation. Arnold (1985:34) and Stone (1991b, 1992) have summarized these studies, including Chisholm's *Rural Settlement and Land Use* (1970), perhaps the most influential study of movement among agriculturalists. Chisholm focused on the distances farmers walked to fields from a nucleated settlement, concluding that distances of less than 1 kilometer were commonly traversed and that these short-distance trips had little effect on farmers' decisions about movement. Farmers did, however, try to limit trips to less than 2 kilometers, and 3 to 4 kilometers was an upper threshold for how far farmers would walk from their residence to an intensively cultivated field. Any cultivation beyond this distance required modification of the settlement system (e.g., the adoption of field houses).

Stone (1991b) addressed this question by examining the movement of Kofyar farmers. His study not only quantified movement more rigorously than did Chisholm's classic study but also measured the movement of farmers living in dispersed, as opposed to nucleated, communities. Whereas Chisholm was concerned with the distances farmers walked from residence to field, Stone measured the distances farmers traveled to be a part of cooperative agricultural work groups. Despite differences in settlement pattern and the motivation for movement, Stone documented distance thresholds similar to those reported by Chisholm. Stone found that Kofyar farmers typically limited travel to 700 meters when taking part in agricultural work groups. Travel beyond 700 meters was less frequent, and 2 kilometers was an effective upper limit on how far people would go in order to participate in agricultural work parties (Stone 1991b:347, 1992:166). Stone's research therefore provides general support for a 2-kilometer radius as a range within which the most *intensive* cultivation occurs and the area of regular interaction among community members.

Finally, an archaeological case from the Mesa Verde region supports the interpretation that a 2-kilometer radius is an appropriately sized catchment for the zone of most intensive cultivation. Kohler and others (1986) examined the distance between habitations and fields for the settlements studied by the Dolores Archaeological Program. They concluded that the maximum one-way distance between habitations and fields, averaged for all households, was 1.7 kilometers in the A.D. 880–920 period (Kohler et al. 1986:536). Distances were greatest during the period when people were living in aggregated villages and traveling farthest to fields. In other periods, when settlement was more dispersed, the distance from habitations to fields was less, with a minimum average one-way distance of 0.24 kilometer in the A.D. 600–720 period.

Chisholm's study indicates that catchment areas for more extensive agriculture can exceed this 2-kilometer threshold for intensive cultivation. Along these lines, Arnold (1985:34) summarizes studies from around the world and reports that the fields of subsistence agriculturalists are regularly exploited when they are within a 3- to 5-kilometer radius from a residence, and a distance of 7 to 8 kilometers is the maximum distance that people regularly travel to fields. Puebloan agricultural catchments may have been on the upper end of this range. Bradfield (1971:21) acknowledges that Hopi farmers traveled great distances to fields in the historic period but argues that traveling long distances to fields was feasible only after the introduction of burros. He presents an argument that the distance to fields would have been limited to approximately 7 kilometers before the introduction of the burro.

Arnold (1985:51–56) reports similar-sized catchments for resource procurement for pottery manufacture. Using cross-cultural data, he found that 7 kilometers was an upper limit for the distance traveled to obtain raw clay, 6 to 9 kilometers for obtaining temper, and 10 kilometers for

obtaining glaze, slip, and paint resources. Even among highly mobile foragers, there are limits to the distance traveled on foot to obtain resources on
a regular basis. Lee (1969:61), for example, reports that !Kung hunter-
gatherers regularly travel no more than 10 kilometers from a residential
camp to obtain resources.

A final consideration is that the large sites and public architecture
analyzed here may represent centers of religious and economic activity and
may have been visited by people from more distant locations. A day's travel
on foot can be estimated at 36 kilometers (Drennan 1984; Wilcox 1996).
Traveling to and from one of these centers in a day would therefore be
limited to an area with a cost-equivalent radius of 18 kilometers, the area
from which the center could be visited on a relatively regular basis.

Distance and travel time clearly condition resource use and interaction.
Three areas provide a useful heuristic means of evaluating the distribution
of community centers. The area of most intensive cultivation and regular
interaction among community members is approximated by a 2-kilometer
cost-equivalent radius (13 square kilometers on perfectly flat terrain). A 7-
kilometer cost-equivalent radius (154 square kilometers on flat terrain)
approximates an area in which wild food and nonfood resources were
gathered on a regular basis and an area of more extensive agriculture.
Finally, a catchment in which people could have traveled to and from a
center in one day's walk is estimated by an 18-kilometer radius (1,018 square
kilometers on flat terrain).

Community Centers and Polygons

In this study, polygons are constructed around community centers straight-
forwardly: each polygon surrounds a particular community center and
encloses the land that is closer to this community center than to any other.
In defining the boundaries between polygons, distance is measured in
terms of cost-equivalence. In the analyses that follow, the centers are listed
beginning with those in the southeast and moving to the west, and the areas
within polygons are measured in square kilometers without considering the
cost-equivalent distance.

There are 36 community centers in Period 2 (table 7.1). Figure 7.3
illustrates how the polygon boundaries around these centers are shaped by
major topographic features—something that becomes more pronounced in

Table 7.1 Period 2 Community Centers and Associated Polygons

MAP NO.	SITE	POLYGON AREA (KM²)	COMPLETELY BOUNDED? (YES/NO)
1	Morris 20	709.5	N
2	O'Bryan's Weber Canyon Pueblo	399.7	N
3	O'Bryan's Prater Canyon Pueblo	98.7	Y
4	Far View House	149.8	Y
5	Mouth of Navajo Canyon great house	363.7	N
6	Red Pottery Mound	856.5	N
7	Yucca House	375.0	Y
8	Wallace Ruin	115.8	Y
9	Haynie Ruin	71.1	Y
10	Ida Jean Ruin	39.6	Y
11	Emerson Ruin	481.7	N
12	Reservoir Ruin	708.1	N
13	Escalante Ruin	333.1	N
14	Hartman Draw	103.8	Y
15	Mitchell Springs	164.6	Y
16	Yellow Jacket Pueblo	352.9	N
17	Goodman Point great house	107.0	Y
18	Casa Negra	375.4	Y
19	Uncle Albert Porter	170.6	Y
20	Carvell Ruin	320.6	N
21	Ansel Hall	84.1	Y
22	North Lowry great house	94.6	Y
23	Lowry Pueblo	68.5	Y
24	Casa de Valle	40.6	Y
25	Upper Squaw Mesa Village	419.4	Y
26	Carhart Ruin	186.1	N
27	Hedley West Hill Ruin	196.6	Y
28	Three-Kiva Ruin	505.4	Y
29	Montezuma Village I	212.4	N
30	Jackson's Montezuma Creek Bench Site #1	1,633.5	N
31	Moki Island	324.4	N
32	Edge of the Cedars	224.0	N
33	Bluff Cemetery	1,344.5	N
34	Cottonwood Falls	472.0	N
35	Arch Canyon	539.3	N
36	Et al. Ruin	1,364.2	N

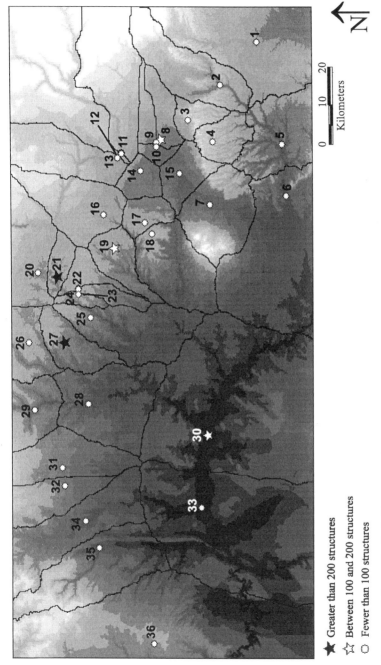

Figure 7.3 Polygons for Period 2 community centers.

★ Greater than 200 structures
☆ Between 100 and 200 structures
○ Fewer than 100 structures

0   10   20
Kilometers

subsequent periods. Polygon boundaries in the western portion of the region are shaped by Comb Ridge, which in places rises 1,000 feet (305 meters) above Comb Wash. Between Comb Ridge and McElmo Creek, polygon boundaries are shaped by a series of deeply incised canyons. South of McElmo Creek, Ute Mountain affects the boundaries of the surrounding community centers, and the precipitous north rim of Mesa Verde (approximately 1,700 feet [520 meters] high) also contributes to the shape of polygon boundaries.

The same major physiographic features shape polygon boundaries for the 44 community centers identified for Period 3 (table 7.2, fig. 7.4), and this effect is even more pronounced for the 59 community centers in Period 4 (table 7.3, fig. 7.5). In Period 4, the north rim of Mesa Verde defines polygon boundaries for all of the communities in Mesa Verde National Park. Sleeping Ute Mountain separates the community centers south of it (Moqui Spring Pueblo and Cowboy Wash) from those to the north. Many of the polygon boundaries between McElmo Creek and Squaw Mesa follow the northeast-to-southwest-trending canyons in this area, and farther west, in southeastern Utah, polygon boundaries are shaped by the north-south-trending canyons in that area. Finally, the polygon boundary on the west end of the study area runs along Comb Ridge. These polygons show how major physiographic features impede pedestrian movement, a factor that presumably played a role in shaping the social landscape and interaction in the Mesa Verde region.

The polygons also illustrate how settlement became more clustered through time. Community centers are relatively evenly spaced in Period 2 but become more clustered in Period 3,[11] and clustering is even more pronounced in Period 4.[12] This results in a decrease in the sizes of polygons in the central Mesa Verde region through time. Table 7.4 summarizes the data on polygon size. The mean size of *all* polygons decreases through time because the number of polygons increases, but the *range* of polygon size increases through time. This pattern is highlighted by contrasting the polygons defined entirely by surrounding community centers with those that have boundaries defined by the edge of the study. The percentage of polygons with boundaries defined by other sites increases steadily through time, and the sizes of these polygons decrease substantially through time. On the other hand, polygons for which one or more boundaries are defined by the edge of the study area increase in size through time.

These data illustrate two general characteristics of the changing social

Table 7.2 Period 3 Community Centers and Associated Polygons

MAP NO.	SITE	POLYGON AREA (KM²)	COMPLETELY BOUNDED? (YES/NO)
1	Lion House	977.2	N
2	Hoy House	54.5	Y
3	Battleship Rock cluster	63.7	Y
4	Kiva Point	408.9	N
5	Site 34	37.5	Y
6	Far View House	93.8	Y
7	Mitchell Springs	1,162.9	N
8	Mud Springs	641.8	N
9	Yellow Jacket Pueblo	1,328.0	N
10	Goodman Point Great Kiva	38.7	Y
11	Shields Pueblo	79.2	Y
12	Griffey Ruin	40.0	Y
13	Casa Negra	179.6	Y
14	Rich's Ruin	25.2	Y
15	Bass complex	42.4	Y
16	Lancaster/Pharo Ruin	100.2	Y
17	Carvell Ruin	344.0	N
18	Herren Farms	31.6	Y
19	Head of Hovenweep Mesa-Top Ruin	33.8	Y
20	Finley Farm/Charnel House/Ray Ruin complex	23.9	Y
21	Pigg Site	13.9	Y
22	Mockingbird Mesa-Top Ruin	226.8	Y
23	Kristie's Ruin	8.8	Y
24	Carol's Ruin	15.2	Y
25	Kearns Site	140.0	Y
26	Lower Cow Canyon Ruin	31.6	Y
27	Brewer Pueblo	83.2	Y
28	Lower Squaw Mesa Village	123.6	Y
29	Hedley Middle Ruin	323.1	N
30	Nancy Patterson Pueblo	378.7	Y
31	Montezuma Village I	296.9	N
32	Tsitah Wash complex	995.1	N
33	Aneth Archaeological District	285.3	N

continued on next page

MAP NO.	SITE	POLYGON AREA (KM²)	COMPLETELY BOUNDED? (YES/NO)
34	Greasewood Flat Ruin	284.4	Y
35	Ten-Acre Ruin	144.2	Y
36	Brew's #1	146.2	Y
37	Jackson's Montezuma Creek Bench Site #2	995.3	N
38	Five-Acre Ruin	152.6	Y
39	Gravel Pit	193.5	Y
40	Parker Site	159.9	Y
41	Decker Ruin	970.2	N
42	Black Mesa Quartzite Pueblo	139.8	Y
43	Red Knobs	712.2	N
44	Mouth of Mule Canyon complex	1,479.6	N

landscape in the Mesa Verde region: (1) community centers became more closely spaced in the central Mesa Verde region (Lipe 1995:143),[13] meaning that there would have been greater competition for resources in this central area; and (2) the large-site communities of the Mesa Verde region became increasingly isolated from large-site communities in surrounding regions. Analyzing the catchment areas associated with each community center illustrates these changes in greater detail.

COMMUNITY CENTER CATCHMENTS

Figures 7.6 through 7.9 illustrate the changing social landscape in the Mesa Verde region by showing the 2-, 7-, and 18-kilometer cost-equivalent catchments around each community center in Periods 1 through 4. Following the model of the Sand Canyon locality, the cost-equivalent 2-kilometer radius is the core of each community. This catchment is the zone of densest residential settlement, the zone with the most frequent interaction among community members, and the zone of most intensive agricultural activity. Within the 2-kilometer catchment, community members had to allocate access to one of the most valuable natural resources: arable land. This 2-kilometer cost-equivalent catchment approximates the community boundary defined as the area where there was regular interaction and shared access to land for the most intensive agriculture.

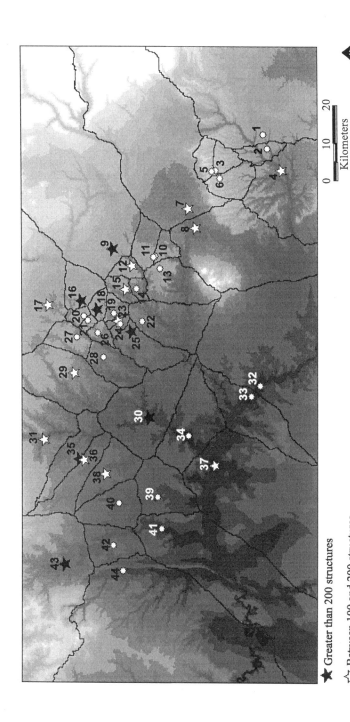

Figure 7.4 Polygons for Period 3 community centers.

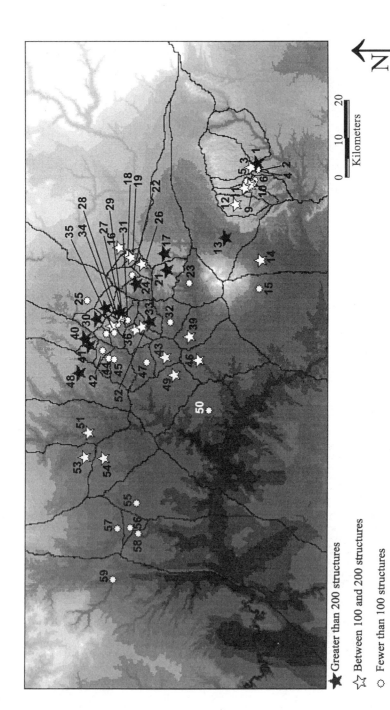

Figure 7.5 Polygons for Period 4 community centers.

★ Greater than 200 structures

☆ Between 100 and 200 structures

○ Fewer than 100 structures

N

0   10   20
Kilometers

Table 7.3 Period 4 Community Centers and Associated Polygons

MAP NO.	SITE	POLYGON AREA (KM²)	COMPLETELY BOUNDED? (YES/NO)
1	Cliff Palace	137.9	Y
2	Oak Tree House	1,056.7	N
3	Spruce Tree House	131.6	Y
4	Square Tower House	7.7	Y
5	Site 20½	23.2	Y
6	Double House	43.9	Y
7	Spring House	1.6	Y
8	Kodak House	1.9	Y
9	Long House	2.0	Y
10	Ruin 16	23.3	Y
11	Mug House	17.9	Y
12	Bowman's Pueblo	62.6	Y
13	Yucca House	593.2	Y
14	Moqui Spring Pueblo	401.2	N
15	Cowboy Wash	617.2	N
16	Yellow Jacket Pueblo	2,034.1	N
17	Goodman Point Pueblo	263.8	Y
18	Rohn 84	10.3	Y
19	Stevenson Site	13.4	Y
20	Easter Ruin	19.0	Y
21	Sand Canyon Pueblo	71.0	Y
22	Rohn 150	32.1	Y
23	Castle Rock Pueblo	128.2	Y
24	Woods Canyon Pueblo	40.3	Y
25	Lancaster/Pharo Ruin	339.1	N
26	Beartooth Ruin	30.2	Y
27	Gardner Ruin	25.4	Y
28	Miller Pueblo	3.3	Y
29	McVicker Homestead Ruin	2.4	Y
30	Little Cow Canyon Pueblo	32.2	Y
31	Thompson Site	15.8	Y
32	Yellow Jacket Floodplain Mesita Ruin	67.8	Y

continued on next page

MAP NO.	SITE	POLYGON AREA (KM²)	COMPLETELY BOUNDED? (YES/NO)
33	Seven Towers	36.9	Y
34	Fuller Ruin	11.9	Y
35	Ruin Canyon Rim Pueblo	8.7	Y
36	Big Spring Ruin	34.5	Y
37	Cow Mesa 40	15.5	Y
38	Cottonwood Ruin	13.0	Y
39	Cannonball Ruin	112.1	Y
40	Berkeley Bryant Site	134.5	N
41	Bob Hampton Ruin	24.3	Y
42	Brewer Well Site	19.4	Y
43	Horseshoe/Hackberry	57.2	Y
44	Papoose Canyon Talus Pueblo	15.7	Y
45	Spook Point Pueblo	57.3	Y
46	Morley-Kidder 1917	221.2	N
47	Pedro Point	53.8	Y
48	Hedley Main Ruin	331.2	N
49	Hovenweep Square Tower	221.8	Y
50	Hovenweep Cajon Ruin	1,476.9	N
51	Coalbed Village	291.2	N
52	Hibbets Pueblo	20.1	Y
53	Bradford Canyon-Head Ruin	313.0	N
54	Deadman's Canyon-Head Ruin	213.6	Y
55	Ute Gravel Pit Site	390.6	Y
56	Ruin Spring Ruin	31.2	N
57	Radon Spring Ruin	320.3	Y
58	Wetherill's Chimney Rock	984.4	N
59	Arch Canyon Pueblo	2,357.2	N

Community members undoubtedly negotiated economic and social relationships outside of this core area. The 7-kilometer radius includes agricultural lands that may have been less intensively cultivated than fields in the 2-kilometer zone, and it includes the area from which wild resources were regularly obtained. Thus, community members who lived within the 2-kilometer cost-equivalent catchment shared access to resources in the 7-kilometer cost-equivalent catchment. There almost certainly are residential sites in the 7-kilometer zone, but the greater size of this catchment would

Table 7.4 Summary Descriptive Statistics for Cost-Based Polygons for Community Centers in All Periods

PERIOD	NO.	%	MEAN SIZE (KM²)	STANDARD DEVIATION (KM²)	RANGE (KM²)
All Polygons					
Period 2 sites	36	100	389.1	383.3	39.6–1,633.5
Period 3 sites	44	100	318.3	396.0	8.8–1,479.7
Period 4 sites	59	100	237.4	464.4	1.1–2,357.2
Polygons Bounded by Other Sites					
Period 2 sites	17	47	157.4	119.4	39.6–419.4
Period 3 sites	31	70	108.8	92.3	8.8–378.7
Period 4 sites	46	78	72.8	112.9	1.1–593.2
Polygons Extending to Study Area Boundaries					
Period 2 sites	19	53	569.4	420.6	186.1–1,633.5
Period 3 sites	13	30	818.1	395.7	296.9–1,479.7
Period 4 sites	13	22	819.8	724.3	134.5–2,357.2

have served to limit the regular face-to-face interaction between people living in this area. Additional research is needed to determine whether households living in the 7-kilometer zone were integrated into or differentiated from the communities defined by each community center and its 2-kilometer cost-equivalent boundary.

The 18-kilometer cost-equivalent catchment encompasses the one-day, round-trip walking distance that surrounds each community center. This catchment enables us to visualize the connectedness and potential for interaction between centers and their associated core communities in the Mesa Verde–region settlement system. It also encompasses the buffer zone surrounding the more heavily used area around each community center or group of community centers. Finally, this catchment illustrates the degree to which the large-site communities of the Mesa Verde region became increasingly isolated from large sites in surrounding regions.

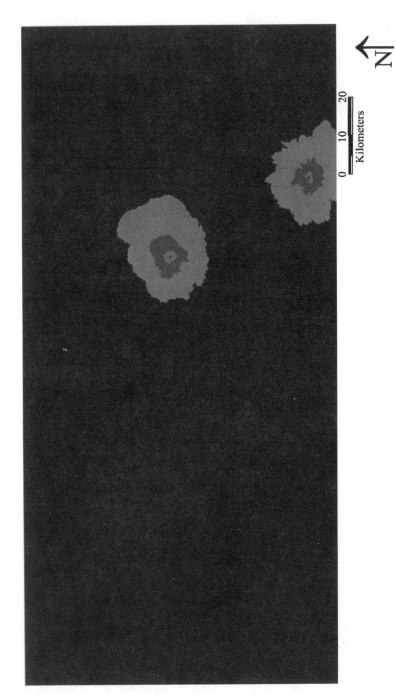

Figure 7.6 Period 1 community centers and their 2-, 7-, and 18-kilometer cost-equivalent catchments.

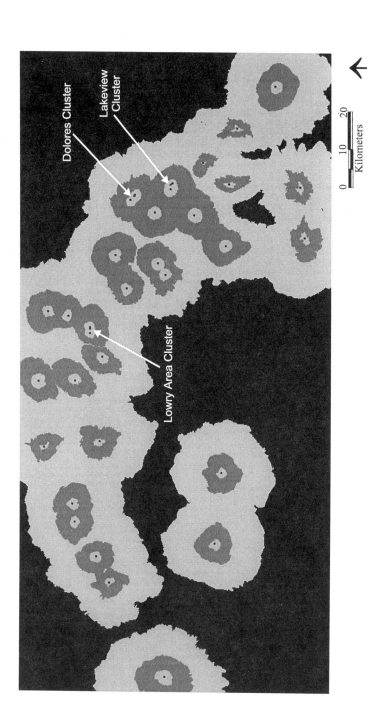

Figure 7.7 Period 2 community centers and their 2-, 7-, and 18-kilometer cost-equivalent catchments.

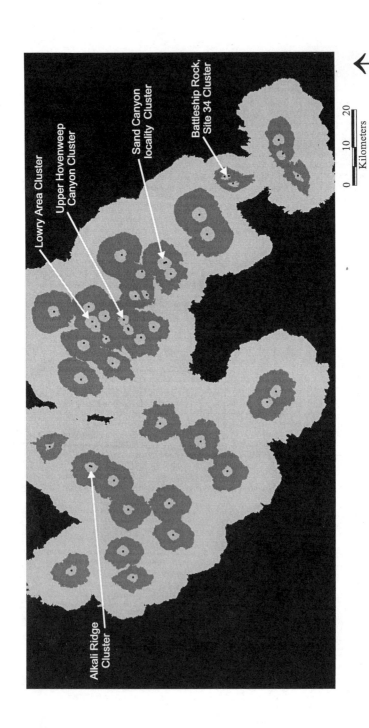

Figure 7.8 Period 3 community centers and their 2-, 7-, and 18-kilometer cost-equivalent catchments.

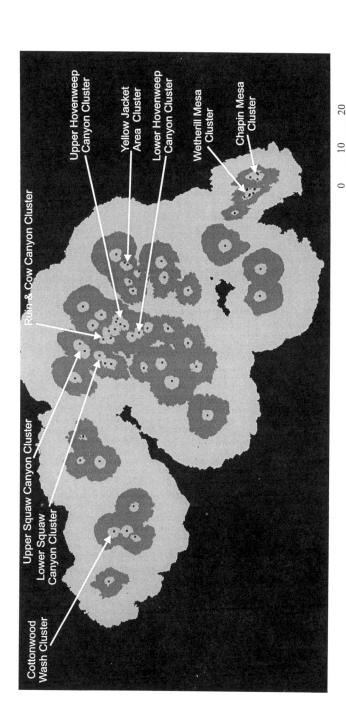

Figure 7.9 Period 4 community centers and their 2-, 7-, and 18-kilometer cost-equivalent catchments.

Table 7.5 Areas of Cost-Based Catchments for Period 1 Communities

SITE	AREA (KM²) IN 2-KM RADIUS	AREA (KM²) IN 7-KM RADIUS	AREA (KM²) IN 18-KM RADIUS
Mancos Canyon great kiva	4.2	45.9	300.8
Sand Canyon locality great kiva	8.1	65.0	375.3

Note: Radius = cost-equivalent radius.

Catchment Overlap

For Period 1, there are only two sites at which public architecture has been documented and no sites with more than 50 structures. The two public buildings are the great kiva in the Sand Canyon locality and a great kiva at site 5MT2350, at the confluence of Ute, Grass, and Mancos Canyons.[14] Only two great kivas are known for this period, but it is clear that there were more than two Period 1 communities. Virtually every intensive survey in the central Mesa Verde region has identified residential sites dating to the early A.D. 1000s (Adler 1990; Fetterman and Honeycutt 1987; Greubel 1991; Hayes 1964; Neily 1983; Rohn 1977; Smith 1987), and residential sites with tree-ring dates in the early 1000s have been excavated. Areas for the catchments of Period 1 communities appear in table 7.5.

When adjusted for the energy it takes to walk over variable terrain, the areas of these catchments are considerably smaller than the areas of circles with actual 2-, 7-, and 18-kilometer radii (13, 154, and 1,018 kilometers, respectively). This is because the terrain surrounding the Mancos Canyon great kiva, which is located in the bottom of Mancos Canyon, is much more difficult to traverse than the area surrounding the Sand Canyon locality great kiva, which is located on a relatively level mesa top. These catchment areas illustrate how physiography affects the social landscape in the region and how the catchment overlap documented for Periods 2 through 4, by taking physiography into account, actually presents a conservative estimate for the increasing competition for resources in the area.

Visual inspection of figures 7.6 through 7.9 shows how the community catchments increasingly overlap through time; this overlap is quantified by measuring the total area in each of the catchment zones (table 7.6). There

Table 7.6 Areas of Cost-Based Catchment Zones Surrounding Community Centers in the Mesa Verde Region

PERIOD	NO. OF CENTERS	Area (km²) in 2-km Radius		Area (km²) in 2–7-km Radius		Area (km²) in 7–18-km Radius		AREA (KM²) BEYOND 18-KM RADIUS
		TOTAL	PER SITE	TOTAL	PER SITE	TOTAL	PER SITE	
Period 2	36	224	6.2	1,950	54.2	5,223	145.1	6,609
Period 3	44	260	5.9	2,008	45.6	4,753	108.0	6,986
Period 4	59	284	4.8	1,804	30.6	3,793	64.3	8,126

Note: Radius = cost-equivalent radius.

was a modest increase in the total area within the 2-kilometer cost-equivalent radii of community centers through time, owing to the increasing number of community centers in Periods 2 through 4. But when that total area is divided by the number of centers, the average area within the 2-kilometer zones actually decreases through time. This reduction is due to the increasing overlap of the 2-kilometer catchments around community centers. This overlap could result only in increasing competition for the resources in these areas.

The same trend occurs in the cost-equivalent 2- to 7-kilometer catchment zones. The overlap is so substantial that in spite of the increase in the number of community centers through time, there is only a slight rise in the *total* area of the 2- to 7-kilometer catchment zones between Periods 2 and 3, and the figure actually drops between Periods 3 and 4. The increasing overlap of catchment zones is also reflected in the dramatic decrease in size shown when the total area in the 2- to 7-kilometer zones is divided by the number of community centers in each time period. Again, this could only result in increased competition for resources in these areas.

The trend is even more dramatic for the 7- to 18-kilometer cost-equivalent catchments: there the catchment overlap is so substantial that the total area in these zones drops in every period. In contrast, the peripheral area lying outside the 18-kilometer catchment zones of the large-site settlement system became larger through time. These data illustrate that the large-site communities within the central Mesa Verde–region settlement system became more closely spaced through time. Simultaneously, the large-site settlement system became increasingly isolated from peripheral small-site communities in the Mesa Verde region and from the large-site communities in adjacent regions.[15]

Community Clusters

The increasing overlap of community catchments, particularly the 2-kilometer catchments, produced clusters of several closely spaced community centers, for which there are at least three possible interpretations. First, they may represent sequential occupations and, therefore, the short-distance movement of community centers during a single period. Second, they may represent contemporaneously occupied communities that were independent but closely related, given their proximity and potential for regular interaction. Third, they may represent a distinct category of community within the Mesa Verde–region social landscape: contemporaneously occupied macrocommunities organized around multiple community centers.

Community centers in Period 2 are relatively evenly spaced (figs 7.3 and 7.7), but there are three notable exceptions: the Lake View group (Wallace, Haynie, and Ida Jean Ruins), the cluster of sites around Lowry Pueblo (including Lowry, North Lowry, and Casa de Valle), and the Dolores group, consisting of Escalante, Reservoir, and Emerson Ruins. In all areas, three community centers are located less than 1 kilometer apart. Available evidence indicates that some of the centers in these clusters were sequentially occupied but that others were contemporaneously occupied.[16] These clusters of community centers may have played a different role in the regional social landscape than the other first-order communities in the region.

Overlap of the 2-kilometer cost-equivalent catchments is still limited in Period 3, but there are five multicommunity clusters (fig. 7.8).[17] These appear to be community centers that were occupied contemporaneously, and they may be organizationally different from the other first-order communities in Period 3.

Overlap of the 2-kilometer catchments increases dramatically in Period 4 (fig. 7.9). On Mesa Verde this includes the Chapin Mesa cluster (four community centers) and the Wetherill Mesa cluster (seven community centers). There are six multicommunity centers (composed of 17 centers in all) in the area between McElmo Creek and Montezuma Creek, and one in southeastern Utah (composed of two community centers).[18]

Determining the social, economic, and political organization of these multicommunity clusters and how it might differ from that of the other first-order communities in the region is beyond the scope of this study. However, the overlapping catchments in these multicommunity clusters would have resulted in increased competition for resources within this area. Individuals living in these communities would have had to negotiate their access to resources not only with members of their own first-order community but also with members of adjacent communities. In addition, the distance to more extensively used resources areas—the 7-kilometer catchments—was greater, and the total area in the 7-kilometer catchments was smaller. The increased competition for resources could have resulted in conflict or the development of new mechanisms for cooperation and sharing of resources. Increased population density would have reduced the options for residential mobility within these areas.

Increased competition and reduced options for residential movement might have contributed to the intensification of subsistence economies and the development of more formal systems of land tenure.

COMMUNITY CENTERS AND TREE-RING-DATED SITES

The distribution of community centers for each period, along with the distribution of all sites with tree-ring cutting dates from that period, is examined next, in order to evaluate how the large-site settlement system compares with the locations of smaller sites.

Period 1 Tree-Ring-Dated Sites

7.10 illustrates the distribution of the 33 sites with cutting dates that fall into Period 1, including the Mancos Canyon community center. Ten sites have cutting dates in the A.D. 950 to 999 interval, and 22 date between 1000 and 1049. These small, dispersed sites were parts of communities that either had no public architecture or, quite possibly, had public buildings that have not been located and recorded. Figure 7.10 illustrates a pattern that characterized settlement in the subsequent periods: there is a cluster of dates from sites on Mesa Verde and another cluster in the area between Yellow Jacket and Cross Canyons. These areas are densely settled zones in the periods that follow. Further, the distribution of sites with tree-ring cutting dates in Period 1 suggests that some Period 2 communities developed in preexisting communities.

Period 2 Tree-Ring-Dated Sites

There are 75 sites with cutting dates that fall in Period 2, including 8 of 36 community centers (fig. 7.11). In addition, nine sites with cutting dates from Period 2 become community centers in the subsequent periods, indicating that construction of these later community centers began in Period 2 or, perhaps more likely, the later community centers were constructed with timbers salvaged from earlier buildings located within the community. In either case, these cutting dates indicate that Period 2 communities were located near these Period 3 centers, demonstrating the persistence of occupation in these localities.

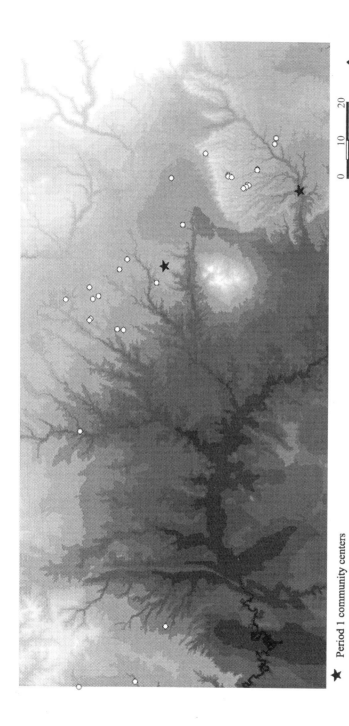

★ Period 1 community centers

○ Sites with Period 1 tree-ring cutting dates

Figure 7.10 Period 1 community centers and sites with tree-ring cutting dates.

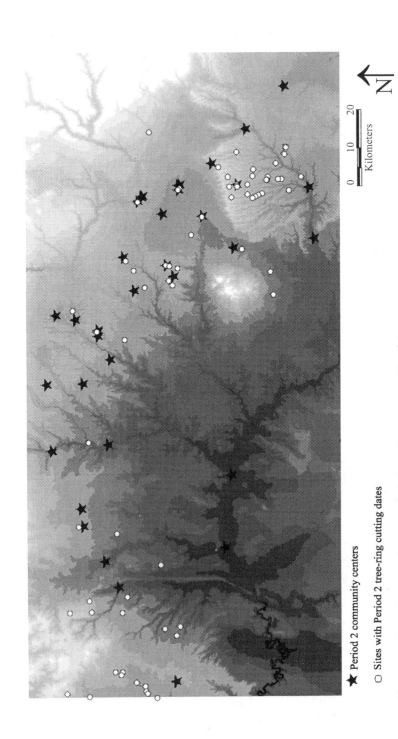

★ Period 2 community centers

○ Sites with Period 2 tree-ring cutting dates

0   10   20
Kilometers

N

Figure 7.11 Period 2 community centers and sites with tree-ring cutting dates.

Figure 7.11 illustrates a general pattern that holds for each of the subsequent periods. The distribution of tree-ring-dated, mostly small sites is largely coterminous with the distribution of large community centers. The exception is in southeastern Utah, especially in the area west of Comb Ridge. There, many small sites are located substantial distances from known large community centers, indicating that some communities in this area consisted entirely of small sites or that their community centers have not been found.

Period 3 Tree-Ring-Dated Sites

Figure 7.12 illustrates the distribution of all sites, large and small, with Period 3 cutting dates along with the Period 3 community centers. Seven of the 77 sites that have cutting dates are Period 3 community centers. Ten sites with cutting dates from Period 3 are also Period 4 community centers, indicating there were Period 3 communities in the vicinity of the Period 4 community centers and demonstrating community persistence in these localities (compare fig. 7.12 with fig. 7.13). As in Period 2, the distribution of sites with Period 3 tree-ring cutting dates is basically coterminous with the distribution of community centers, except west of Comb Ridge, where there are many small sites with no known large community center nearby.

Period 4 Tree-Ring-Dated Sites

Figure 7.13 illustrates the distribution of all sites with Period 4 cutting dates and the distribution of Period 4 community centers. There are only 65 large and small sites with cutting dates, despite the fact that there are many more cutting dates for Period 4 than for all the earlier periods (53 percent of all cutting dates between A.D. 900 and 1300 come from Period 4 sites). Twelve of the sites with Period 4 cutting dates are community centers. Two Period 3 community centers, Lion House and Far View House in the Mesa Verde area, have cutting dates from Period 4 as well, indicating they were not fully abandoned during this period.

In the central Mesa Verde region, the distribution of tree-ring-dated sites is almost coterminous with the distribution of community centers. Figure 7.13 shows that although the community centers on Mesa Verde proper were confined to a small area, there were many smaller sites with tree-ring cutting dates in the surrounding areas, including the Mancos River valley and the canyons immediately south of the Mancos River. Comparing

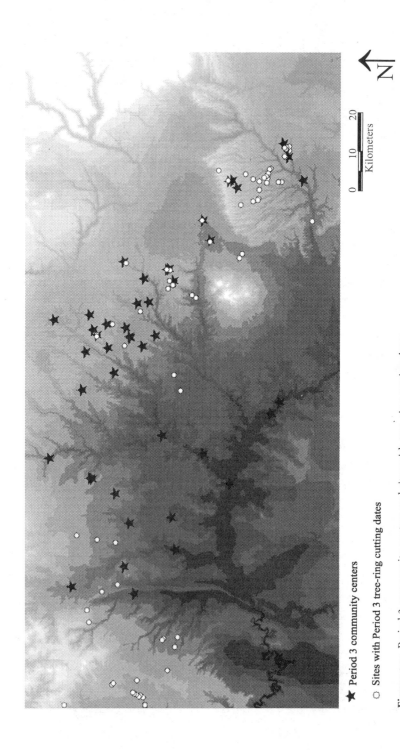

★ Period 3 community centers

○ Sites with Period 3 tree-ring cutting dates

0   10   20
Kilometers

N

Figure 7.12 Period 3 community centers and sites with tree-ring cutting dates.

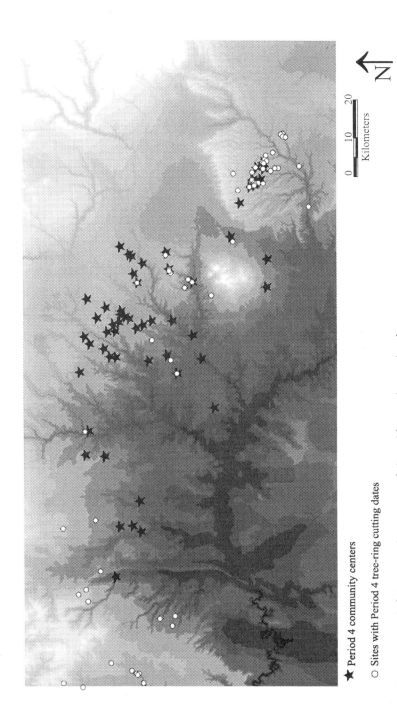

★ Period 4 community centers

○ Sites with Period 4 tree-ring cutting dates

N

0   10   20
Kilometers

Figure 7.13 Period 4 community centers and sites with tree-ring cutting dates.

figures 7.11, 7.12, and 7.13 shows that there are fewer Period 4 dated sites from the eastern edge of the Mesa Verde region, suggesting that there may have been an abandonment of this portion of the region in Period 4. There continues to be a wide geographic distribution of tree-ring-dated sites in southeastern Utah, especially west of Comb Ridge, indicating that small-site settlement remains common in the western Mesa Verde region.

COMMUNITY MOVEMENT

Community movement within the Mesa Verde region is documented by examining the location of each community center in one period and identifying the community center that is its nearest neighbor in the subsequent period. The cost-equivalent distance between the community centers is used to measure the scale of movement.

New community centers are interpreted as having continued to serve the existing community when the movement between community centers in two sequential time periods is less than 2 kilometers. This is consistent with the definition of communities as spatially restricted areas where there was regular, face-to-face interaction and shared access to local resources. When movement is within 7 kilometers, the zone of regular resource use, continuity in community membership remains likely but is less clear than for moves of less than 2 kilometers. When the distance between centers is greater than 7 kilometers, there is a greater chance that the earlier community dissolved, and the relationship to the nearest neighbor of the subsequent period is less certain. In some cases, a community center in one period had two nearest neighbors in the subsequent period that were almost equal distances away; both nearest neighbors are listed in these cases.

Period 1 to Period 2 Community Movement

Little can be said about the general character of community movement between Periods 1 and 2 because Period 1 communities are so few in number (table 7.7). Continuity in the Sand Canyon community is indicated by the short-distance move between the Period 1 great kiva and the Period 2 community center, Casa Negra (Adler 1994). The Mancos Canyon great kiva is within the regular resource use area of the later Mouth of Navajo Canyon community center, indicating that continuity in this Mancos Canyon community

Table 7.7 Cost-Equivalent Distances between Period 1 Community Centers and Their Period 2 Nearest Neighbors

PERIOD 1 COMMUNITY CENTER	PERIOD 2 NEAREST NEIGHBOR	DISTANCE TO NEAREST NEIGHBOR (ADJUSTED KM)
Mancos Canyon great kiva	Mouth of Navajo Canyon great house	5.2
Sand Canyon locality great kiva	Casa Negra	0.3

is also likely. As noted earlier, tree-ring data suggest that other Period 2 community centers also developed in preexisting Period 1 communities, even though there are few public buildings that date to Period 1.

Period 2 to Period 3 Community Movement

Distances between Period 2 and Period 3 community centers vary considerably, from several cases in which the move was less than 100 meters to a maximum distance of 45.6 cost-equivalent kilometers (table 7.8, fig. 7.14). Eleven of the 36 Period 2 community centers (30 percent) are within the 2-kilometer zone of a Period 3 center, indicating a short-distance move and likely continuity in the community. Six Period 2 centers are within the 7-kilometer radius of a Period 3 center (17 percent), a moderate distance over which continuity in community membership is still considered possible. Two Period 2 centers have Period 3 centers that fall just beyond the 7-kilometer threshold, and community continuity between periods is possible in these cases.

There are 19 Period 2 community centers (53 percent) with Period 3 nearest neighbors farther than 7 kilometers away; these moves range from just over 7 kilometers to 45.6 kilometers. Interpreting community movement at these greater distances is difficult. One possible interpretation is that Period 2 communities persisted through time but migrated greater distances to settle new, empty localities. Another possibility is that the Period 2 communities dissolved and segments of them migrated to become members of other preexisting communities. It is also possible that the nature of community organization changed such that Period 3 communities

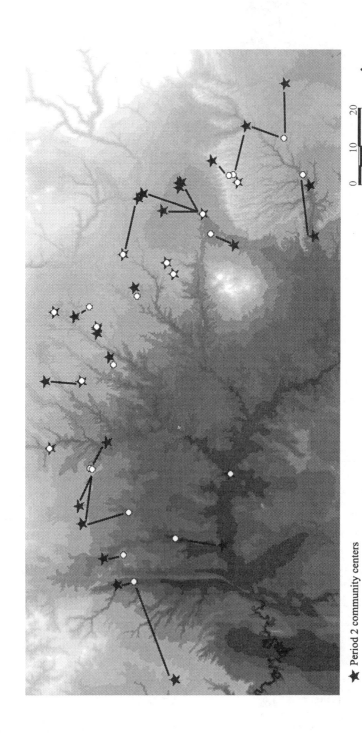

Figure 7.14 Period 2 community centers and their Period 3 nearest neighbors.

★ Period 2 community centers

○ Period 3 nearest neighbors

N

0   10   20
Kilometers

Table 7.8 Cost-Equivalent Distances between Period 2 Community Centers and Their Period 3 Nearest Neighbors

PERIOD 2 COMMUNITY CENTER	PERIOD 3 NEAREST NEIGHBOR	DISTANCE TO NEAREST NEIGHBOR (ADJUSTED KM)
Morris 20	Lion House	15.9
O'Bryan's Weber Canyon Pueblo	Lion House, Battleship Rock cluster	17.2
O'Bryan's Prater Canyon Pueblo	Mitchell Springs, Site 34	17.3
Far View House	Far View House	0.0
Mouth of Navajo Canyon great house	Kiva Point	3.5
Red Pottery Mound	Kiva Point	27.9
Yucca House	Mud Springs	6.9
Wallace Ruin	Mitchell Springs	10.4
Haynie Ruin	Mitchell Springs	10.4
Ida Jean Ruin	Mitchell Springs	9.6
Emerson Ruin	Mitchell Springs	17.6
Reservoir Ruin	Mitchell Springs	17.7
Escalante Ruin	Yellow Jacket Pueblo	17.2
Hartman Draw	Mitchell Springs	11.2
Mitchell Springs	Mitchell Springs	0.0
Yellow Jacket Pueblo	Yellow Jacket Pueblo	0.0
Goodman Point great house	Shields Pueblo	0.2
Casa Negra	Casa Negra	0.0
Uncle Albert Porter	Bass complex	2.8
Carvell Ruin	Carvell Ruin	0.0
Ansel Hall	Carvell Ruin, Lancaster	7.1
North Lowry	Pigg Site	0.0
Lowry Pueblo	Pigg Site	0.7
Casa de Valle	Pigg Site	2.5
Upper Squaw Mesa Village	Lower Squaw Mesa Village	2.3
Carhart Ruin	Hedley Middle Ruin	12.9
Hedley West Ruin	Hedley Middle Ruin	0.2
Three-Kiva Ruin	Ten-Acre Ruin	11.7
Montezuma Village I	Montezuma Village II	0.6

continued on next page

PERIOD 2 COMMUNITY CENTER	PERIOD 3 NEAREST NEIGHBOR	DISTANCE TO NEAREST NEIGHBOR (ADJUSTED KM)
Jackson's Montezuma Creek Bench #1	Jackson's Montezuma Creek Bench #2	0.4
Moki Island	Brew's Site #1	12.4
Edge of the Cedars	Brew's Site #1, Parker Site	18.0
Bluff Cemetery	Decker Ruin	16.0
Cottonwood Falls	Black Mesa Quartzite Pueblo	7.6
Arch Canyon	Mouth of Mule Canyon Pueblo	5.4
Et al. Ruin	Mouth of Mule Canyon Pueblo	45.6

Note: Community centers are listed beginning with those in the southeast section of the study area and moving toward the northwest.

remained in the vicinity of the abandoned Period 2 community centers but did not have a large community center. Intensive survey in the areas surrounding these abandoned Period 2 community centers would be needed to resolve this question.

Period 2 to 3 community movement is characterized in two general ways. First, movement between community centers is short or moderate in the central Mesa Verde region, where site density is the greatest. Second, community movement over greater distances is more common outside of the central Mesa Verde region.[19]

Period 3 to Period 4 Community Movement

Turning to the Period 3 community centers and distances to Period 4 community centers, 17 of the 44 large sites (39 percent) are within 2 cost-equivalent kilometers of one another (table 7.9, fig. 7.15).

Another eight Period 3 community centers (18 percent) are within 7 cost-equivalent kilometers of a Period 4 community center, and two Period 3 centers are just beyond this 7-kilometer threshold. Nineteen of the 44 Period 3 community centers (43 percent) are more than 7 cost-equivalent kilometers from Period 4 villages. The shortest-distance moves continue to be in the central Mesa Verde region, and the scale of movement is greater on the margins of this densely settled zone.[20]

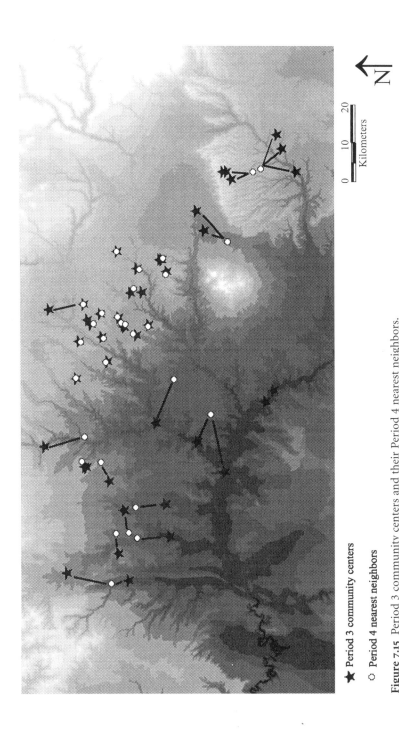

★ Period 3 community centers

○ Period 4 nearest neighbors

Figure 7.15 Period 3 community centers and their Period 4 nearest neighbors.

0   10   20
Kilometers

N

Table 7.9 Cost-Equivalent Distances between Period 3 Community Centers and Their Period 4 Nearest Neighbors

PERIOD 3 COMMUNITY CENTER	PERIOD 4 NEAREST NEIGHBOR	DISTANCE TO NEAREST NEIGHBOR (ADJUSTED KM)
Lion House	Oak Tree House	18.0
Hoy House	Oak Tree House	13.9
Battleship Rock cluster	Spruce Tree House	13.5
Kiva Point	Oak Tree House	13.7
Site 34	Spruce Tree House	13.9
Far View House	Spruce Tree House	7.6
Mitchell Springs	Yucca House	11.2
Mud Springs	Yucca House	6.9
Yellow Jacket Pueblo	Yellow Jacket Pueblo	0.0
Goodman Point great kiva	Goodman Point Pueblo	0.6
Shields Pueblo	Goodman Point Pueblo	1.0
Griffey Ruin	Easter Ruin	1.0
Casa Negra	Sand Canyon Pueblo	1.3
Rich's Ruin	Woods Canyon Pueblo	3.4
Bass complex	Woods Canyon Pueblo	3.2
Lancaster/Pharo Ruin	Lancaster Ruin	0.0
Carvell Ruin	Lancaster Ruin	12.5
Herren Farms	Beartooth Ruin	0.8
Head of Hovenweep Mesa-Top Ruin	Gardner Ruin	0.4
Finley Farm/Charnel House/Ray Ruin complex	Little Cow Canyon Pueblo	2.6
Pigg Site	Little Cow Canyon Pueblo	1.3
Mockingbird Mesa-Top Ruin	Seven Towers Pueblo	0.6
Kristie's Ruin	Thompson Ruin, McVicker Homestead Ruin	1.5
Carol's Ruin	Thompson Ruin, McVicker Homestead Ruin	1.7
Kearns Site	Big Spring Ruin	1.4
Lower Cow Canyon Ruin	Cottonwood Ruin	1.4
Brewer Pueblo	Berkeley Bryant Site	0.6
Lower Squaw Mesa Village	Papoose Canyon Rim Pueblo	0.9

PERIOD 3 COMMUNITY CENTER	PERIOD 4 NEAREST NEIGHBOR	DISTANCE TO NEAREST NEIGHBOR (ADJUSTED KM)
Hedley Middle Ruin	Hedley Main Ruin	0.3
Nancy Patterson Pueblo	Hovenweep Square Tower	13.7
Montezuma Village II	Coalbed Village	14.8
Tsitah Wash complex	Hovenweep Cajon	21.5
Aneth Archaeological District	Hovenweep Cajon	18.6
Greasewood Flat Ruin	Hovenweep Cajon	9.2
Ten-Acre Ruin	Bradford Canyon-Head Ruin	3.2
Brew's #1	Bradford Canyon-Head Ruin, Deadman's Canyon-Head Ruin	3.9
Jackson's Montezuma Creek, Bench Site #2	Hovenweep Cajon	21.9
Five-Acre Ruin	Deadman's Canyon-Head Ruin	7.7
Gravel Pit	Ute Gravel Pit Site	9.8
Parker Site	Ute Gravel Pit Site, Ruin Spring Ruin	4.6
Decker Ruin	Wetherill's Chimney Rock	10.6
Black Mesa Quartzite Pueblo	Radon Spring Ruin	9.0
Red Knobs	Arch Canyon Pueblo	18.8
Mouth of Mule Canyon complex	Arch Canyon Pueblo	5.4

Note: Community centers are listed beginning with those in the southeast section of the study area and moving toward the northwest.

Table 7.10 summarizes the scale of movement between community centers for Periods 2 through 4. These data indicate that the scale of movement decreased through time. The scale of movement was always greater on the margins of the large-site settlement system, and shorter-distance moves characterize the central Mesa Verde region. Thus, the increasing density of communities in the central Mesa Verde region resulted in fewer opportunities for community residential movement. Instead, communities in this area persisted in roughly the same geographic locations through time. This is the area in which there was the greatest overlap in community catchments

Table 7.10 Percentages of Community Centers Moving Various Distances between Periods 2 and 4

TIME PERIOD	< 2 KM (%)	2–7 KM (%)	> 7 KM (%)
Period 2 to Period 3	30	17	53
Period 3 to Period 4	39	18	43

and the greatest competition for resources. Outside the central Mesa Verde region, where the density of community centers was lower, there was more frequent community relocation over greater distances. Options for mobility may have been greater in this area, competition for resources lower, and subsistence economies may have remained more extensive relative to the intensified economies of the Mesa Verde region.

POPULATION MOVEMENT BETWEEN REGIONS

Finally, an even larger scale of population movement can be examined: migration into and out of the Mesa Verde region. This issue is addressed by examining all the tree-ring dates from the region. Although these data are not sufficient to fully understand movement into and out of the region, they are a starting point with which to examine this question.

The method employed in these analyses is straightforward and similar to that employed in chapter 6. The continuous harvesting of timber is taken to indicate continuity in the occupation of the region. Periods of little or no harvesting may indicate site abandonment and emigration.

A plot of the 3,301 cutting dates from the Mesa Verde region that fall before A.D. 1300 (fig. 7.16) illustrates the low number of tree-ring dates in the 900s. Schlanger and Wilshusen (1993) have argued for abandonment of the Dolores River valley in the early 900s, and there appears to have been a more general emigration from the entire Mesa Verde region during this period (Varien 1994; Wilshusen 1995). The reduced number of dates does not conclusively prove a large-scale emigration from the Mesa Verde region during the tenth century, but it suggests that such an abandonment is a strong possibility.

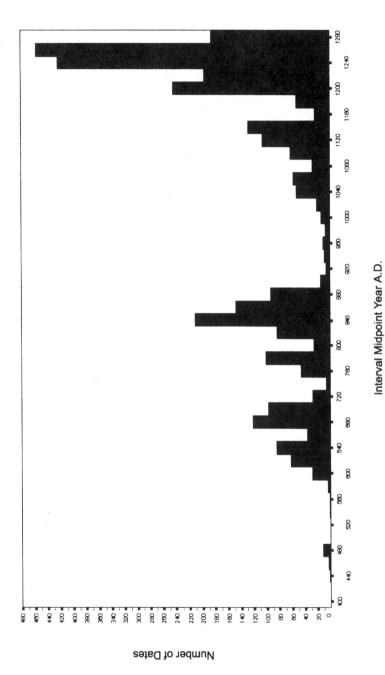

Figure 7.16 All Mesa Verde–region tree-ring cutting dates.

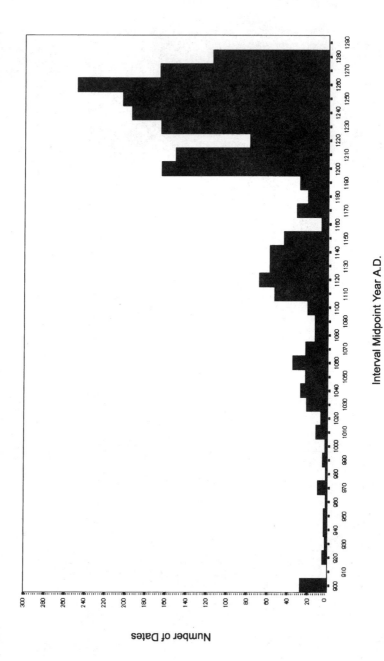

Figure 7.17 Mesa Verde–region tree-ring cutting dates between A.D. 900 and 1300.

Figure 7.17 illustrates the distribution of the 2,087 cutting dates between A.D. 900 and 1300. Perhaps the most important aspect of these data is the continuous distribution of dates. This is evidence that the Mesa Verde region was never entirely abandoned between 900 and 1290. The distribution of dated samples does have distinct modes, but the question remains whether the periods of relatively few dates were also periods when there was at least some emigration from the Mesa Verde region.

Figure 7.17 shows not only that the 900s are characterized by the fewest dates but also that the relatively few dates span almost the entire century. That there are so few dates for so long a time supports the interpretation that the Mesa Verde region witnessed a large decline in population during this century. Such a population decline has important implications for the period of interest in this study: it suggests that the many communities that were present by 1050 formed in part by population movement into the region sometime in the late 900s or early 1000s, meaning that the founding dates of these communities can be placed in this time period.

Two additional periods, both of relatively short duration, have relatively few tree-ring dates. One is between 1070 and 1100, the other between 1150 and 1170. The timing of these intervals is of interest because the first approximates the period when the assumed Chacoan regional system is thought to have expanded into the Mesa Verde region, and the second is the period immediately after the Chacoan system is thought to have collapsed. In addition, there were periods of environmental deterioration between approximately 1090 and 1110 and 1140 and 1180.[21]

In sum, the tree-ring data indicate that the Mesa Verde region was probably depopulated in the early A.D. 900s. This means the Period 2 communities may have formed as a result of immigration into the Mesa Verde region from elsewhere. It is also possible that there was short-term migration between the Mesa Verde region and adjacent areas in the late 1000s and again in the 1150 to 1170 interval. The tree-ring data cannot confirm whether there was widespread abandonment and depopulation during these periods, but they indicate that future research should examine these periods more carefully.

COMMUNITY SEDENTISM AND MOBILITY IN
THE MESA VERDE REGION

The social context in which all residential mobility occurred in the Mesa Verde region was strongly affected by the region's rugged terrain, which impeded the movement of people and thereby influenced human interaction, the formation of community boundaries, and mobility. Spatial analyses reveal three general characteristics of the changing social landscape. First, communities became more tightly spaced in the central Mesa Verde region, indicating the potential for greater competition for resources there through time. Second, community centers on the margins of the large-site settlement system were abandoned over time, so that the large-site communities of the Mesa Verde region became increasingly isolated from adjacent regions. Third, the examination of all sites with tree-ring cutting dates indicates that there were areas, particularly in the western portion of the study area, that had communities consisting entirely of small sites with no known large-site community center.

The analyses also document a wide range in the geographic scale of community movement. There are many cases in which community centers moved over short distances, indicating that a community persisted in the same geographic location through time. There are also a number of cases in which community centers moved over larger distances; in these cases the processes by which communities were abandoned and resettled are more difficult to infer.

The geographic scale of community mobility is variable, but there is a general pattern to this variation. The distance of the moves is greater for large-site communities on the margins of the study area, whereas shorter-distance moves characterize community movement in the central Mesa Verde region. These data indicate that communities in the central Mesa Verde region were occupied for centuries, and their development can be fully understood only by considering this historical context.

Finally, tree-ring data indicate that the Mesa Verde region was never fully abandoned between A.D. 950 and 1290. They do, however, suggest that there was emigration from the region beginning in the late 800s and immigration back into the region in the late 900s and early 1000s. The tree-ring data also indicate that partial, short-term abandonment during periods of environmental deterioration remains a possibility. The most likely intervals for these periods of short-term migration are between 1070 and 1100 and between 1150 and 1170.

MOBILE

HOUSEHOLDS

AND

PERSISTENT

COMMUNITIES

Archaeologists working in the American Southwest have questioned the conventional wisdom that societies became sedentary once they adopted agriculture and pottery. These researchers have demonstrated that agricultural and horticultural societies do not abandon mobility when they adopt food production and pottery making. But much of this research has been couched in either-or terms: societies are argued to be either mobile or sedentary. This perspective fails to recognize a point made by Kelly (1992:60) when he observed that "no society is sedentary. . . . People simply move in different ways."

Influenced by studies of hunter-gatherer mobility, research in the Southwest is almost exclusively focused on identifying *seasonal* mobility at the scale of individual small sites, and no attention is paid to whether or not they were part of a larger-scale community. A few studies have focused on the movement of large, aggregated villages, but without addressing household residential mobility in these communities. Most studies have focused on the ecological determinants of mobility, usually environmental change and resource depletion, while social factors related to mobility have been largely ignored.

Following the research of Kelly (1992) and Eder (1984), I view mobility as a multidimensional phenomenon. This means that groups use several different mobility strategies simultaneously. These strategies can be organized by gender or by age set, can involve individuals or task groups, and can combine elements of residential and logistical mobility. My research addresses one dimension of the mobility strategies practiced by ancient agricultural societies in the Southwest: the *relatively* high-frequency residential movement of households within and among communities that, in themselves, may have persisted continuously within established geographical boundaries for as long as three centuries. Rather than being opposing concepts, sedentism and mobility were strategies that were simultaneously employed.

In the first part of this chapter I summarize the data on residential mobility presented in chapters 4–7 in order to address the initial goal of this research—to provide a sound empirical study that improves our understanding of population movement in the Mesa Verde region. Existing interpretations of Mesa Verde–region mobility are then reviewed in light of these results, including an assessment of how mobility was affected by environmental change, by resource depletion, by social factors, or by some combination of the three. These data also provided insights into the migrations that accompanied the abandonment of the Mesa Verde region.

The main purpose of this chapter, however, is to address the second goal of the research—to build a model of residential mobility that views mobility as a social process. Modeling mobility as a social process benefits from incorporating the concepts of structure and agency and by viewing mobility as part of the mode of production. The frequency of residential movement changed through time, and the patterns of residential movement diverged in different parts of the Mesa Verde region.

Changes in the frequency of household residential movement in the central Mesa Verde region indicate that the system of land tenure was transformed between A.D. 950 and 1300 from a system characterized by usufruct to one characterized by heritable property rights. This change occurred as a result of increased competition for resources through time. During this period, different mobility strategies came to characterize the central Mesa Verde region and the area surrounding it. The central region was increasingly characterized by decreased residential mobility and intensified subsistence economies, but in peripheral areas people continued to practice more frequent residential movement and more extensive movement. It is possible that these differences led to the increasing conflict documented for the region in the late 1200s, which in turn might have contributed to the final migrations from the region.

THE RESIDENTIAL MOBILITY OF MESA VERDE–REGION HOUSEHOLDS

One of the major purposes of this study was to develop a methodology for measuring the occupation duration of residential sites. Previous studies that examined regional settlement patterns and attempted demographic reconstructions either ignored the issue of occupation span or made best-guess estimates for the length of site occupation. Occasionally, architectural style has been used to estimate occupation span (Schlanger 1987), but this is useful only in setting *upper* limits to the occupation spans of sites with *earthen* architecture. Architectural style does not provide occupation span estimates for individual sites and thus cannot document variation in the length of occupation among these sites.

Previous accumulations research developed accumulation rates for *all* pottery; these studies are problematic because they use data from single- and multiple-component sites and they aggregate all pottery, which includes vessels with different use-lives and accumulation rates. In this study I have tried to isolate a functionally specific vessel category ideal for accumulations research—cooking pots—and to develop a cooking-pot sherd accumulation rate using a strong archaeological case.

The accumulation rates developed in chapter 4 should have broad applicability for the northern Southwest, and the general methods for estimating site occupation span should be useful to archaeologists working in many parts of the world. By applying these methods to residential sites in the Sand Canyon locality, considerable variation in site occupation span is documented, but despite this variability there is a general pattern of ever-lengthening occupation span through time.

The sample of Pueblo II habitations in the Sand Canyon locality is limited to two sites; best estimates for their occupation spans are 16 and 26 years, respectively. They contrast with 13 Pueblo III components, for which the average occupation span is 44 years (if Troy's Tower and Mad Dog Tower are excluded, the mean is 50 years). These findings suggest an important shift in the residential mobility patterns of households in the

Sand Canyon locality through time. Occupation span estimates range between 19 and 80 years at the 13 Pueblo III residential sites; it is unlikely that this range is due entirely to sampling error. The estimates indicate that occupation at a few sites was limited to a single generation but that most Pueblo III sites were occupied for multiple generations.

Resource depletion was expected to have caused household residential movement at relatively regular intervals, and well-documented environmental deterioration, including drought, was expected to have caused household movement at specific time periods. Neither seems to have been the case. The variation in the occupation span estimates suggests that residential mobility was stimulated by several factors, and social factors may have been more important than either environmental change or resource depletion in causing the residential movement of households.

The domestic cycle—a social factor—may have been important in determining the frequency of residential movement at sites where occupation was limited to a single generation, which includes both of the two Pueblo II occupations and three of the Pueblo III residential sites. At these sites, new residences may have been built at or near the time that new households formed, and they may subsequently have been abandoned after children had grown and left the households. At the eight Pueblo III residential sites occupied for more than one generation, new households either used the existing residential facilities or added new residential structures so that the site grew by accretion.

Occupation span estimates for the Sand Canyon locality rarely exceed three generations. Gaines and Gaines (1997) have simulated the population dynamics of a hypothetical three-household settlement on a year-by-year basis over a period of 70 years. They found the longevity of such a settlement to be extremely sensitive to the survival schedule and the marriage and residence rules employed in the simulation. Their work indicates that there are limits to the occupation duration of small sites set by the demographic composition of the group. The small residences in the Sand Canyon locality that were occupied for two and three generations may have been abandoned because they were no longer demographically viable.

It is clear that some of the small residential sites in the Sand Canyon locality were occupied through periods of environmental deterioration, judging from their occupation span estimates and their dating. Research has shown that agricultural productivity in the Sand Canyon locality was higher than average for the region as a whole (Van West 1994), and Sand Canyon locality households may have been able to withstand times of environmental deterioration. This may not have been true for areas of lower agricultural productivity; future research in these areas may document greater household movement during periods of environmental deterioration. It is possible that the Sand Canyon locality actually absorbed population during these environmentally stressed times, although this remains a question for future research.

Finally, the occupation span estimates move in a direction opposite to that predicted by simple resource depletion models. That is, resource depletion around the Pueblo III habitations was almost certainly greater than depletion around the Pueblo II residential sites, yet the Pueblo III residences were occupied longer. The Pueblo II and Pueblo III habitation sites located on the mesa top are on the same type of soil, so changing agricultural productivity does not explain why they were occupied for different intervals. In addition, all habitation sites in the Sand Canyon community lie within a few kilometers of one another, so access to wild food resources and other raw materials was similar for all of them. This does not mean that resource depletion in the vicinity of these residential sites did not occur—on the contrary, it almost certainly did. But resource depletion did not dictate household movement in a regular or mechanistic fashion. The decision by a household to move or stay put in response to local resource depletion depended on the social context. This social context included the immediate community to which a household belonged and the other communities in the region.

COMMUNITY SEDENTISM AND MOBILITY

Analyses of community sedentism and mobility within the Sand Canyon locality are anchored by a growing body of middle-range theory that links the abandonment of structures, sites, and regions to particular behaviors. This middle-range theory is relevant to studies of population movement because the distance between an abandoned site and the nearest subsequently occupied site is an important factor determining the size of the artifact assemblage left at the abandoned site. When the distance is short, de facto refuse is salvaged from the abandoned site, but when the distance is long, de facto refuse is left behind. In the research reported here, I have attempted to contribute to this middle-range theory by showing how these general behaviors are influenced by historically contingent practices.

I also examined tree-ring dates in order to determine whether communities in the Sand Canyon locality were occupied continuously or intermittently, offering a new dimension for analyses using tree-ring dates. Traditionally, tree-ring dates have been used to date individual structures and sites. But stratigraphic analysis demonstrates that timbers were commonly salvaged from individual structures for use elsewhere. Tree-ring dates recovered from burned structures provide evidence for the repeated use of the salvaged timbers. By aggregating the tree-ring dates from sites within community boundaries, the history of wood use by a community can be examined.

Before reviewing these analyses, it is useful to return to the definition of community used in this study. Communities have important spatial and temporal dimensions, and these constrain what can be considered a community. Communities are places where individuals have regular face-to-face contact, which sets geographic limits on the size of the community. At a specific point in time, communities have a definite membership—those people residing within the community boundaries. Because community members live in a geographically circumscribed area where they interact on a regular basis, they share the resources within their community catchment. Regular interaction and sharing of local resources within a geographically limited area is therefore fundamental to the definition of an ancient community. The importance of this cannot be overstated, because regular interaction in the context of copresence is critical to the reproduction of society (Giddens 1984:64–72). The form, composition, and organization of the community change through time, but this does not mean that the community itself fails to persist. Instead, understanding these community dynamics becomes one of our primary goals in studying ancient communities.

These Sand Canyon locality data were used to define the geographical, demographical, and sociohistorical dimensions of Mesa Verde–region communities, producing a model for their settlement patterns and organization that differs from models used in previous analyses. The main difference is that communities are seen as having a community center with an associated settlement cluster. The community center is the area of densest residential settlement and public architecture. Each community center is surrounded by a settlement cluster. The individuals and households that occupy the residential sites in this settlement cluster move relatively frequently, probably within their own community and between their community and neighboring communities. The community centers proper, however, have longer durations of occupation and move shorter distances.

Tree-ring dates suggest that the Sand Canyon community was occupied for a minimum of 100 years, and occupation for as long as three centuries is suggested by even earlier tree-ring dates and by the salvaging of pit structure roofs at abandonment. The abandonment of roof timbers as de facto refuse is largely limited to structures abandoned at the time of the final long-distance migration from the region. Timbers were commonly salvaged from earlier structures dating between the late A.D. 1000s and the middle to late 1200s. The salvaging of timbers suggests continuous or nearly continuous occupation of the Sand Canyon locality during this period. That these timbers appear to have been salvaged near the time the structures were abandoned suggests that it was the occupants of the abandoned structures who salvaged and reused the timbers, which implies continuity in the occupation of these communities.

The artifact density in abandoned pit structures suggests that mesa-top habitation sites continued to be used even after they were abandoned as year-round residences. These mesa-top habitation sites are interpreted as having undergone continued use as field houses—a hypothesis that is reasonable in the light of existing data but that clearly needs further research. If these sites did see continued use as field houses, then the residential mobility that resulted from their abandonment as habitations was not due to depletion of soil nutrients. Again, the continuous use of these sites, despite the changing settlement pattern, implies continuity in ownership, which further implies continuity in the occupation of the community.

Evidence for long and continuous occupation of localities is also seen in the tree-ring dates from Chapin and Wetherill Mesas in Mesa Verde National Park. In these areas there was nearly continuous occupation for as long as 300 years and perhaps even more. On Chapin Mesa, which has the largest sample of excavated sites, there is continuous occupation, punctuated by only short periods of possible abandonment, for 600 years. Together these analyses indicate that histories of individual communities in the Sand Canyon locality and on Mesa Verde often spanned centuries. Understanding the organizational dynamics of these communities requires a detailed reconstruction of their histories and a thorough description of the regional social context. Examination of the regional context also permits an evaluation of models of community organization based on Sand Canyon locality research.

The historical development of Mesa Verde–region communities at a regional scale was examined using the existing survey data, the community center database, and a database that included every tree-ring date from the Mesa Verde region. These analyses revealed three general characteristics of the Mesa Verde–region social landscape between A.D. 950 and 1290. First, there was population growth and increased clustering of communities in the central Mesa Verde region. Second, the boundaries of the large-site settlement system as a whole constricted through time, so that these large-site communities became increasingly isolated from adjacent areas. Finally, there were localities in the Mesa Verde region where communities consisted entirely of small sites that apparently were not organized around either a large site or public architecture. Settlement patterns similar to those documented for the Sand Canyon locality characterize many communities in the central Mesa Verde region, but community organization outside of this area may have been more variable.

The frequency and distance that communities moved through time was examined by analyzing the community center database. Community movement—like the household movement already discussed—was characterized by variability. There was variation in the distances that communities moved and in the lengths of time that communities were occupied. There is, however, a general pattern to this variation. Communities on the margins of the large-site settlement system moved the greatest distances and had the shortest histories, whereas shorter-distance moves and longer occupational histories tend to characterize communities in the central Mesa Verde region. The short-distance moves in the central Mesa Verde region are further evidence for the continuity of community organization and the historic development of these communities.

The variation in the distances that communities moved suggests that the stimuli for this movement also varied. It is possible that resource depletion stimulated movement over longer distances on the margins of the large-site settlement system. It is unlikely, however, that resource depletion stimulated the shorter-distance movement in the central Mesa Verde region. This is especially true for the depletion of timber for construction materials and fuel, which has been identified as an important stimulus to mobility in other studies (Kohler and Matthews 1988). In much of the central Mesa Verde region, there were community centers within the same community catchment areas in sequential periods. Even if these communities were periodically abandoned and resettled, the periods of abandonment would have been insufficient to allow full regeneration of local resources, especially of the pinyon-juniper forest.

Tree-ring data indicate that the entire Mesa Verde region was never fully abandoned between A.D. 950 and 1290. There are, however, far fewer tree-ring dates during the late 1000s and again between 1150 and 1170. Droughts occurred during both of these intervals. Households and communities that had access only to marginal resources may have left the region (or been forced out) during these periods. A similar process has been documented in historic-period pueblos (Levy 1992). Determining whether this occurred in the Mesa Verde region requires further research, including better chronologies from a variety of areas within the region. At present, the tree-ring data can suggest only that short-term emigration as a response to climatic deterioration, similar to that proposed for the Dolores River valley between 650 and 920 (Schlanger and Wilshusen 1993), *may* have occurred in the Mesa Verde region during the 950 to 1300 period as well.

Finally, researchers have offered different interpretations of the timing of emigration from the Mesa Verde region. Some suggest emigration began in A.D. 1150 (Eddy, Kane, and Nickens 1984:40), others argue for the early 1200s (Lipe 1995:152), and still others argue that population grew until the last decades of the 1200s, with a large, rapid out-migration at that time (Rohn 1989:166). All three interpretations could be correct. Communities on the margins of the large-site settlement system were being abandoned in 1150, a process that continued in the early 1200s. Some of the members of these communities may have left the region to join communities elsewhere, creating migration streams for subsequent population movement (indeed, movement in the late 1100s may have followed migration streams established by the tenth-century migrations from the region). In the central Mesa Verde region during the same 1150 to 1225 period, there was continuity of occupation in some communities, and new communities formed in this area after 1225. Some localities in the central Mesa Verde region *did* grow until the late 1200s, and undoubtedly there were many thousands of people living in the region in the decade preceding the final migrations.

PERSISTENT COMMUNITIES IN THE MESA VERDE REGION

The data on community movement presented in chapter 7 can be used to identify the most persistently occupied places in the Mesa Verde region and, by extension, the communities with the longest histories. For the most part, these persistent communities are identified by grouping community centers that moved fewer than 7 kilometers from one time period to the next; however, a few cases in which the move was just above this 7-kilometer threshold are also included. These persistent communities are listed in table 8.1, beginning with communities located in the southeast portion of the study area and moving toward the northwest.

Figure 8.1 illustrates these 27 persistent places, showing the 2- and 7-kilometer cost-equivalent radii around each community center (see figs. 7.2–7.5 for the locations and names of individual community centers). On the south, there is a persistent community in Mancos Canyon, and to the north of it is one on Chapin Mesa (there are almost certainly additional persistent communities on Mesa Verde—for example, on Wetherill Mesa—but they do not show up because earlier communities on Mesa Verde were not organized around large sites). There are three persistent communities between Mesa Verde and McElmo Creek: the Yucca House, Mud Springs, and Mitchell Springs communities. The largest concentration of persistent communities occurs in the area between McElmo Creek and Squaw Mesa, where there are 16 persistent communities. Farther west, there is a persistent community in Montezuma Canyon and another just to the west on Alkali Ridge.

The 7-kilometer threshold was relaxed in the area to the west of Alkali Ridge. At this slightly larger scale of movement, there is persistent use of

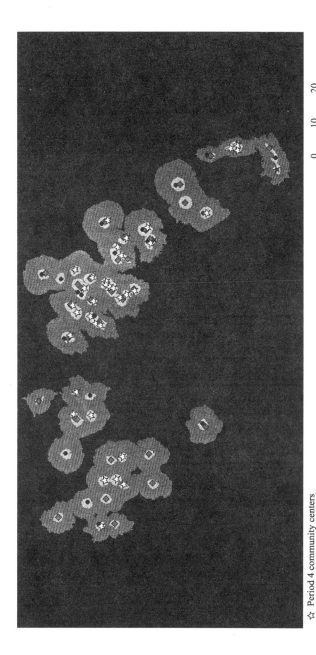

☆ Period 4 community centers

◆ Period 3 community centers

● Period 2 community centers

★ Period 1 community centers

Figure 8.1 Locations of 27 persistent communities, showing their associated community centers and their 2- and 7-kilometer cost-equivalent catchments.

Table 8.1 Mesa Verde–Region Persistent Places, A.D. 900–1290

NO.	PERSISTENT COMMUNITY	PERIOD 1 COMMUNITY CENTER (A.D. 950–1049)	PERIOD 2 COMMUNITY CENTER (A.D. 1050–1149)	PERIOD 3 COMMUNITY CENTER (A.D. 1150–1224)	PERIOD 4 COMMUNITY CENTER (A.D. 1225–1290)
1	Mancos Canyon area	Mancos Canyon great kiva	Navajo Canyon great house	Kiva Point	
2	Mesa Verde–Chapin Mesa area		Far View House	Far View House	Spruce Tree, Cliff Palace, Oak Tree, Square Tower
3	Yucca House–Mud Springs area		Yucca House	Mud Springs	Yucca House
4	Mitchell Springs area		Mitchell Springs	Mitchell Springs	
5	Sand Canyon area	Sand Canyon great kiva	Casa Negra	Casa Negra	Sand Canyon Pueblo
6	Goodman Point area		Goodman Point great house	Shields Pueblo, Goodman Point great kiva	Goodman Point Pueblo
7	Yellow Jacket area		Yellow Jacket Pueblo great house	Yellow Jacket Pueblo	Yellow Jacket Pueblo
8	Easter Ruin area			Griffey Ruin	Easter Ruin
9	Woods Canyon area		Uncle Albert Porter	Bass complex, Rich's Ruin	Woods Canyon Pueblo, Rohn 150

No.	Area			
10	Carvell area		Carvell Ruin	Carvell Ruin
11	Lancaster area	Ansel Hall	Lancaster/Pharo Ruin	Lancaster Ruin
12	Ruin Canyon area		Herren Farm Ruin	Beartooth Ruin
13	Lowry area	Lowry Pueblo, North Lowry, Casa de Valle	Pigg Site, Finley Farm/Ray Ruin/Charnel	Little Cow Canyon Pueblo
14	Mockingbird Mesa area		Mockingbird Mesa-Top Ruin	Seven Towers Ruin
15	Upper Hovenweep Canyon area		Upper Hovenweep Canyon Mesa-Top, Kristie's Ruin, Carol's Ruin	Gardner Ruin, Miller Pueblo, Thompson Ruin, McVicker Homestead Ruin
16	Middle Cajon Mesa area		Kearns Site	Big Spring Ruin, Hibbets Pueblo
17	Lower Cow Canyon area		Lower Cow Canyon Ruin	Cottonwood Ruin
18	Brewer area		Brewer Pueblo	Berkeley Bryant Site
19	Middle Squaw Mesa area	Upper Squaw Mesa Village	Lower Squaw Mesa Village	Papoose Canyon Pueblo, Brewer Well, Spook Point Pueblo
20	Hedley area	Hedley West Ruin	Hedley Middle Ruin	Hedley Main Ruin

Table 8.1 (continued)

NO.	PERSISTENT COMMUNITY	PERIOD 1 COMMUNITY CENTER (A.D. 950–1049)	PERIOD 2 COMMUNITY CENTER (A.D. 1050–1149)	PERIOD 3 COMMUNITY CENTER (A.D. 1150–1224)	PERIOD 4 COMMUNITY CENTER (A.D. 1225–1290)
21	Montezuma Canyon area		Montezuma Village I	Montezuma Village II	Coalbed Village
22	Alkali Mesa area		Three-Kiva Ruin	Ten-Acre Ruin, Brew's Site #1	Bradford Canyon-Head Ruin, Deadman's Canyon
23	Montezuma Creek area		Jackson's Montezuma Creek #1	Jackson's Montezuma Creek #2	
24	Recapture Wash area		Moki Island	Parker Ruin, Gravel Pit Ruin	Ute Gravel Pit Site
25	Upper Cottonwood Wash area		Cottonwood Falls great house	Red Knobs, Black Mesa Quartzite Pueblo	Radon Spring Ruin, Ruin Spring Ruin
26	Middle Cottonwood Wash area			Decker Ruin	Wetherill's Chimney Rock
27	Upper Comb Wash area		Arch Canyon Pueblo	Mouth of Mule Canyon	Arch Canyon Pueblo

each of the major north-south drainages: Recapture Wash, Cottonwood Wash, and Comb Wash. The persistent use of these drainages indicates historical continuity in the occupation of the western edge of the Mesa Verde region, but on a spatially more extensive scale. Environmental conditions may help explain why these communities are spatially extensive: the area west of Alkali Ridge is lower in elevation, is drier, and has shallower soils than the central Mesa Verde region. There is a final persistent community identified on Montezuma Creek near the San Juan River. These persistent communities were not the only communities in the region that had histories, but they are the largest communities with the longest histories. As such, they would have structured in important ways the social landscape in which individuals and households moved.

SEDENTISM AND MOBILITY AS A SOCIAL PROCESS

To explain the variation and patterns documented for household and community mobility in the Mesa Verde region, residential movement needs to be considered as a socially negotiated activity. Modeling mobility as a social process requires social theory—that is, theory concerned with the nature of human action (practice and agency) and the relation of this behavior to historically derived structure. The relationship between practice/agency and structure has been one of the chief problems addressed by anthropologists since the 1960s (Ortner 1984). But cultural anthropology, because it typically examines behavior over a limited time frame, is best suited to understanding agency and, to a lesser degree, how structure enables and constrains agency. The research reported here, however, examines the dynamic interplay between structure and practice/agency over a period of more than 300 years in order to analyze changes in residential mobility in the Mesa Verde region. Archaeology is unique among the social sciences in its potential for understanding structure as being historically constituted and in its ability to show how practice/agency both reproduces *and* transforms this structure.

Individuals and households, and probably some suprahousehold groups, were the agents who negotiated residential movement. This movement was negotiated in a social landscape defined in part by the communities illustrated in figure 8.1, as well as by other, smaller communities not identified there. Structure in the Mesa Verde region developed in the context of these historically constituted communities. The practice of residential mobility, an example of human agency, reproduced and transformed the system of land tenure. Land tenure systems were an important part of the social structure in the Mesa Verde region and were negotiated by individuals at the social scale of the community.

Residential Mobility, Agricultural Production, and Land Tenure

It is useful to conceive of residential mobility as an element of a group's mode of production. This helps us envision individuals and households as strategic actors who negotiate their self-interest when making residential moves. Residential mobility is an important part of the mode of production because it directly affects how individuals and households gain access to the most critical resources in agricultural production: land and labor.

Small residential sites in the Mesa Verde region in the early Pueblo II period were associated with the best soils for dryland agriculture, but as population grew, some increasing numbers of residences were located on soils that were less agriculturally productive (Adler 1990:239, 1996b; Fetterman and Honeycutt 1987:103, 125; Hayes 1964:93, 109; Rohn 1977:237, 241–243). The only period when there was no direct association between arable land and residential sites was when the large, canyon-oriented villages were settled in the middle to late 1200s. Thus, the placement of residential sites appears to have been a means by which households claimed land, probably farming areas close to their residence. In addition, residential mobility was the means by which individuals and households gained access to social resources—that is, by placing residential sites in proximity to those of other community members.

Kelly (1992:48) lists many factors that cause mobility, including economic, social, and political considerations. The proximate cause for every move cannot be known, but these moves, when they occurred, were the means by which people gained access to natural and social resources. Even though we cannot know the cause for every move, the changing frequency of residential movement can be documented and used to examine the social context in which it occurred.

People maintain their access to productive resources through systems of land tenure. Adler (1996b) sees land tenure as a complex, risk-buffering strategy; land tenure assures one's access to productive resources, thereby reducing uncertainty, but it also denies one access to lands held in tenure by other groups, thereby increasing risk. Land tenure varies considerably, from relatively communal access (which does not mean equal access by everyone but rather ownership by groups larger than either individuals or households) to heritable property rights vested in particular individuals. In relatively unrestrictive land tenure systems, people own land only so long as they are actively using it—a form of ownership termed *usufruct*— but with more formal land tenure people retain ownership to land that is not in active use.

Adler (1996b) documents a cross-cultural pattern in which small groups have primary access to productive resources for short periods of time in situations requiring low agricultural labor investment. An example is that of swidden agriculturalists for whom land ownership is defined by usufruct. Larger primary-access groups, composed of many households, are found where there are moderate levels of agricultural intensification. At high levels of agricultural intensification, small primary-access groups are again typical, but they maintain rights to land over long periods of time through inheritance. Adler (1996b) uses this cross-cultural pattern to interpret changing settlement patterns in the Sand Canyon locality. He argues that increasing population density stimulated moderate levels of agricultural intensification and an increase in the sizes of primary-resource access groups, as evidenced by increasing site size and aggregation through time.

I view land tenure as an important part of what Cowgill (1993a) calls local rules and therefore as an important part of the structure that enabled and constrained the residential mobility of strategic actors. Focusing on land tenure systems links the social scales examined in this study. Individuals and households used the practice of residential movement to gain access to productive resources. This access, however, was negotiated at a larger social scale, because individuals and households lived close to many others who sought access to the same productive resources. In the larger region, individuals and households not only negotiated among themselves for access to local resources but also, as communities, they acted to perpetuate their collective land-use rights in the larger regional landscape composed of many communities. The collective role of communities in the social reproduction and protection of land-use rights becomes increasingly important as the land-use rights of individuals and households become more exclusionary (Adler 1996b). The multicommunity clusters identified in chapter 7 may indicate that the social reproduction and protection of land-use rights occurred on an even larger social scale in the final period of occupation in the Mesa Verde region.

Land tenure systems are socially mediated, historically constituted, and highly flexible; their flexibility stems from their being the product of active social negotiations. Adler (1996b) notes that land tenure systems exist in the minds of individuals, and as such they cannot be unearthed from the archaeological record. I argue that the frequency of residential movement provides archaeological evidence from which we can make inferences about land tenure, illuminating how land tenure was both reproduced and transformed.

The process of residential mobility includes the construction of houses, which are more than just places to live. Especially with dispersed settlement patterns, the location of a residence marks the ownership of resources in the area immediately surrounding it. Pit structures and kivas, even if they were used primarily for domestic activities, also served important ritual and symbolic ends (Lipe 1989). In addition, residential sites were used as burial grounds, which may have further enhanced their symbolic importance. It is unlikely that meaning associated with these places simply vanished when they were abandoned as permanent residences. Even if we cannot decode the specific meaning that subsequent inhabitants of the area gave to these abandoned residential sites, we can be sure that they were a recognizable part of the social landscape. Indeed, they remain a part of the social landscape today.

The symbolic importance of these abandoned residences is especially relevant when the long history of many of the communities is considered. During the historical development of these communities, through the practice of residential movement, the social landscape became increasingly filled with these symbols of past ownership and land use. The changing social landscape of the Mesa Verde region was not characterized simply by increasing population density but also by an increasing density of abandoned residences, which I suggest were highly charged symbols. These abandoned residences and burial grounds might have been important *symbolic* resources that individuals and households drew upon as they negotiated their claims to *productive* resources through the practice of residential mobility.

Although land tenure systems existed in the minds of individuals, the *practice* of residential movement materialized them. Estimates of occupation span and frequency of household residential movement indicate that Pueblo II residences were occupied for a single generation each. It is likely that residential mobility during this period was linked to the domestic cycle. Land was plentiful relative to later periods, and each generation may have claimed new land on which to reside and farm when forming new households. Length of occupation was measured at only two habitation components during this period, but the inference that habitations at this time were limited to a single generation is supported by their having consisted of earthen architecture; several researchers have demonstrated that earthen buildings in temperate climates have a maximum use-life of 30 years (Ahlstrom 1985:83–84, 638; Cameron 1990; Diehl 1992; McIntosh 1974; Schlanger 1987:586).

Elsewhere I have argued that the earth-to-masonry architectural transition had important implications for changing patterns of residential mobility (Varien 1998), a point supported by Diehl's (1992) cross-cultural research. A review of Mesa Verde–region architectural trends shows that almost all residences before A.D. 1050 were constructed as earthen buildings (Varien 1998). The transition to masonry buildings occurred between 1050 and 1150, apparently developing earlier on Mesa Verde proper and later in other areas in the region (Varien 1998). Thus, single-generation occupations characterize the 950 to 1050/1150 period, a time when residential sites have the closest association with the most productive soils.

The Sand Canyon locality residential sites that postdate 1150 include some habitations that were occupied for a single generation and others that were almost certainly occupied for at least two and perhaps three generations. There was increasing overlap of community catchments in the central Mesa Verde region in the post-1150 period, resulting in greater competition for resources there. Increasing population, increasing competition for resources, and decreasing potential for mobility are related to the development of increasingly formal and exclusionary land tenure systems (Adler 1996b; Netting 1993; Stone 1993, 1996; Stone, Netting, and Stone

1990). The occupation of residential sites for multiple generations is evidence of a transformation in land tenure systems in the Mesa Verde region. Particular residences and the resources associated with them appear to have been passed down through several generations. These cases, in which the transmission of resources is so apparent, reinforce Halperin's (1989) point: residential mobility, or the lack thereof, represents not only changing places but also changing hands.

To restate and summarize the foregoing argument, land tenure, as an institution, was reproduced and transformed through the practice of residential mobility. Between A.D. 950 and 1300, individuals and households gained access to natural and social resources via the construction and placement of residential sites. Population density and competition for resources was low when Mesa Verde–region communities were first formed between 950 and 1050, and land tenure was probably characterized by usufruct. Through time, population density and competition for resources increased. Negotiation for land-use rights would have become more competitive as well, and people may have begun to use historic claims to use-rights in order to claim access to land that was not in constant production. Historic connections to abandoned residential sites and burial grounds may have been important symbols in this process of negotiation. Eventually, population density and competition for resources increased to the point at which residential sites changed from earthen to masonry buildings and some residential sites began to be occupied for multiple generations. A land tenure system based on usufruct was transformed into one based on some form of heritable property rights.

The historical development of these land tenure systems may have been an important factor enabling the dramatic residential mobility that characterized the settlement pattern changes of the 1200s, in which households moved from their mesa-top farms into canyon-oriented villages. Centuries of residential mobility may have resulted in more formal and exclusionary land tenure systems, and the social landscape may have been socially formatted to the degree that groups no longer needed to live directly on their farms in order to protect their claims to productive land (Adler 1990). Households within communities may have recognized the historic claims to land by other community members, and communities may have taken on a much more important role in protecting these land-use claims in a context of greater regional competition for resources. If access to productive land within the community was ensured through this historically constituted land tenure system, the movement to aggregated, canyon-oriented villages may signal a point at which accessing social resources—including those used for defense in a time of conflict—had become more important than claiming productive resources. The development of multi-community clusters may have been a means by which the land use rights of individuals and households were ensured at a social scale larger than that of the single community.

Occupation span estimates for the post-1150 habitations also exhibit considerable variation. This variability indicates that households pursued different strategies of residential movement, and it is likely that some households were more successful than others when they negotiated this movement as a means of gaining access to natural and social resources. Future research should measure changes in residential mobility through time and across space, improving our understanding of the variation in occupation span. It will be particularly important to measure the frequency of household movement in a number of the persistent communities and in communities that were less persistent.

Marriage, Residence, and the Movement of Individuals

Local marriage and postmarital residence rules were another important aspect of structure that affected residential mobility in the Mesa Verde region. Given the reconstruction of the population size of Sand Canyon locality communities (Adler 1990, 1992, 1996b; Adler and Varien 1994), it is clear that it was not until after A.D. 1150 that single communities were large enough to have provided a viable mating network internally. Before 1150, marriages would almost certainly have been between individuals from different communities, and residential mobility linked to the domestic cycle would have required the movement of individuals across community boundaries. This was probably important in building relationships between households in different communities, thereby facilitating interaction within the region. Residential mobility was a means of gaining access to productive natural and social resources, but the movement of individuals between communities affected political life as well.

EXTENSIFIERS AND INTENSIFIERS

To conclude this study, I focus on a final aspect of the variation and patterning revealed by these analyses—the increasing contrast between communities in the central Mesa Verde region and those on the periphery. In the central Mesa Verde region, community centers were larger, many had longer occupation spans, and there were shorter-distance moves between community centers of successive periods. This resulted in greater catchment overlap and more persistent communities in the central Mesa Verde region, as illustrated in figure 8.1. Outside of this central area, communities were spatially more extensive, and there were some communities that were not organized around large sites and public architecture.

To borrow terminology from Stone (1993), the people inhabiting the persistent communities in figure 8.1 increasingly became "intensifiers," and those living outside these persistent communities remained "extensifiers." If intensification is measured in terms of increasing population, material, information, or energy per unit area or per capita (Lipe 1992:128), then the inhabitants of the central Mesa Verde region became intensifiers simply as a result of their increasing population density through time. More specifically, there is evidence that the technology of agricultural production was intensified to a greater degree in the area associated with the persistent communities.

Ecological variables undoubtedly played a role in defining the area occupied by these intensifiers. This area corresponds roughly with the location of the most productive agricultural land today—the deepest mesa-top soils that are best suited to dryland agriculture. It is also the area that provides the best mix of mesa-top and canyon environments, a combination that increased the opportunities for a mixed agricultural strategy combining dryland agriculture on the mesa tops and canyon-oriented floodwater irrigation. And this area is at an elevation that offers the best trade-off between frost-free growing season and precipitation. Outside of this area—in the portion of the region occupied by groups who remained extensifiers—soils are shallower, precipitation is less in the areas of lower elevation, and the growing season is shorter in areas of higher elevation.

The Ute Mountain Archaeological Project (Breternitz and Robinson 1996) provides an example of mobility and sedentism in the area occupied by extensifiers. This project examined communities on the southern pied-mont of Ute Mountain, with a focus on Cowboy Wash, a drainage that flows only during periods of rainfall runoff (see fig. 7.2 for the location of Ute Mountain and fig. 7.5 for the location of Cowboy Wash Pueblo). Between A.D. 1025 and 1280 there were three occupations in this area, each with a different settlement strategy (Billman 1997, 1998).

The first was short-lived, dating sometime between 1050 and 1075. Small habitations with a single pit structure each were widely dispersed, and there was no community center with public architecture. The residential sites show evidence of year-round occupation, but the middens are shallow, indicating short occupation spans. This occupation is interpreted as the result of individual households homesteading a wide area on the southern piedmont, where they took advantage of a period of higher than normal summer precipitation to practice dry farming. This attempt at homestead-ing apparently failed, and the homesteads were abandoned by 1075 (Billman 1998).

The second occupation occurred sometime between 1075 and 1150. Resi-dential sites were still predominantly single-household occupations, but they were distributed in recognizable settlement clusters along three drain-ages: Navajo Wash, West Navajo Wash, and Cowboy Wash. Again there was no community center or public architecture associated with these settlement clusters. Settlement occurred as a result of the nearly synchro-nous movement of entire communities into the area, communities that settled in the most productive area for floodwater agriculture (Billman 1998; Huckleberry and Billman n.d.). Population in the Cowboy Wash community grew rapidly between 1075 and 1125. It declined significantly between 1125 and 1150, and the community appears to have met a violent end at around 1150. Many of the pit structure floors were littered with disarticulated, intensively fractured human remains.

During the final period of occupation, dating between 1225 and 1280, two communities were founded, one on Cowboy Wash and one near Moqui Springs in West Navajo Wash. Each community was organized around a community center with public architecture, the Cowboy Wash and Moqui Springs Pueblos (table 7.3, fig. 7.5). Again, these communities appear to have been settled as a result of community mobility. Individual sites have longer occupation spans, some lasting two generations. The longevity of these communities, compared with those of previous occupations, is attributed to intensified ceremonialism and agricultural production (Billman 1997). Evidence of violence is also present in the human remains of this period, but rather than disarticulated remains on pit structure floors, this violence is evidenced by an increasing number of individuals with heavy trauma to the cranium, not unlike that documented for the Sand Canyon locality and other areas of the Mesa Verde region during this period (Lightfoot and Kuckelman n.d.). Thus, the final inhabitants of the southern piedmont of Ute Mountain were more like the intensifiers of the central Mesa Verde region.

Through time, settlement in the Mesa Verde region increasingly diverged into these two different strategies. Intensifiers developed more persistent communities by intensifying ceremonialism and agricultural production. The result was lower-frequency residential movement. Extensifiers continued to rely on more frequent and more spatially extensive residential movement.

These two groups may have come to use the area outside the immediate catchments of the persistent communities in different ways. Intensifiers may have organized logistically to exploit this periphery as a secondary sustaining area, particularly if their immediate catchments became depleted of resources such as large game. Extensifiers, on the other hand, continued to use the area on the periphery of the central Mesa Verde region as their primary sustaining area, with more extensive land use and a higher frequency of residential movement. These two differing modes of production, exploiting the same area in different ways, may have produced tensions between those living in the two areas. It is possible that such tensions contributed to the increasing conflict documented for the Mesa Verde region during the late 1200s. This conflict may have contributed to the residential movement that brought the residential occupation of the Mesa Verde region to its dramatic end: the final migrations from the region.

NOTES

CHAPTER 1. SEDENTISM AND MOBILITY IN HORTICULTURAL AND AGRICULTURAL SOCIETIES

1. Many studies use accumulations research to understand questions of assemblage formation. Good examples include Aldenderfer 1981a, 1981b; Ammerman and Feldman 1974; David 1972; de Barros 1982; DeBoer 1974, 1985; Hatch, Whittington, and Dyke 1982; Kintigh 1984; Lightfoot 1994; Mills 1989a; Orton 1982; and Schlanger 1990, 1991.

CHAPTER 3. SEDENTISM AND MOBILITY IN THE MESA VERDE REGION

1. Petersen (1986, 1987a, 1988) also evaluates changes in the length of the growing season by examining the bristlecone pine tree-ring record from the Almagre Mountains in the central Colorado Rockies. These data are not included because the Almagre Mountain bristlecone pine chronology is poorly suited for reconstructing temperature in southwestern Colorado for the following reasons: (1) it is a tree-ring sequence with poor time-sequence properties, (2) there is no proof that such tree-ring sequences are sensitive to mean annual temperature, and (3) Four Corners climate is not related to that of the Front Range (Jeffrey S. Dean, personal communication, 1996).

2. Force and Howell's reconstruction is virtually identical to Karlstrom's (1988) for the Black Mesa region, and the local processes emphasized by Force and Howell do not explain the synchroneity of arroyo cutting across the entire southern Colorado Plateau.

3. Force and Howell (1997) also argue that ancient farmers in McElmo Canyon took advantage of the aggrading conditions for floodwater farming between A.D. 900 and 1300. Floodwater farming focused on manipulating water from the side canyons entering McElmo Canyon from the north, but evidence also exists for water control features on the main channel of McElmo Creek. Minimum sediment accumulation rates were between 1.5 and 2.5 meters per 100 years, a figure that could not be representative of the entire Holocene because this would have produced deposits more than 150 to 250 meters thick (Force and Howell 1997). The rapid deposition was due in part to agricultural practices; ancient farmers were selecting areas of rapid aggradation, and their agricultural practices intensified the process of aggradation. Habitations were located close to these agriculturally desirable places but on the less active parts of the aggrading system: high spots on alluvial fans, old terrace remnants on valley flanks, valley edge talus and bedrock exposures, and other inactive portions of the floodplain.

Force and Howell suggest these agricultural activities might have triggered another period of entrenchment in the following ways: (1) floodwater farming areas along the

McElmo increased the size of the northside fans, which in turn constricted the main channel, thereby increasing its gradient; (2) habitation and agriculture would have cleared vegetation, resulting in reduced bottom cohesion and increased susceptibility of the main channel to entrenchment; and (3) sediment impoundment behind agricultural features would have decreased the sediment load. It is clear, however, that entrenchment did not occur until well into the A.D. 1200s, and these localized human activities do not explain why arroyo cutting occurred at the same time across the entire southern Colorado Plateau.

Pueblo III habitation sites and agricultural features located on the fans just above the active floodplain were abandoned in the early 1200s. The post-abandonment stratigraphy at these sites clearly indicates that the hydrologic system continued to aggrade *after* these small sites were abandoned. Their abandonment was not the result of changing hydrological conditions but instead seems to have been a part of regionwide changes in settlement patterns that characterized the Mesa Verde region beginning in the early to middle 1200s. These changes included the shift to aggregated settlement, canyon environments, and defensible site locations (Varien 1998; Varien et al. 1996). In sum, entrenchment did not begin until at least the middle 1200s and occurred over many decades. It is therefore unlikely that it was the sole cause of abandonment and mobility in McElmo Canyon or in the other drainages of the Mesa Verde region.

4. Nelson and Anyon (1996) argue that this fallow valley pattern can be expected under the following conditions: (1) relatively intensive agriculture such that a portion of the community works in fields throughout the growing season, (2) low regional population density, and (3) a situation in which resources other than agricultural land constrain the length of the stay, requiring long-distance population movement in order to allow the regeneration of critical resources.

CHAPTER 4. MEASURING HOUSEHOLD RESIDENTIAL MOBILITY

1. Cook's contributions to accumulations research can be found in the following publications: Cook 1946, 1972a, 1972b; Cook and Heizer 1965, 1968; Cook and Treganza 1947, 1950; Treganza and Cook 1948.

2. Kleindienst and Watson (1956) were also among the first to challenge archaeologists to study living communities, but they were concerned with establishing a more secure basis for analogical interpretations of archaeological materials. Binford's research was particularly influential in shaping these early studies; his interest in both cultural and natural formation processes spans decades (Binford 1962, 1968, 1976, 1978a, 1978b, 1979, 1981a, 1981b).

3. Among other topics, these studies examined the function, use-life, and discard of artifacts (Arnold 1990; Coles 1979; Deal 1985; Gould, Koster, and Sontz 1971; Hayden and Cannon 1983; Murray 1980; Tani 1994); the factors that structure site layout (Arnold 1991; Kent 1991a, 1992; Killion 1990); and how social organization and activity areas can

be inferred at occupied or recently abandoned sites (Bonnichsen 1973; David 1971; Longacre and Ayres 1968).

4. Aldenderfer (1981a, 1981b), Ammerman and Feldman (1974), Hatch, Whittington, and Dyke (1982), Kintigh (1984), Lightfoot (1992a), Orton (1982), Schlanger (1990), and Shott (1989) all used simulations to examine aspects of this relationship.

5. Much of this work has been pioneered by Kohler and his colleagues (Kohler 1978; Kohler and Blinman 1987; Nelson, Kohler, and Kintigh 1994). Kohler (1978) used the principles of the discard equation in a simulation to estimate population size and growth rate and to evaluate political complexity at a site in Florida. Kohler and Blinman (1987) examined the total accumulation of pottery on Basketmaker III and Pueblo I sites in the Dolores River valley in southwestern Colorado, using these data to evaluate the seasonality of site occupation. Nelson, Kohler, and Kintigh (1994) refined these earlier estimates and employed pottery accumulations in estimating the occupation span of Dolores-area sites. Schlanger also focused on artifact accumulations in Dolores sites to simulate the effects of occupation span on assemblage composition (Schlanger 1990) and to examine the accumulation of ground stone artifacts (Schlanger 1991). Wallace (1995) used similar techniques to estimate pottery accumulation for Tonto Basin households to address the question of the scale of pottery production and exchange.

6. See Arnold 1988; Bedaux 1987; Birmingham 1975; David 1972; David and Hennig 1972; Deal 1983; DeBoer 1974, 1983, 1985; DeBoer and Lathrap 1979; Gill 1981; Hagstrum 1987; Kramer 1985; Longacre 1985; Longacre and Skibo 1994; Miller 1985; Nelson 1981, 1991; Pastron 1974; Stark 1985; Weigand 1969.

7. The temperature gradient between the heated and unheated portions of the vessel can range between 300° and 600° C (Pierce 1998). The external surface of the vessel expands more than the interior of the vessel, and the base expands more than the upper portions of the vessel (Pierce 1998). The cooler portions of the vessel act as a restraining force to the vertical and horizontal expansion of surfaces. This results in compressive stress on the exterior surfaces, tensile stress on the interior surfaces, and shear stress vertically within the vessel wall (Pierce 1998). The opposite occurs as the vessel cools (Rye 1981:27; Rice 1987:229). This stress is relieved by micro-cracking (Rye 1981; Pierce 1998), and spalling or catastrophic macro-cracking can occur when these stresses exceed the vessel's strength (Bronitsky 1986:250).

8. Several experimental studies have examined how potters could control pore space and manipulate temper as a means of controlling crack propagation (Braun 1983, 1987; Bronitsky and Hamer 1986; Rye 1976; Steponaitis 1983; West 1992). These experiments report a number of contradictory conclusions, including whether the addition of fine temper or coarse temper is the better means of promoting thermal stress resistance. West (1992) has conducted the most comprehensive experiment evaluating how temper relates to thermal stress resistance. He separates strength from toughness as distinct properties of pottery. Strength is resistance to initial cracking due to impact, whereas toughness is the ability to absorb substantial amounts of energy (West 1992:18). He argues that cooking pots may have been the first pottery designed to maximize toughness

by absorbing fracture energy through crack deflection, branching, and blunting so that cracking occurs in a stable, as opposed to catastrophic, manner (West 1992:19). West's experiment addresses how toughness is achieved through the addition of temper.

9. The magnitude of error is illustrated by substituting the mean values for size of the San Mateo household cooking pot inventory and the use-lives of these vessels (Nelson 1991:177) into the discard equation. The equation predicts that 81 vessels would be discarded in a single year, whereas Nelson reports that only 12 vessels are replaced each year.

10. Lightfoot presented slightly different numbers in earlier publications interpreting the dating at Duckfoot (Lightfoot 1992b, 1993). The differences are due to the fact that only dates with a *vv* suffix were interpreted as noncutting dates in the earlier publication. In his most recent publication, Lightfoot also considers dates with the suffix ++ to be noncutting dates. Thus, a date of 851++B was interpreted as a cutting date in the earlier publications but as a noncutting date in his most recent publication.

11. There are earlier clusters of cutting dates present at this site, beginning in the A.D. 820s. These could be interpreted as initial site occupation, thereby extending the estimate of length of occupation to 50 or 60 years. Lightfoot (1992b, 1994), however, interpreted the timbers that provided the 820s dates as wood that was salvaged from abandoned sites in the immediate vicinity of Duckfoot. His interpretation is supported by cross-cultural studies of earthen architecture similar to that found at Duckfoot. These studies indicate that earthen buildings typically last between 6 and 12 years, rarely exceed 15 years without extensive remodeling, and have an upper limit of 20–30 years even with remodeling (Ahlstrom 1985:82–90, 638; Cameron 1990; Diehl 1992; McIntosh 1974; Schlanger 1987:589). Extensive remodeling of Duckfoot structures—including the complete rebuilding of pit structure roofs—was documented (Lightfoot, Etzkorn, and Varien 1993; Lightfoot 1994:23). Therefore, site use-life of 20–25 years is possible, but the longer estimate of 50–60 years is unlikely. The pottery from this site is also consistent with a site occupied between A.D. 850 and 880; if site occupation began in the 820s, higher frequencies of earlier types would be expected (see Blinman 1986a:69–79; 1988c). In sum, the available evidence overwhelmingly supports the interpretation that the minimum length of time Duckfoot was occupied was 20 years, and that the maximum duration of occupation was no greater than 25 years.

12. Pit structure 4 may have replaced pit structure 2—which was the only pit structure with an unburned roof and some secondary refuse on the floor—in the last years of occupation at Duckfoot.

13. In the analyses that follow, sherd weights are used when available. This is because sherd counts vary dramatically with the degree of vessel fragmentation, but weights do not (Egloff 1973; Evans 1973; Gifford 1916; Solheim 1960; see Pierce et al. 1998 for a discussion of the systematic differences between counts and weights in pottery assemblages from tested sites in the Sand Canyon locality).

14. The rim-arc analysis uses polar coordinate graph paper and follows the methods outlined by Egloff 1973. Polar coordinate graph paper has graduated concentric circles

and radial lines that mark angles in increments from 0° to 360°. Rim sherds are matched to the concentric circles on the graph paper to determine the size of the vessel orifice, and these measurements are used to determine size classes of vessels. When the rim sherd is matched to the correct concentric circle on the graph paper, the proportion of the vessel can be estimated using the graduated radial lines. Lightfoot (1994:75) also devised a method for counting and measuring the lengths of rim sherds that could not be matched to the polar coordinate graph paper because they were too small or had an irregular shape. He then wrote a simple computer program (1994:75) to accumulate the total degrees of arc represented by each size class, and these arc totals were divided by 360 to produce the minimum number of vessel estimates for each size category. Finally, the length totals for each form class were incorporated by summing the lengths and then dividing by the average rim circumference for that form class, as calculated from the reconstructed vessel assemblage from Duckfoot.

15. The weight estimate was produced by taking the number of vessels for each form and size category, multiplying it by the average weight of that vessel class in the reconstructed vessel assemblage, and then summing the results for all gray wares.

16. Lightfoot's definition of the household differs from that offered by archaeologists working on the Dolores Archaeological Project (Kohler and Blinman 1987:7; Wilshusen 1988b). DAP archaeologists argued that pit structures during the A.D. 850–880 period were shared by two to three households, each household having its residence in the surface room suite. Lightfoot's analysis of Duckfoot architecture and floor artifact assemblages support his interpretation. Seen in this light, the architectural suite as defined by Lightfoot has continuity through time, and the kiva units of the later Pueblo II and III periods would be analogous residential units (Lipe 1989).

17. Lightfoot (1994:79, table 4.5) reports the estimated number of small, medium, and large cooking pots discarded at Duckfoot. I divided these numbers by the estimate of the occupation span (20 to 25 years) and the number of households (3), which yields the number of cooking pots in each size category discarded per year per household. The inverse of this is the use-life of an individual cooking pot.

18. These numbers are taken from Kohler and Blinman's figure 2 (1987:8). The rate per pit structure corresponds to Lightfoot's annual rate per household.

19. The difference between the Kohler and Blinman (1987) accumulation rate and the Nelson, Kohler, and Kintigh (1994) accumulation rates stems primarily from the fact that Kohler and Blinman used data only from Grass Mesa Village, whereas Nelson and colleagues used data from nine sites in the Dolores River valley. This produced slightly different figures for the estimates of total discard and the average sherd weight.

20. Dolores data are from Nelson, Kohler, and Kintigh (1994:126–127). On the basis of data from Duckfoot, I determined that cooking pot sherds were 57.5 percent of the *total* pottery assemblage; I reduced the point estimates for the amount of *total* pottery at the Dolores sites to this amount (i.e., 57.5 percent) to determine the number of cooking pot sherds. Duckfoot data include material from the midden only (Lightfoot and Etzkorn 1993:318, 336), which ensures that only screened contexts are used. At

Duckfoot, cooking pots were 62.4 percent of the total *gray wares;* I reduced the number of total gray wares in the midden to this amount (i.e., 62.4 percent) to determine the number of cooking pot sherds in the midden.

CHAPTER 5. HOUSEHOLD RESIDENTIAL MOVEMENT IN THE SAND CANYON LOCALITY

1. For each sampling stratum, I calculated the percentages (using counts) of Pueblo II versus Pueblo III decorated white wares that were assigned to traditional types. These percentages were then used to partition the corrugated sherds in each sampling unit into Pueblo II and III portions. This procedure was used for the sampling strata in the centers of the 13 tested sites, but the outer periphery sampling strata typically had too few decorated white ware sherds to enable this procedure to be followed. The outer periphery contained two sampling strata; the northern outer periphery sampling stratum surrounded the architecture and inner periphery sampling strata, and the southern outer periphery sampling stratum surrounded the midden sampling stratum (Varien 1998). I used the relative percentages of Pueblo II and III decorated white wares from the architecture and inner periphery sampling strata to divide corrugated sherds in the northern outer periphery, and the relative percentages of Pueblo II and Pueblo III decorated white wares from the midden to divide the corrugated sherds in the southern outer periphery.

2. Lightfoot (1994:146) distinguishes between the family, which is a unit of kinship, and the household, which is a coresidential group—a distinction prevalent in anthropology since the 1950s (Bender 1967; Fortes 1958). As noted by Lightfoot, the household is the preferred unit of analysis in archaeology because it is recognized on the basis of the activities it performs rather than on the basis of the kin relations of its members. This behavioral definition of the household has been promoted by a number of archaeologists and anthropologists because it emphasizes "activities and patterned associations between activity groups" (Lightfoot 1994:146), which we can potentially reconstruct from the archaeological record. While acknowledging that we do not know the kin relations between members of Duckfoot households, Lightfoot (1994:158) suggests that each pit structure suite might have housed an extended family that included smaller, infrahousehold groups. Lightfoot (1994:162) argues that the Pueblo I pit structure suite as the architectural correlate of a large household is a pattern that persisted in the form of kiva suites in the subsequent Pueblo II and III periods.

3. If these point estimates are correct, the original interpretation of these sites (Varien 1998) must be reconsidered. I previously argued that these sites were constructed in the early A.D. 1200s and abandoned by the middle 1200s, when the major period of construction at Sand Canyon Pueblo occurred (Bradley 1993). The pottery assemblages from these sites support the interpretation that they were occupied earlier than Sand Canyon Pueblo (Hegmon 1991; Varien 1998). Thus, the sites were originally interpreted as having been constructed between 1210 and 1220 and abandoned by sometime between

1240 and 1250, giving the sites a 20–40 year period of occupation. The point estimates suggest that either the initial occupation of the site was earlier than previously interpreted or the occupation of these sites overlapped to a greater degree with Sand Canyon Pueblo. The tree-ring dates may therefore represent remodeling events rather than initial construction, and the true beginning date for these sites could be as early as 1180. This early construction date, in combination with the long site occupations, would still be consistent with the pottery assemblages present.

CHAPTER 6. COMMUNITY PERSISTENCE IN THE SAND CANYON LOCALITY

1. These strata are interpreted as culturally deposited unburned roof fall for several reasons. First, the sediments lack any of the sorting by particle size that would have occurred had they been transported by wind or water and deposited gradually as an intact roof deteriorated. Second, adobe, calcium carbonate, and artifactual inclusions within the stratum are too large to have been transported there by wind, and the inclusions are not eroded as would be the case had they been transported by water. Third, there is no evidence of bedding planes within the strata; instead, inclusions are oriented at random angles to one another. Fourth, chunks of unburned adobe, many with beam impressions, are present as inclusions. Finally, it is important to remember that the timbers in kiva roofs are below the courtyard surface. This means that if the roofs were abandoned and left intact to decay naturally, *all* of the roof timbers would eventually have to be incorporated in the structure fill. The absence of any evidence for roof timbers—either rotting wood or stratigraphic dislocation structures—in the strata covering the floor or anywhere in the structure fill sequence is further evidence that the timbers were salvaged at the time these structures were abandoned.

2. In the case of Sand Canyon locality structures, I believe the most important factor conditioning whether timbers were salvaged or abandoned was distance to the next occupied site. In the general model of abandonment behaviors outlined earlier, the presence or absence of de facto refuse was also conditioned by whether the abandonment was planned or unplanned and gradual or rapid. The burned Sand Canyon locality kivas, where there is abundant de facto refuse, do not appear to have been rapid/unplanned abandonments; instead, the burning appears to have been planned. The long-distance move that accompanied the abandonment of these structures did not permit people to salvage timbers or return to the abandoned site repeatedly to salvage materials.

3. The cultural fill includes one case from Lookout House where household refuse (i.e., ashy sediments, charcoal, abundant and varied charred botanical remains, discarded artifacts, and discarded animal bone) was deposited in an abandoned kiva; there the artifact density was over 1,300 artifacts per cubic meter. The other cases of cultural fill include small, abandoned, earth-walled pit structures at Kenzie Dawn Hamlet that were deliberately filled with refuse lacking the ashy sediments and botanical remains that

characterize most household refuse. There artifact density was approximately 400 artifacts per cubic meter. These cases provide examples of artifact density in different types of culturally deposited fill, providing a baseline for the interpretation of artifact density in natural and mixed fills.

4. The fill was judged to be naturally deposited (largely due to the absence of ashy sediments), but the artifact density in these cases indicates that people were depositing artifacts in these strata.

5. The criteria that distinguish mixed fills from natural deposits include the presence of inclusions not oriented to the bedding planes and the absence of clearly defined sorting by particle size. Mixed fills do not include the ashy sediments or construction debris that characterize trash fills.

6. Whether cutting or noncutting, the date is derived from the outermost ring on the tree-ring sample. Cutting and noncutting dates are distinguished from each other by codes provided by the tree-ring laboratory. Following commonly accepted practice, I identify cutting dates as those specimens with the suffix *B, G, L, c, r,* or *v* (or a combination of these suffixes), so long as the ++ code is not attached. Conversely, all samples with the suffix *vv* or samples with ++ attached to any suffix are classified as noncutting dates (Ahlstrom 1985:31; Dean 1985; Robinson, Harrill, and Warren 1975:6). Tree-ring dating is accurate because the tree-rings correspond to annual events (at times even seasonal accuracy is possible), and they are precise because replication of the dating process invariably produces identical results. With cutting dates that are labeled *B, G, L, c,* or *r,* the "dated event" is the last ring produced by the tree and therefore the date of the death of a particular tree or limb (Ahlstrom 1985:38; Dean 1978a:226; Lightfoot 1994:25). In the case of samples coded *v* or samples with + attached to the suffix, the relationship of the last ring to the death of the tree or limb is less certain, and the sample may be slightly earlier than the last recorded tree ring. I include *v* and + dates as cutting dates because the potential early bias of these samples is minimal and is always less than five years (Ahlstrom 1985:35, 38–39, 611–614; Dean 1985).

7. A noncutting date results when rings are missing from the outermost surface of a specimen. The relationship of the last dated ring (the noncutting date) to the true death date of the tree is unknown. In dating individual structures, large clusters of noncutting dates are interpreted as resulting from specimens missing only a few rings, and therefore cutting dates can still be approximated (Ahlstrom 1985:58; Dean 1978b:146).

Noncutting dates (n = 1,126) from the Sand Canyon locality provide a much larger sample that can be used to examine gaps in the cutting-date record. There are multiple modes, or clusters, in the distribution of noncutting dates, suggesting that timbers were harvested throughout the A.D. 950 to 1290 period (Varien 1997:155). The 712 noncutting dates from Chapin Mesa further support the usefulness of clusters of noncutting dates; periods with the fewest noncutting dates correspond roughly to periods with the fewest cutting dates, including the early 700s, the early 900s, the late 1000s to 1150, and the 1220s (Varien 1997:157–159). Clusters of noncutting dates suggest that timbers were harvested relatively continuously over a long period on Chapin Mesa. Together, the cutting and noncutting dates suggest that timber was harvested continuously for a minimum of 300 years (between 1000 and 1300), and nearly continuously for 600 years (between 600 and 1300).

CHAPTER 7. THE SOCIAL LANDSCAPE IN THE MESA
VERDE REGION

1. Conference participants were asked to examine the regions in which they did fieldwork and to locate all known sites larger than 50 structures that dated between A.D. 1150 and 1300. My colleagues and I at Crow Canyon, with the help of many archaeologists and local landowners, began to gather these data for the Mesa Verde region in southwestern Colorado and southeastern Utah. (Although many consider the Mesa Verde region to include the part of New Mexico that lies north of San Juan River, that area, the Totah region [McKenna and Toll 1992], was treated as a separate region at the conference.) Data collection included archival research, networking with archaeologists and others, aerial coverage of the study area, and a reconnaissance of a majority of the known large sites. The results of this conference, including the settlement pattern data, have recently been reported (Adler 1996a; Varien et al. 1996).

2. I would like to thank Kristie Arrington, David Breternitz, Jerry Fetterman, Steve Fuller, Linda Honeycutt, Winston Hurst, Jim Judge, Sandy Thompson, and Bill Lipe for contributing to the final review of the community center database.

3. The sites are Far View, Casa Negra, Yellow Jacket Pueblo, Mitchell Springs Pueblo, Yucca House, Lancaster Ruin, the Carvell Ruin, and Hedley Ruin.

4. Oak Tree House is a good example. Tree-ring dates indicate that initial construction occurred in the late A.D. 1100s and early 1200s, or during Period 3. However, I infer that its peak occupation dates to the period after 1225 and include it only in Period 4.

5. Wilshusen (1991, 1995) has tracked population movement out of the Dolores Valley in the north-central Mesa Verde region in the late A.D. 800s, and also the settlement of large, dispersed communities in the Cedar Hill area near the Colorado–New Mexico border on the southern edge of the Mesa Verde region. These Cedar Hill communities formed in the decade after the large, aggregated communities of the Dolores Valley were abandoned. Wilshusen's (1995:43–73) description of the Cedar Hill communities provides the most thorough discussion of the settlement patterns and community organization for the early 900s in the northern San Juan region. These community settlement patterns also appear to describe the Period 1 communities that formed in the central Mesa Verde region between 950 and 1050.

The Cedar Hill communities are dispersed settlement clusters in which residential sites are grouped around a great kiva. Wilshusen (1995:73–80) argues that these communities—when compared with the large, aggregated villages found throughout the Mesa Verde region in the middle to late 800s—represent a dramatic reformatting of the social landscape and political economy of these northern San Juan communities.

There are also indications that the Chuska Valley and Chaco Canyon, located to the south of the Mesa Verde region, experienced population growth and the development of new communities during the 900s (Thompson 1994; Windes and Ford 1992). In addition to the Cedar Hill area, the Chuska Valley and the Chaco drainage may be areas that received immigrants from the Mesa Verde region in the early 900s, and these groups may have returned to the Mesa Verde region in the late 900s and early 1000s.

6. Observations about site size and settlement pattern in Period 1 are supported by every intensive survey in the central portion of the Mesa Verde region (Fetterman and Honeycutt 1987; Greubel 1991; Hayes 1964; Neily 1983; Rohn 1977). Survey on Cedar Mesa, Utah—the western edge of the Mesa Verde region as defined in this study—documented a hiatus in occupation during this period (Matson, Lipe, and Haase 1988). Excavations yielding tree-ring dates have confirmed the presence of habitation sites dating to late in this period in the Sand Canyon locality (Kent 1991b) and in many other localities in the central Mesa Verde region (Gillespie 1976; Hill 1985; Kuckelman and Morris 1988; Lancaster et al. 1954; O'Bryan 1950). It is worth noting, however, that most of these small habitation sites date to the early 1000s, not the 900s.

7. Mesa Verde–region sites that have been labeled Chacoan outliers include Escalante Ruin (Thompson 1994), Lowry Pueblo (Martin 1936), Yucca House, and the Lake View Group, which comprises three sites: Wallace (Bradley 1988), Haynie, and Ida Jean Ruins. These sites have many of the attributes traditionally used to identify Chacoan great houses: a compact, symmetrical, planned layout; massive construction; banded, core-veneer masonry; blocked-in, above-ground kivas; and large rooms (Lekson 1991; Marshall et al. 1979; Powers, Gillespie, and Lekson 1983).

8. Surveys in the central portion of the Mesa Verde region all document trends similar to those reported by Adler for the Sand Canyon locality: increased household clustering that resulted in some larger roomblock-kiva complexes; increased clustering of roomblocks to produce multiroomblock sites; and a greater disparity in site size between the largest and smallest residential sites. Looking beyond the Mesa Verde region, these trends characterize settlement in other areas on the Colorado Plateau. For example, this type of settlement pattern is similar to what has been termed the Scribe S phase in the Zuni region (Watson, LeBlanc, and Redman 1980:203–205). Considerable variation in settlement pattern is present in Period 3, however. On Cedar Mesa, for example, site size remains small, and large, multiroomblock sites are not present in the surveyed areas of the mesa.

9. The Bass Complex is a good example of this type of multiroomblock site. In the Sand Canyon community in Period 3, the largest multiple roomblock site remains centered on Casa Negra, which is a Period 2 community center. In the Goodman Point community, there are several large multiroomblock sites, including Shields Pueblo, which is located in the same general area as a possible Period 2 great house and great kiva (Adler 1990:258–261). Tree-ring dates from Shields Pueblo indicate that it was occupied in both Periods 2 and 3. There is also a large great kiva that probably dates to Period 3 located approximately 500 meters south of Shields Pueblo.

10. To calculate cost-equivalent kilometers, I used IDRISI and the same map algebra that I used to create the friction surface for the Mesa Verde region. With them I created a new friction surface of nearly level terrain (a 2-degree slope was used because I assumed that no terrain would be entirely level). I determined the cost (in terms of energy) of moving across 1 kilometer on this nearly level terrain. The cost-equivalent distance between two points anywhere in the Mesa Verde region was then calculated simply by dividing the cost of moving between any two points in the Mesa Verde region by the value of moving across 1 kilometer on the nearly level terrain. The method for calculating cost-equivalent kilometers is presented in greater detail in Varien 1997: Appendix B.

11. One cluster of Period 3 community centers (containing four sites with small polygons, and six polygons in all) occurs in the area centered on Mesa Verde National Park. The second, and larger, cluster (18 relatively small polygons) is in the area between McElmo Creek and Squaw Canyon. An area with two larger polygons separates these two concentrations of denser settlement. A final, less distinct cluster of large sites occurs in southeastern Utah between Montezuma Canyon and Comb Ridge (eight sites with relatively small polygons).

12. One group on Mesa Verde proper includes 13 sites of greater than 50 rooms. One of these villages, Oak Tree House, is the community center located in the southeast-ernmost portion of the study area, and its location results in this center's having a large polygon. Yucca House is located on the western edge of the large polygon that separates the Mesa Verde group of large sites from the concentration of large villages north of McElmo Creek. A total of 36 villages is located in this group, which stretches north from McElmo Creek on the south to Lancaster Ruin on the north, and from Yellow Jacket Pueblo on the east to Montezuma Creek in southeastern Utah on the west.

13. Ian Thompson first pointed out to me that the largest Mesa Verde sites occurred in a narrow axis running southeast to northwest through the region, and he pointed out that this axis became narrower through time. Identification of a core area within the Mesa Verde region (termed the central Mesa Verde region) owes a great deal to Thompson's observations about Mesa Verde–region settlement patterns.

14. The Mancos Canyon site (5MT2350) was excavated and found to be a multiple component habitation. Stratigraphically, the great kiva and two associated masonry rooms were the last buildings constructed at the site. The great kiva burned, and the latest cutting date was A.D. 973, indicating that construction occurred at approximately this time (Farmer 1977:284, 302). The great kiva was interpreted as an intercommunity integrative structure that probably replaced similar structures dating slightly earlier, in the late 800s and early 900s (Farmer 1977:285; Gillespie 1976:69). The Mancos Canyon group of sites is important because it is in one of the few areas in the Mesa Verde region where there appears to have been continuity of occupation from the late 800s through the late 900s. The use of masonry architecture at site 5MT2350 is also interesting because buildings found elsewhere in the Mesa Verde region at this time still had predominantly earthen construction (Varien 1998). The buildings at this community

center are larger and more substantial than architecture at surrounding residential sites in Period 1, a pattern that characterizes settlement patterns in the later periods.

15. The spatial contraction of the most densely populated areas in the Mesa Verde region further isolated the population from other large-site settlement systems in surrounding regions (see Adler 1996a for the locations of large sites in the surrounding regions). There are almost certainly no large sites to the north or east of the Mesa Verde region. To the southeast, the closest large sites are those of the Totah region. The nearest large Totah sites are located along the lower La Plata River approximately 30 linear kilometers southeast of Oak Tree House. Aztec Ruin, the largest site in the Totah region, is approximately 55 linear kilometers from Oak Tree House. To the northwest there is a large site in Fable Valley, approximately 70 linear kilometers from Arch Canyon Pueblo in the northwest corner of the study area. To the west, survey on Cedar Mesa indicates that population peaked during Period 4, but residential sites remained small, occurring in loosely clustered aggregates (Matson, Lipe, and Haase 1988:253, 258). The large sites in the Kayenta region are located over 100 linear kilometers to the southwest. And to the south, large sites are scattered in an area south of the San Juan River and west of the Carrizo, Lukachukai, and Chuska Mountains. The closest is Pancho House, located over 80 linear kilometers away. Sites PE-8 and PE-9 in Alcove Canyon in the Carrizo Mountains and Mummy Cave and White House in Canyon de Chelly, along with Kinlichee, Klagetoh, and Kin Tiel, are other prominent large sites in this area; all are located between 100 and 200 linear kilometers to the south. Thus, the central Mesa Verde region became increasingly isolated from other concentrations of large sites in the decades prior to abandonment of the region, which is an important factor to consider when discussing the population movement that accompanied this abandonment.

16. On the basis of Dean Wilson's examination of surface pottery, Thompson (1994:17) argued that Reservoir and Emerson Ruins dated from the middle of the eleventh century to the early twelfth century. Tree-ring dates from Escalante Ruin indicate that it was constructed later, in the A.D. 1120 to 1140 period. For the Lake View group, Bradley (1988:8–14) interpreted tree-ring dates to argue that the initial construction at Wallace Ruin dated to approximately 1045 (and perhaps earlier) and that construction continued into the 1120s (this site also has a reoccupation dating to the 1200s [Bradley 1988:16]). Wallace Ruin, therefore, was almost certainly contemporaneous with at least portions of the occupations at the other two community centers in the Lake View group, Ida Jean and Haynie. Thus these multicommunity clusters do not appear to have been entirely sequential occupations.

17. These include the Finley Farm complex and the Pigg Site in the Lowry area; Ten-Acre Ruin and Brew's Site number 1 on Alkali Ridge; Carol's Ruin and Kristie's Ruin in upper Hovenweep Canyon; Casa Negra, the Goodman Point great kiva, and Shields Pueblo in the Sand Canyon locality; and the Battleship Rock and Site 34 community centers on Mesa Verde.

18. These include Stevenson Pueblo and Rohn 84 in the Yellow Jacket Canyon area; the Thompson, McVicker, Miller, Gardner, and Fuller sites in the upper Hovenweep

Canyon area; Big Spring Ruin and Hibbets Pueblo in the lower Hovenweep Canyon area; Lew's Site, Ruin Canyon Pueblo and Cow Mesa 40 in the Ruin and Cow Canyon area; the Spook Point, Papoose Canyon, and Brewer Well sites in the lower Squaw Canyon area; the Berkeley Bryant and Bob Hampton sites in the upper Squaw Canyon area; and Ruin Spring Ruin and Wetherill's Chimney Rock in the middle section of Cottonwood Wash in southeastern Utah.

19. There were 10 community centers on the eastern edge of the study area that were abandoned by the end of Period 2. There is also abandonment by the end of Period 2 of community centers on the south edge of the study area (Red Pottery Mound, Bluff Cemetery), on the west edge of the study area (Et al. Site), and on the north edge of the study area (Edge of the Cedars, Carhart Ruin). A major topic for future empirical studies will be whether these abandoned communities were incorporated into other Mesa Verde–region communities or whether community members emigrated from the Mesa Verde region.

20. We can begin to understand what happens to communities on the edge of the Mesa Verde region by examining the specific cases. In the area surrounding Mesa Verde National Park, the nearest Period 4 neighbors for the Period 3 large sites are either Oak Tree House or Spruce Tree House. Survey in the areas around Oak Tree House and Spruce Tree House indicates that these two villages probably formed from local populations living in dispersed communities on the mesa tops in the period before the Period 4 large sites were formed (Rohn 1977). It is unlikely that the more distant Period 3 communities in this area (Lion House, Hoy House, Battleship Rock, Kiva Point, and Site 34) moved to form the large, aggregated communities in Period 4. Survey of the eastern portion of Mesa Verde National Park indicates that it was largely abandoned in Period 4 (Smith 1987:67). But many small Period 4 cliff dwelling have been documented in the western portion of the park and in the canyons just south of the Mancos River.

In the southwestern portion of the study area, the Period 3 community centers near the San Juan River (Jackson's Montezuma Bench Site number 2, Tsitah Wash complex, Aneth Archaeological District, and Greasewood Flat Ruin) all have a Period 4 nearest neighbor of the Hovenweep Cajon Ruin. Hovenweep Cajon Ruin is the smallest of the Period 4 community centers, with approximately 40 to 50 structures, and it therefore could not account for all of the community members emigrating from the Period 3 large-site communities along the San Juan River. Thus, these Period 3 communities may have remained in place with no aggregated site, or community members may have emigrated to other communities either within or outside of the Mesa Verde region.

On the western edge of the study area on Cedar Mesa, survey has documented many small sites dating to Period 4 (Matson, Lipe, and Haase 1988), and it is likely that these small sites were organized into some type of community. Population estimates for Cedar Mesa during this period range between 500 and 1,500 people (Matson, Lipe, and Haase 1988:253). In the area between Comb Wash and Montezuma Canyon, the distance between community centers in successive periods is not much greater than 7 kilometers. Here I am referring to the Period 3 community centers Mouth of Mule Canyon Ruin,

Nancy Patterson, Five-Acre Ruin, Gravel Pit, Decker, and Black Mesa Quartzite Pueblo and their Period 4 nearest neighbors. Thus we may see relative continuity of communities in this area, but with catchment areas and movement at a slightly greater scale than we see along the densely settled axis in the central Mesa Verde region.

On the northern edge of the study area, the Period 3 Red Knobs site is interpreted as having been abandoned in Period 4. There are small Period 4 cliff dwellings and tree-ring-dated sites in the area around Red Knobs, and the community in this area may have remained in place as a dispersed community with no large Period 4 site. The Carvell Ruin was another large Period 3 community center located on the northern edge of the study area. The nearest neighbor to Carvell is Lancaster Ruin, but it is unlikely that Lancaster received emigrants from Carvell because Lancaster itself had a Period 3 occupation, and Lancaster appears to have declined in size between Periods 3 and 4.

21. To examine the tree-ring data further, I looked at the distribution of the 3,405 noncutting dates from the A.D. 900 to 1300 interval (Varien 1997:220). It is interesting that the decades with the fewest noncutting dates generally correspond to periods when there were also few cutting dates: the 910 and 930 intervals, the decades of the 1090s and 1100s, and the 1150 to 1170 interval. That the histograms showing more than 5,000 cutting and noncutting dates are similar suggests an important point: that the low modes truly are periods when fewer trees were harvested.

REFERENCES

Adams, K. R.

1992   The Environmental Archaeology Program. In *The Sand Canyon Archaeo-logical Project: A Progress Report,* edited by W. D. Lipe, pp. 99–104. Occasional Papers no. 2, Crow Canyon Archaeological Center, Cortez, Colorado.

1998   Chapter 16: Tested Sites Macrobotanical Remains. In *The Sand Canyon Archaeological Project: The Site Testing Program,* edited by M. D. Varien. Crow Canyon Archaeological Center, Cortez, Colorado. In press.

Adler, M. A.

1989   Ritual Facilities and Social Integration in Nonranked Societies. In *The Architecture of Social Integration in Prehistoric Pueblos,* edited by W. D. Lipe and M. Hegmon, pp. 35–52. Occasional Papers no. 1, Crow Canyon Archaeological Center, Cortez, Colorado.

1990   *Communities of Soil and Stone: An Archaeological Investigation of Population Aggregation among the Mesa Verde Region Anasazi, A.D. 900–1300.* Ph.D. dissertation, Department of Anthropology, University of Michigan, Ann Arbor.

1992   The Upland Survey. In *The Sand Canyon Archaeological Project: A Progress Report,* edited by W. D. Lipe, pp. 11–23. Occasional Papers no. 2, Crow Canyon Archaeological Center, Cortez, Colorado.

1994   Population Aggregation and the Anasazi Social Landscape: A View from the Four Corners. In *The Ancient Southwestern Community: Models and Methods for the Study of Prehistoric Social Organization,* edited by W. H. Wills and R. D. Leonard, pp. 85–101. University of New Mexico Press, Albuquerque.

1996a   *The Prehistoric Pueblo World, A.D. 1150–1350.* University of Arizona Press, Tucson.

1996b   Land Tenure, Archaeology, and the Ancestral Pueblo Social Landscape. *Journal of Anthropological Archaeology* 15(4):337–371.

Adler, M. A., and M. D. Varien

1994   The Changing Face of the Community in the Mesa Verde Region A.D. 1000–1300. In *Proceedings of the Anasazi Symposium 1991,* compiled by J. E. Smith and A. Hutchinson, pp. 83–97. Mesa Verde Museum Association, Inc., Mesa Verde National Park, Mesa Verde, Colorado.

Adler, M. A., and R. H. Wilshusen

1990   Large-Scale Integrative Facilities in Tribal Societies: Cross-cultural and Southwestern US Examples. *World Archaeology* 22:133–145.

Ahlstrom, R.V.N.

1985   *The Interpretation of Tree-Ring Dates.* Ph.D. dissertation, University of Arizona, Tucson.

Ahlstrom, R.V.N., J. S. Dean, and W. J. Robinson

1991   Evaluating Tree-Ring Interpretations at Walpi Pueblo, Arizona. *American Antiquity* 56:628–644.

Ahlstrom, R.V.N., C. R. Van West, and J. S. Dean

1995   Environmental and Chronological Factors in the Mesa Verde–Northern Rio Grande Migration. *Journal of Anthropological Archaeology* 14(2):125–142.

Aldenderfer, M. S.

1981a   Computer Simulation for Archaeology: An Introductory Essay. In *Simulations in Archaeology,* edited by J. A. Sabloff, pp. 11–49. University of New Mexico Press, Albuquerque.

1981b   Creating Assemblages by Computer Simulation: The Development and Use of ABSIM. In *Simulations in Archaeology,* edited by J. A. Sabloff, pp. 67–117. University of New Mexico Press, Albuquerque.

Ames, K. M.

1981   The Evolution of Social Ranking on the Northwest Coast of North America. *American Antiquity* 46:789–805.

Ammerman, A. J.

1981   Surveys and Archaeological Research. *Annual Reviews in Anthropology* 10:63–88.

Ammerman, A. J., and M. W. Feldman

1974   On the "Making" of an Assemblage of Stone Tools. *American Antiquity* 39(4):610–616.

Arnold, D. E.

1985   *Ceramic Theory and Cultural Process.* Cambridge University Press, Cambridge.

Arnold, J. E.

1993   Labor and the Rise of Complex Hunter-Gatherers. *Journal of Anthropological Archaeology* 12:75–119.

Arnold, P. J. III

1988   Household Ceramic Assemblage Attributes in the Sierra de los Tuxtlas, Veracruz, Mexico. *Journal of Anthropological Research* 44: 357–383.

1990   The Organization of Refuse Disposal and Ceramic Production within Contemporary Mexican Households. *American Anthropologist* 92:915–932.

1991   *Domestic Ceramic Production and Spatial Organization: A Mexican Case Study in Ethnoarchaeology.* Cambridge University Press, New York.

Ascher, R.

1961　　Analogy in Archaeological Interpretation. *Southwestern Journal of Anthropology* 17:317–325.

1968　　Time's Arrow and the Archaeology of a Contemporary Community. In *Settlement Archaeology,* edited by K. C. Chang, pp. 43–52. National Press Books, Palo Alto, California.

Baumhoff, M. A., and R. F. Heizer

1959　　Some Unexploited Possibilities in Ceramic Analysis. *Southwestern Journal of Anthropology* 15:308–316.

Beardsley, R. K., P. Holder, A. D. Krieger, B. J. Meggers, J. B. Rinaldo, and P. Kutsche

1956　　Functional and Evolutionary Implications of Community Patterning. In *Seminars in Archaeology: 1955,* edited by R. Wauchope, pp. 129–157. SAA Memoirs no. 11, Society for American Archaeology, Salt Lake City.

Bedaux, R.

1987　　Aspects of Life Span of Dogon Pottery. In *A Knapsack Full of Pottery: Archaeo-Ceramological Miscellanea Dedicated to H. J. Franken,* pp. 137–153. Newsletter of the Department of Pottery Technology, vol. 5, Leiden, Netherlands.

Bender, B.

1979　　Gatherer-Hunter to Farmer: A Social Perspective. *World Archaeology* 10:204–222.

1985　　Emergent Tribal Formations in the American Midcontinent. *American Antiquity* 49:393–400.

1990　　The Dynamics of Nonhierarchical Societies. In *The Evolution of Political Systems: Sociopolitics in Small-Scale Societies,* edited by S. Upham, pp. 247–263. Cambridge University Press, Cambridge.

Bender, D. R.

1967　　A Refinement of the Concept of the Household: Families, Co-residence, and Domestic Functions. *American Anthropologist* 69:493–504.

Berry, M. S.

1982　　*Time, Space, and Transition in Anasazi Prehistory.* University of Utah Press, Salt Lake City.

Billman, B. R.

1997　　*The Puebloan-Period Occupation of the Ute Mountain Piedmont: Synthesis and Conclusions.* Soil Systems Publications in Archaeology no. 22, vol. 7.

1998　　Puebloan Settlement in the Southern Piedmont. Manuscript in possession of the author.

Binford, L. R.

1962　　Archaeology as Anthropology. *American Antiquity* 28:217–225.

1968	Archaeological Theory and Method. In *New Perspectives in Archaeology,* edited by S. R. Binford and L. R. Binford, pp. 1–3. Aldine, Chicago.
1976	Forty-seven Trips: A Case Study in the Character of Some Formation Processes. In *Contributions to Anthropology: The Interior Peoples of Northern Alaska,* edited by E. S. Hall, Jr., pp. 299–351. National Museum of Man, Mercury Series, Paper no. 49, Ottawa.
1978a	*Nunamiut Ethnoarchaeology.* Academic Press, New York.
1978b	Dimensional Analysis of Behavior and Site Structure: Learning from an Eskimo Hunting Stand. *American Antiquity* 43:330–361.
1979	Organization and Formation Processes: Looking at Curated Technologies. *Journal of Anthropological Research* 35:255–273.
1980	Willow Smoke and Dogs' Tails: Hunter-gatherer Settlement Systems and Archaeological Site Formation. *American Antiquity* 45:4–20.
1981a	Behavioral Archaeology and the "Pompeii Premise." *Journal of Anthropological Research* 37:195–208.
1981b	*Bones: Ancient Men and Modern Myths.* Academic Press, New York.
1982	The Archaeology of Place. *Journal of Anthropological Archaeology* 1:5–31.
1983	Long-Term Land-Use Patterning: Some Implications for Archaeology. In *Working at Archaeology.* Academic Press, New York.
1990	Mobility, Housing, and Environment: A Comparative Study. *Journal of Anthropological Research* 46:119–152.

Birmingham, J.

1975	Traditional Potters of the Katmandu Valley: An Ethnoarchaeological Study. *Man* 10:370–386.

Blalock, H. M., Jr.

1979	*Social Statistics* (revised 2d ed.). McGraw-Hill, New York.

Blinman, E.

1986a	Additive Technologies Group Final Report. In *Dolores Archaeological Program: Final Synthetic Report,* compiled by D. A. Breternitz, C. K. Robinson, and G. T. Gross, pp. 53–101. Bureau of Reclamation, Engineering and Research Center, Denver.
1986b	Technology: Ceramic Containers. In *Dolores Archaeological Program: Final Synthetic Report,* compiled by D. A. Breternitz, C. K. Robinson, and G. T. Gross, pp. 595–609. Bureau of Reclamation, Engineering and Research Center, Denver.
1988a	*The Interpretation of Ceramic Variability: A Case Study from the Dolores Anasazi.* Ph.D. dissertation, Washington State University, Pullman.
1988b	Ceramic Vessels and Vessel Assemblages in Dolores Archaeological Program Collections. In *Dolores Archaeological Program, Supporting Studies: Additive and Reductive Technologies,* compiled by E. Blinman, C. J. Phagan, and R. H. Wilshusen, pp. 449–482. Bureau of Reclamation, Engineering and Research Center, Denver.

1988c Justification and Procedures for Ceramic Dating. In *Dolores Archaeological Program, Supporting Studies: Additive and Reductive Technologies,* compiled by E. Blinman, C. J. Phagan, and R. H. Wilshusen, pp. 501–544. Bureau of Reclamation, Engineering and Research Center, Denver.

1993 Anasazi Pottery: Evolution of a Technology. *Expedition,* 35(1):14–22.

Bonnichsen, R.

1973 Millie's Camp: An Experiment in Archaeology. *World Archaeology* 4:277–291.

Boserup, E.

1965 *The Conditions of Agricultural Growth.* Aldine, Chicago.

Bourdieu, P.

1990 *The Logic of Practice.* Stanford University Press, Stanford, California.

Bradfield, M.

1971 *The Changing Pattern of Hopi Agriculture.* Royal Anthropological Institute of Great Britain and Ireland.

Bradley, B. A.

1988 Wallace Ruin Interim Report. *Southwestern Lore* 54(2):8–33.

1992 Excavations at Sand Canyon Pueblo. In *The Sand Canyon Archaeological Project: A Progress Report,* edited by W. D. Lipe, pp. 79–97. Occasional Papers no. 2, Crow Canyon Archaeological Center, Cortez, Colorado.

1993 Planning, Growth, and Functional Differentiation at a Prehistoric Pueblo: A Case Study from Southwest Colorado. *Journal of Field Archaeology* 20:23–42.

Braun, D. P.

1983 Pots as Tools. In *Archaeological Hammers and Theories,* edited by J. A. Moore and A. S. Keene, pp. 107–134. Academic Press, New York.

1987 Coevolution of Sedentism, Pottery Technology, and Horticulture in the Central Midwest, 200 B.C.–A.D. 600. In *Emergent Horticultural Economies of the Eastern Woodlands,* edited by W. F. Keegan, pp. 153–181. Occasional Paper 7, Center for Archaeological Investigations, Southern Illinois University, Carbondale.

Braun, D. P., and S. Plog

1982 Evolution of "Tribal" Social Networks: Theory and Prehistoric North American Evidence. *American Antiquity* 47:504–525.

Breternitz, C. D., and C. K. Robinson

1996 Cultural Dynamics in the Four-Corners Region: Results of the Ute Mountain Ute Irrigated Lands Archaeological Project. Paper presented at the 61st annual meeting of the Society for American Archaeology, New Orleans.

Breternitz, D. A.

1993 The Dolores Archaeological Project: In Memoriam. *American Antiquity* 58:118–125.

Bronitsky, G.

1986   The Use of Materials Science Techniques in the Study of Pottery Con-
        struction and Use. In *Advances in Archaeological Method and Theory,* vol.
        9, edited by M. B. Schiffer, pp. 209–276. Academic Press, New York.

Bronitsky, G., and R. Hamer

1986   Experiments in Ceramic Technology: The Effects of Various Tempering
        Materials on Impact and Thermal Shock Resistance. *American Antiquity*
        51(1):89–101.

Bronson, B.

1972   Farm Labor and the Evolution of Food Production. In *Population Growth:
        Anthropological Implications,* edited by B. Spooner, pp. 190–218. MIT
        Press, Cambridge, Mass.

1977   The Earliest Farming: Demography as Cause and Consequence. In *Origins
        of Agriculture,* edited by C. A. Reed, pp. 23–48. Mouton Press, The Hague,
        Netherlands.

Brookfield, H. C.

1972   Intensification and Disintensification in Pacific Agriculture. *Pacific View-
        point* 13:30–48.

1984   Intensification Revisited. *Pacific Viewpoint* 25:15–44.

Brown, J. A.

1985   Long-Term Trends to Sedentism and the Emergence of Complexity in
        the American Midwest. In *Prehistoric Hunter-Gatherers: The Emergence
        of Cultural Complexity,* edited by T. D. Price and J. A. Brown, pp. 201–231.
        Academic Press, New York.

Brown, P., and A. Podolefsky

1976   Population Density, Agricultural Intensity, Land Tenure, and Group Size
        in the New Guinea Highlands. *Ethnology* 15:211–238.

Brumfiel, E. M.

1992   Distinguished Lecture in Archaeology: Breaking and Entering the Ecosys-
        tem—Gender, Class, and Faction Steal the Show. *American Anthropologist*
        94:551–567.

Brush, S. B., and B. L. Turner II

1987   The Nature of Farming Systems and Views of Their Change. In *Compara-
        tive Farming Systems,* edited by B. L. Turner II and S. B. Brush, pp. 11–48.
        Guilford Press, New York.

Burns, B. T.

1983   *Simulated Anasazi Storage Behavior Using Crop Yields Reconstructed from
        Tree-Rings: A.D. 652–1968.* Ph.D. dissertation, University of Arizona. Uni-
        versity Microfilms, Ann Arbor, Michigan.

Cameron, C. M.

1990   Pit Structure Abandonment in the Four Corners Region of the American

Southwest: Late Basketmaker III and Pueblo I Periods. *Journal of Field Archaeology* 17(1):27–37.

1991   Structure Abandonment in Villages. In *Archaeological Method and Theory,* vol. 3, edited by M. B. Schiffer, pp. 155–194. University of Arizona Press, Tucson.

1993   Abandonment and Archaeological Interpretation. In *Abandonment of Settlements and Regions: Ethnoarchaeological and Archaeological Approaches,* edited by C. M. Cameron and S. A. Tomka, pp. 3–7. Cambridge University Press, Cambridge.

Cameron, C. M., and S. A. Tomka

1993   *The Abandonment of Settlements and Regions: Ethnoarchaeological and Archaeological Approaches.* Cambridge University Press, Cambridge.

Carmichael, D. L.

1990   Patterns of Residential Mobility and Sedentism in the Jornada Mogollon. In *Perspectives on Southwestern Prehistory,* edited by P. E. Minnis and C. L. Redman, pp. 122–134. Westview Press, Boulder, Colorado.

Cashdan, E.

1985   Coping with Risk: Reciprocity among the Basarwa of Northern Botswana. *Man* 20:454–474.

Cater, J. D., and M. L. Chenault

1988   Kiva Use Reinterpreted. *Southwestern Lore* 54(3):19–32.

Charles, D. K., and J. E. Buikstra

1983   Archaic Mortuary Sites in the Central Mississippi Drainage: Distribution, Structure, and Behavioral Implications. In *Archaic Hunters and Gatherers in the American Midwest,* edited by J. Phillips and J. Brown, pp. 117–145. Academic Press, New York.

Chayanov, A. V.

1966   *The Theory of Peasant Economy.* Edited by D. Thorner, B. Kerblay, and R.E.F. Smith. Richard D. Irwin, Homewood, Illinois. Reprint, 1986, University of Wisconsin Press, Madison.

Chisholm, M.

1970   *Rural Settlement and Land Use.* Aldine, Chicago.

Clarke, D. L.

1972   *Models in Archaeology.* Methuen, London.

Coles, J.

1979   *Experimental Archaeology.* Academic Press, New York.

Conklin, H. C.

1961   The Study of Shifting Cultivation. *Current Anthropology* 2:27–61.

Connolly, M. R.

1992   The Goodman Point Historic Land-Use Study. In *The Sand Canyon Archaeological Project: A Progress Report,* edited by W. D. Lipe, pp. 33–44.

Occasional Papers no. 2, Crow Canyon Archaeological Center, Cortez, Colorado.

Cook, S. F.

1946   A Reconsideration of Shell Mounds with Respect to Population and Nutrition. *American Antiquity* 12(1):51–53.

1972a   *Prehistoric Demography.* Addison-Wesley Modular Publications in Anthropology, 16. Addison-Wesley, Reading, Massachusetts.

1972b   Can Pottery Residues Be Used as an Index to Population? In *Contributions of the University of California Archaeological Research Facility: Miscellaneous Papers on Archaeology,* no. 14, pp. 17–39. Department of Anthropology, University of California, Berkeley.

Cook, S. F., and R. F. Heizer

1965   *The Quantitative Approach to the Relation between Population and Settlement Size.* Archaeological Research Facility, Report no. 64, University of California, Berkeley.

1968   Relationship among Houses, Settlement Areas, and Population in Aboriginal California. In *Settlement Archaeology,* edited by K. C. Chang, pp. 76–116. National Press, Palo Alto, California.

Cook, S. F., and A. E. Treganza

1947   The Quantitative Investigation of Aboriginal Sites: Comparative Physical and Chemical Analysis of Two California Shell Mounds. *American Antiquity* 13:135–141.

1950   The Quantitative Investigation of Indian Mounds: With Special Reference to the Relation of the Physical Components to the Probable Material Culture. *University of California Publications in American Archaeology and Ethnology,* vol. 40, no. 5, pp. 223–262. Berkeley.

Cowgill, G. L.

1975   On the Causes and Consequences of Ancient and Modern Population Changes. *American Anthropologist* 77:505–525.

1993a   Distinguished Lecture in Archaeology: Beyond Criticizing New Archaeology. *American Anthropologist* 95(3):551–573.

1993b   Equality Is Never Perfect, Domination Never Total. Paper presented at the Chacmool Conference, Calgary, Alberta.

1996   Population, Human Nature, Knowing Actors, and Explaining the Onset of Complexity. In *Debating Complexity: Proceedings of the 26th Annual Chacmool Conference,* edited by D. A. Meyer, P. C. Dawson, and D. T. Hanna. Archaeological Association of the University of Calgary, Calgary, Alberta.

Cushing, F. H.

1979   *Zuni Breadstuff.* Indian Notes and Monographs, Museum of the American Indian, Heye Foundation, New York.

David, N.
1971   The Fulani Compound and the Archaeologist. *World Archaeology* 3:111–131.
1972   On the Life Span of Pottery, Type Frequencies, and Archaeological Infer-
         ence. *American Antiquity* 37(1):141–142.
David, N., and H. Hennig
1972   *The Ethnography of Pottery: A Fulani Case Seen in Archaeological Perspec-
         tive.* Addison Wesley Modular Publications in Anthropology, 21. Addison-
         Wesley, Reading, Massachusetts.
Deal, M.
1983   *Pottery Ethnoarchaeology among the Tzeltal Maya.* Ph.D. dissertation,
         Department of Archaeology, Simon Fraser University, Burnaby, British
         Columbia.
1985   Household Pottery Disposal in the Maya Highlands: An Ethnoarchaeolog-
         ical Interpretation. *Journal of Anthropological Archaeology* 4:243–291.
Dean, J. S.
1969   *Chronological Analysis of Tsegi-Phase Sites in Northeastern Arizona.* Paper
         no. 3, Laboratory of Tree-Ring Research, Tucson, Arizona.
1970   Aspects of Tsegi-Phase Social Organization: A Trial Reconstruction. In
         Reconstructing Prehistoric Pueblo Societies, edited by W. A. Longacre, pp.
         140–174. University of New Mexico Press, Albuquerque.
1978a   Independent Dating in Archaeological Analysis. In *Advances in Archaeo-
         logical Method and Theory,* vol. 1, edited by M. B. Schiffer, pp. 223–255.
         Academic Press, New York.
1978b   Miscellaneous Paper Number 24: Tree-Ring Dating in Archaeology. In
         University of Utah Anthropological Papers Number 99, pp. 129–163. Univer-
         sity of Utah Press, Salt Lake City.
1985   Review of Michael S. Berry's *Time, Space, and Transition in Anasazi
         Prehistory. American Antiquity* 50:704–705.
1996   Demography, Environment, and Subsistence Stress. In *Evolving Complex-
         ity and Environmental Risk in the Prehistoric Southwest,* edited by J. A.
         Tainter and B. B. Tainter, pp. 25–56. Santa Fe Institute Studies in the
         Sciences of Complexity, Proceedings vol. 24. Addison-Wesley, Reading,
         Massachusetts.
Dean, J. S., R. C. Euler, G. J. Gumerman, F. Plog, R. H. Hevly, and T.N.V. Karlstrom
1985   Human Behavior, Demography, and Paleoenvironment on the Colorado
         Plateaus. *American Antiquity* 50:537–554.
de Barros, P.L.F.
1982   The Effects of Variable Site Occupation Span on the Results of Frequency
         Seriation. *American Antiquity* 47(2):291–315.
DeBoer, W. R.
1974   Ceramic Longevity and Archaeological Interpretation. *American Antiq-
         uity* 39(2): 335–343.

1983   The Archaeological Record as Preserved Death Assemblage. In *Archaeological Hammers and Theories*, edited by J. A. Moore and A. S. Keene, pp. 19–36. Academic Press, New York.

1985   Pots and Pans Do Not Speak, Nor Do They Lie: The Case for Occasional Reductionism. In *Decoding Prehistoric Ceramics*, edited by B. A. Nelson, pp. 347–357. Southern University Press, Carbondale.

DeBoer, W. R., and D. W. Lathrap

1979   The Making and Breaking of Shipibo-Conibo Ceramics. In *Ethnoarchaeology*, edited by C. Cramer, pp. 102–138. Columbia University Press, New York.

Decker, K. W., and K. L. Petersen

1987   Sediment and Chemical Analyses of Soil Conservation Service Designated Soils. In *Dolores Archaeological Program, Supporting Studies: Settlement and Environment*, compiled by K. L. Petersen and J. D. Orcutt, pp. 133–143. Bureau of Reclamation, Engineering and Research Center, Denver, Colorado.

Dewar, R. E.

1991   Incorporating Variation in Occupation Span into Settlement-Pattern Analysis. *American Antiquity* 56:604–620.

Diehl, M. W.

1992   Architecture as a Material Correlate of Mobility Strategies: Some Implications for Archaeological Interpretation. *Behavior Science Research* 26:1–35.

Drennan, R. D.

1984   Long-Distance Transport Costs in Pre-Hispanic Mesoamerica. *American Anthropologist* 86(1):105–112.

Driver, J. C.

1995   Social Complexity and Hunting Systems in Southwestern Colorado. In *Debating Complexity: Proceedings of the Twenty-Sixth Annual Chacmool Conference*, edited by D. A. Meyer, P. C. Dawson, and D. T. Hanna, pp. 364–374. Archaeological Association of the University of Calgary, Alberta.

Duff, A. I.

1994   The Structure of Economic Interaction through Ceramic Sourcing: Implications for Social Organization. In *Exploring Social, Political, and Economic Organization in the Zuni Region*, edited by T. L. Howell and T. Stone, pp. 25–45. Anthropological Research Papers 46, Arizona State University, Tempe.

n.d.   Scale, Interaction, and Regional Analysis in Late Pueblo Prehistory. In *The Archaeology of Regional Interaction in the Prehistoric Southwest*, edited by M. Hegmon. University Press of Colorado, Boulder. In Press.

Dykeman, D. D., and K. Langenfeld

1987   *Prehistory and History of the La Plata Valley, New Mexico*. San Juan College Cultural Resource Management Program, Farmington, New Mexico.

Earle, T.

1991   Toward a Behavioral Archaeology. In *Processual and Postprocessual Archaeologies: Multiple Ways of Knowing the Past,* edited by R. W. Preucel, pp. 83–95. Occasional Paper no. 10, Center for Archaeological Investigations, Southern Illinois University, Carbondale.

Eddy, F. W.

1977   *Archaeological Investigations at Chimney Rock Mesa: 1970–1972.* Memoirs no. 1, Colorado Archaeological Society, Boulder.

Eddy, F. W., A. E. Kane, and P. R. Nickens

1984   *Southwest Colorado Prehistoric Context: Archaeological Background and Research Directions.* Office of Archaeology and Historic Preservation, Colorado Historical Society, Denver.

Eder, J. F.

1984   The Impact of Subsistence Change on Mobility and Settlement Pattern in a Tropical Forest Foraging Economy: Some Implications for Archaeology. *American Anthropologist* 86:837–853.

Egloff, B. J.

1973   A Method for Counting Ceramic Rim Sherds. *American Antiquity* 38:351–353.

Erdman, J. A.

1970   *Piñon-Juniper Succession after Natural Fires on Residual Soils of Mesa Verde, Colorado.* Brigham Young University Science Bulletin, Biological Series, vol. 9, no. 3. Provo, Utah.

Euler, R. C., G. Gumerman, T.N.V. Karlstrom, J. S. Dean, and R. Hevly

1979   The Colorado Plateaus: Cultural Dynamics and Paleoenvironment. *Science* 205:1089–1101.

Evans, J. D.

1973   Sherd Weights and Sherd Counts. In *Archaeological Theory and Practice,* edited by D. E. Strong, pp. 131–149. Seminar Press, London.

Fairchild-Parks, J. A., and J. S. Dean

1993   Analysis of Tree-Ring Dates from Balcony House, Mesa Verde National Park, Colorado. Ms. on file, Laboratory of Tree-Ring Research, Tucson, Arizona.

Farmer, T. R.

1977   *Salvage Excavations in Mancos Canyon, Colorado, 1975.* Master's thesis, University of Colorado, Boulder.

Feathers, J. K.

1990   *Explaining the Evolution of Prehistoric Ceramics in Southeastern Missouri.* Ph.D. dissertation, University of Washington. University Microfilms, Ann Arbor, Michigan.

Ferguson, T. J., and B. J. Mills

1988   Wood Reuse in Puebloan Architecture: Evidence from Historic Zuni Settlements. Paper presented at the 53d annual meeting of the Society for American Archaeology, Phoenix, Arizona.

Fetterman, J., and L. Honeycutt

1987   *The Mockingbird Mesa Survey, Southwestern Colorado.* Cultural Resource Series no. 22, Bureau of Land Management, Denver.

Fish, S. K., and P. R. Fish

1984   *Prehistoric Agricultural Strategies in the Southwest.* Anthropological Research Papers no. 33, Arizona State University.

Force, E. R., and W. K. Howell

1997   *Holocene Depositional History and Anasazi Occupation in McElmo Canyon, Southwestern Colorado.* Arizona State Museum Archaeological Series, no. 188. University of Arizona Press, Tucson.

Forge, A.

1972   Normative Factors in the Settlement Size of Neolithic Cultivators (New Guinea). In *Man, Settlement, and Urbanism,* edited by P. J. Ucko, R. Tringham, and G. W. Dimbley, pp. 363–376. Duckworth, London.

Fortes, M.

1958   Introduction. In *The Developmental Cycle in Domestic Groups,* edited by J. Goody, pp. 1–15. Papers in Social Anthropology, no. 1, Cambridge University, Cambridge.

Foster, G. M.

1960   Life Expectancy of Utilitarian Pottery in Tzintzuntzan, Mexico. *American Antiquity* 25(4):606–609.

Fowler, A. P., and J. R. Stein

1992   The Anasazi Great House in Space, Time, and Paradigm. In *Anasazi Regional Organization and the Chaco System,* edited by D. E. Doyel, pp. 101–122. Anthropological Papers no. 5, Maxwell Museum of Anthropology, Albuquerque, New Mexico.

Fowler, A. P., J. R. Stein, and R. Anyon

1987   *An Archaeological Reconnaissance of West-Central New Mexico: The Anasazi Monuments Project.* State of New Mexico Office of Cultural Affairs, Historic Preservation Division, Santa Fe.

Fried, M. H.

1967   *The Evolution of Political Society: An Essay in Political Anthropology.* Random House, New York.

Friedman, J.

1974   Marxism, Structuralism and Vulgar Materialism. *Man* 9:444–469.

Gaines, S. W., and W. M. Gaines

1997   Simulating Success or Failure? Another Look at Small-Population Dynamics. *American Antiquity* 62(4):683–697.

Giddens, A.

1979   *The Central Problems of Social Theory.* University of California Press, Berkeley.

1984   *The Constitution of Society: Outline of the Theory of Structuration.* University of California Press, Berkeley.

Gifford, E. W.

1916   Composition of California Shellmounds. *Publications in American Archaeology and Ethnology,* vol. 12, pp. 1–29. University of California, Berkeley.

Gill, G. M.

1981   *The Potter's Mark: Contemporary and Archaeological Pottery of the Kenyan Southeastern Highlands.* Ph.D. dissertation, Boston University.

Gillespie, W. B.

1976   *Culture Change at the Ute Canyon Site: A Study of the Pithouse-Kiva Transition in the Mesa Verde Region.* Master's thesis, Department of Anthropology, University of Colorado, Boulder.

Gilman, P. A.

1987   Architecture as Artifact: Pit Structures and Pueblos in the American Southwest. *American Antiquity* 52:538–564.

1988   Seasonality/Mobility, Seasonality, and Tucson Basin Archaeology. In *Recent Research on Tucson Basin Prehistory: Proceedings of the Second Tucson Basin Archaeological Conference,* edited by W. Doelle and P. Fish, pp. 411–418. Institute for American Research, Anthropological Papers 10, Tucson, Arizona.

Gleichman, C. L., and P. J. Gleichman

1992   The Lower Sand Canyon Survey. In *The Sand Canyon Archaeological Project: A Progress Report,* edited by W. D. Lipe, pp. 25–31. Occasional Papers no. 2, Crow Canyon Archaeological Center, Cortez, Colorado.

Goodenough, W. H.

1956   Residence Rules. *Southwest Journal of Anthropology* 12:22–37.

Goody, J.

1958   *The Developmental Cycle in Domestic Groups.* Papers in Social Anthropology, no. 1, Cambridge University, Cambridge.

1972   *Domestic Groups.* Addison-Wesley Modular Publications in Anthropology, 28. Addison-Wesley, Reading, Massachusetts.

Gould, R. A., D. K. Koster, and A.H.L. Sontz

1971   The Lithic Assemblage of the Western Desert Aborigines of Australia. *American Antiquity* 36:149–169.

Gould, R. R.

1982   *The Mustoe Site: The Application of Neutron Activation Analysis in the Interpretation of a Multi-component Archaeological Site.* Ph.D. dissertation, Department of Anthropology, University of Texas, Austin.

Graham, M.

1993   Settlement Organization and Residential Variability among the Rarámuri. In *Abandonment of Settlements and Regions: Ethnoarchaeological and Archaeological Approaches,* edited by C. M. Cameron and S. A. Tomka, pp. 25–42. Cambridge University Press, Cambridge.

1994   *Mobile Farmers: An Ethnoarchaeological Approach to Settlement Organization among the Rarámuri of Northwestern Mexico.* International Monographs in Prehistory, Ethnoarchaeological Series 3. Ann Arbor, Michigan.

Graves, M. W., W. A. Longacre, and S. J. Holbrook

1982   Aggregation and Abandonment at Grasshopper Pueblo, Arizona. *Journal of Field Archaeology* 9:193–206.

Graves, M. W., and J. J. Reid

1984   Social Complexity in the American Southwest: A View from East Central Arizona. In *Recent Research in Mogollon Archaeology,* edited by S. Upham, F. Plog, D. G. Batcho, and B. E. Kauffman, pp. 266–275. University Museum Occasional Papers no. 10, New Mexico State University, Las Cruces.

Green, S. W.

1980   Toward a General Model of Agricultural Systems. In *Advances in Archaeological Method and Theory,* vol. 3, edited by M. B. Schiffer, pp. 311–355. Academic Press, New York.

Greubel, R. A.

1991   *Hovenweep Resource Protection Zone Class III Cultural Resource Inventory, Montezuma County, Colorado, and San Juan County, Utah.* Alpine Archaeological Consultants. Submitted to Bureau of Land Management, Colorado and Utah.

Grigg, D.

1979   Ester Boserup's Theory of Agrarian Change: A Critical Review. *Progress in Human Geography* 3:64–84.

Haas, J.

1990   Warfare and the Evolution of Tribal Polities in the American Southwest. In *The Anthropology of War,* edited by J. Haas, pp. 171–189. Cambridge University Press, Cambridge.

Haas, J., and W. Creamer

1993   *Stress and Warfare among the Kayenta Anasazi of the Thirteenth Century A.D.* Fieldiana Anthropology, new series, no. 21, publication 1450, Field Museum of Natural History, Chicago.

1996   The Role of Warfare in the Pueblo III Period. In *The Prehistoric Pueblo World: A.D. 1150–1350,* edited by M. A. Adler, pp. 205–213. University of Arizona Press, Tucson.

Haase, W. R.

1985   Domestic Water Conservation among the Northern San Juan Anasazi. *Southwestern Lore* 51(2):15–27.

Hagstrum, M. B.

1987   Supply and Demand of Ceramic Products: An Ethnoarchaeological Study of Community Specialization in the Central Andes, Peru. Paper presented at the 52d annual meeting of the Society for American Archaeology, Toronto, Canada.

Halperin, R. H.

1989   Ecological versus Economic Anthropology: Changing "Place" versus Changing "Hands." *Research in Economic Anthropology* 11:15–41.

Hammel, E. A.

1984   On the *** of Studying Household Form and Function. In *Households: Comparative and Historical Studies of the Domestic Group,* edited by R. M. Netting, R. R. Wilk, and E. J. Arnould, pp. 29–43. University of California Press, Berkeley.

Hard, R. J., and W. L. Merrill

1992   Mobile Agriculturalists and the Emergence of Sedentism: Perspectives from Northern Mexico. *American Anthropologist* 94:601–620.

Harris, D. R.

1973   The Prehistory of Tropical Agriculture: An Ethnoecological Model. In *The Explanation of Culture Change: Models in Prehistory,* edited by C. Renfrew, pp. 391–417. Duckworth, London.

Hatch, J. W., S. L. Whittington, and B. Dyke

1982   A Simulation Approach to the Measurement of Change in Ceramic Frequency Seriation. *North American Archaeologist* 3:333–350.

Haury, E. W.

1935   Tree Rings: The Archaeologist's Time-Piece. *American Antiquity* 1:98–108.

Hayden, B., and A. Cannon

1983   Where the Garbage Goes: Refuse Disposal in the Maya Highlands. *Journal of Anthropological Archaeology* 2:117–163.

Hayes, A. C.

1964   *The Archeological Survey of Wetherill Mesa, Mesa Verde National Park, Colorado.* Archeological Research Series no. 7-A, National Park Service, Washington, D.C.

Hegmon, M.

1989   Risk Reduction and Variation in Agricultural Economies: A Computer Simulation of Hopi Agriculture. *Research in Economic Anthropology* vol. 2, pp. 89–121. JAI Press.

1991   Six Easy Steps to Dating Pueblo III Ceramic Assemblages: Working Draft. Ms. on file, Crow Canyon Archaeological Center, Cortez, Colorado.

Hildebrand, J. A.
1978   Pathways Revisited: A Quantitative Model of Discard. *American Antiquity*
            43(2):274–279.

Hill, B.
1995   *Ecological Variability and Economic Specialization.* Master's thesis, Arizona
            State University, Tempe.
n.d.   Ecological Variability in Agricultural Specialization among the Late Pre-
            historic Pueblos of Central New Mexico. *Journal of Field Archaeology.* In
            press.

Hill, D. V.
1985   Pottery Making at the Ewing Site (5MT927). *Southwestern Lore* 51(1):19–31.

Hovezak, M. J.
1992   *Construction Timber Economics at Sand Canyon Pueblo.* Master's thesis,
            Department of Anthropology, Northern Arizona University, Flagstaff.

Huber, E. K.
1993   *Thirteenth-Century Pueblo Aggregation and Organizational Change in
            Southwestern Colorado.* Ph.D. dissertation, Department of Anthropology,
            Washington State University, Pullman.

Huber, E. K., and W. D. Lipe
1992   Excavations at the Green Lizard Site. In *The Sand Canyon Archaeological
            Project: A Progress Report,* edited by W. D. Lipe. Occasional Papers no.
            2, Crow Canyon Archaeological Center, Cortez, Colorado.

Huckleberry, G. A., and B. R. Billman
n.d.   Floodwater Farming, Discontinuous Ephemeral Streams, and Puebloan
            Abandonment in Southwestern Colorado. *American Antiquity.* In press.

Jenkins, R.
1992   *Pierre Bourdieu.* Routledge, London.

Jewett, R. A., and K. G. Lightfoot
1986   The Intra-site Spatial Structure of Early Mogollon Villages: A Comparison
            of Seasonal and Year-Round Settlements. In *Mogollon Variability,* edited
            by C. Benson and S. Upham, pp. 45–77. University Museum Occasional
            Papers no. 15, New Mexico State University, Las Cruces.

Judge, W. J.
1991   Chaco: Current Views of Prehistory and the Regional System. In *Chaco
            and Hohokam: Prehistoric Regional Systems in the American Southwest,*
            edited by P. L. Crown and W. J. Judge, pp. 13–30. School of American
            Research Press, Santa Fe, New Mexico.

Karlstrom, T.N.V.
1988   Alluvial Chronology and Hydrologic Change of Black Mesa and Nearby
            Regions. In *The Anasazi in a Changing Environment,* edited by G. J.
            Gumerman, pp. 45–91. Cambridge University Press, Cambridge.

Keegan, W. F.
1986   The Optimal Foraging Analysis of Horticultural Production. *American Anthropologist* 88:92–107.

Keeley, L. H.
1988   Hunter-Gatherer Economic Complexity and "Population Pressure": A Cross-cultural Perspective. *Journal of Anthropological Archaeology* 7(4):373–411.

Kelley, J.
1996   Woods Canyon Pueblo: A Late Pueblo III Period Canyon-Oriented Site in Southwest Colorado. Master's thesis, Department of Anthropology, Washington State University, Pullman.

Kelly, R. L.
1983   Hunter-Gatherer Mobility Strategies. *Journal of Anthropological Research* 39:277–306.
1992   Mobility/Sedentism: Concepts, Archaeological Measures, and Effects. *Annual Review of Anthropology* 21:43–66.

Kent, S.
1989   Cross-cultural Perceptions of Farmers and Hunters and the Value of Meat. In *Farmers as Hunters: The Implications of Sedentism,* edited by S. Kent, pp. 1–17. Cambridge University Press, Cambridge.
1991a   The Relationship between Mobility Strategies and Site Structure. In *The Interpretation of Spatial Patterning within Stone Age Archaeological Sites,* edited by E. Kroll and T. D. Price, pp. 33–59. Plenum, New York.
1991b   Excavations at a Small Mesa Verde Pueblo II Anasazi Site in Southwestern Colorado. *Kiva* 57:55–75.
1992   Studying Variability in the Archaeological Record: An Ethnoarchaeological Model for Distinguishing Mobility Patterns. *American Antiquity* 57:635–660.

Kent, S., and H. Vierich
1989   The Myth of Ecological Determinism—Anticipated Mobility and Site Spatial Organization. In *Farmers as Hunters: The Implications of Sedentism,* edited by S. Kent, pp. 96–134. Cambridge University Press, Cambridge.

Kenzle, S. C.
1997   Enclosing Walls in the Northern San Juan: Sociophysical Boundaries and Defensive Fortifications in the American Southwest. *Journal of Field Archaeology* 24(2):195–210.

Kidder, A. V.
1927   Southwestern Archaeological Conference. *Science* 68:489–491.

Kilby, J. D.
1998   A Geoarchaeological Analysis of Ten Pueblo III Pit Structures in the

Sand Canyon Locality, Southwest Colorado. Master's thesis, Eastern New Mexico University, Portales.

Killion, T. W.

1990   Cultivation Intensity and Residential Site Structure: An Ethnoarchaeological Examination of Peasant Agriculture in the Sierra de los Tuxtlas, Veracruz, Mexico. *Latin American Antiquity* 1:191–215.

Kintigh, K. W.

1984   Measuring Archaeological Diversity by Comparison with Simulated Assemblages. *American Antiquity* 49(1):44–54.

1985   *Settlement, Subsistence, and Society in Late Zuni Prehistory.* Anthropological Papers of the University of Arizona, no. 44. University of Arizona Press, Tucson.

1994   Chaco, Communal Architecture, and Cibolan Aggregation. In *The Ancient Southwestern Community: Methods and Models for the Study of Prehistoric Social Organization,* edited by W. H. Wills and R. Leonard, pp. 131–140. University of New Mexico Press, Albuquerque.

1996   The Cibola Region in the Post-Chacoan Era. In *The Prehistoric Pueblo World: A.D. 1150–1350,* edited by M. A. Adler, pp. 131–144. University of Arizona Press, Tucson.

Kintigh, K. W., T. L. Howell, and A. I. Duff

1996   Post-Chacoan Social Integration at the Hinkson Site. *Kiva* 61(3):257–274.

Kleidon, J. H.

1998a   Chapter 12: Saddlehorn Hamlet: 5MT262. In *The Sand Canyon Archaeological Project: The Site Testing Program,* edited by M. D. Varien. Crow Canyon Archaeological Center, Cortez, Colorado. In press.

1998b   Chapter 13: Mad Dog Tower 5MT181. In *The Sand Canyon Archaeological Project: The Site Testing Program,* edited by M. D. Varien. Crow Canyon Archaeological Center, Cortez, Colorado. In press.

1998c   Chapter 14: Castle Rock Pueblo 5MT1825. In *The Sand Canyon Archaeological Project: The Site Testing Program,* edited by M. D. Varien. Crow Canyon Archaeological Center, Cortez, Colorado. In press.

Kleindienst, M. R., and P. J. Watson

1956   "Action Archaeology": The Archaeological Inventory of a Living Community. *Anthropology Tomorrow* 5(1):75–78.

Kohler, T. A.

1978   Ceramic Breakage Rate Simulation: Population Size and the Southeastern Chiefdom. *Newsletter of Computer Archaeology* 14:1–18.

1988   The Probability Sample at Grass Mesa Village. In *Dolores Archaeological Program. Anasazi Communities at Dolores: Grass Mesa Village,* compiled by W. D. Lipe, J. N. Morris, and T. A. Kohler, pp. 51–74. Bureau of Reclamation, Engineering and Research Center, Denver.

1992a   Field Houses, Villages, and the Tragedy of the Commons in the Early Northern Anasazi Southwest. *American Antiquity* 57:617–634.

1992b   Prehistoric Human Impact on the Environment in the Upland North American Southwest. *Population and Environment: A Journal of Interdisciplinary Studies* 13:255–268.

Kohler, T. A., and E. Blinman

1987   Solving Mixture Problems in Archaeology: Analysis of Ceramic Materials for Dating and Demographic Reconstruction. *Journal of Anthropological Archaeology* 6(1):1–28.

Kohler, T. A., and M. Matthews

1988   Long-Term Anasazi Land Use and Forest Reduction: A Case Study from Southwest Colorado. *American Antiquity* 53:537–564.

Kohler, T. A., J. D. Orcutt, E. Blinman, and K. L. Petersen

1986   Anasazi Spreadsheets: The Cost of Doing Agricultural Business in Prehistoric Dolores. In *Dolores Archaeological Program: Final Synthetic Report,* compiled by D. A. Breternitz, C. K. Robinson, and G. T. Gross, pp. 525–538. Bureau of Reclamation, Engineering and Research Center, Denver, Colorado.

Kohler, T. A., and C. R. Van West

1996   The Calculus of Self-interest in the Development of Cooperation: Sociopolitical Development and Risk among the Northern Anasazi. In *Evolving Complexity and Environmental Risk in the Prehistoric Southwest,* edited by J. Tainter and B. B. Tainter. Santa Fe Institute Studies in the Science of Complexity, Proceedings vol. 24, Addison-Wesley, Reading, Massachusetts.

Kosse, K.

1990   Group Size and Societal Complexity: Thresholds in the Long-Term Memory. *Journal of Anthropological Archaeology* 9(3):275–303.

1992   Middle-Range Societies from a Scalar Perspective. Paper presented at the Third Southwest Symposium, Tucson, Arizona.

Kramer, C.

1985   Ceramic Ethnoarchaeology. *Annual Review of Anthropology* 14:77–102.

Kuckelman, K. A.

1998a   Chapter 2: G and G Hamlet 5MT11338. In *The Sand Canyon Archaeological Project: The Site Testing Program,* edited by M. D. Varien. Crow Canyon Archaeological Center, Cortez, Colorado. In press.

1998b   Chapter 5: Kenzie Dawn Hamlet 5MT5152. In *The Sand Canyon Archaeological Project: The Site Testing Program,* edited by M. D. Varien. Crow Canyon Archaeological Center, Cortez, Colorado. In press.

1998c   Chapter 8: Lester's Site 5MT10246. In *The Sand Canyon Archaeological Project: The Site Testing Program,* edited by M. D. Varien. Crow Canyon Archaeological Center, Cortez, Colorado. In press.

1998d   Chapter 9: Lookout House 5MT10459. In *The Sand Canyon Archaeological Project: The Site Testing Program,* edited by M. D. Varien. Crow Canyon Archaeological Center, Cortez, Colorado. In press.

Kuckelman, K. A., and J. N. Morris

1988   *Archaeological Investigations on South Canal.* 2 vols. Four Corners Archaeological Project Report no. 11. Complete Archaeological Service Associates, Cortez, Colorado.

Lancaster, J. A., J. M. Pinkley, P. F. Van Cleave, and D. Watson

1954   *Archeological Excavations in Mesa Verde National Park, Colorado, 1950.* Archeological Research Series no. 2, National Park Service, Washington, D.C.

LeBlanc, S. A.

1978   Settlement Patterns in the El Morro Valley, New Mexico. In *Investigations of the Southwestern Anthropological Research Group: An Experiment in Archaeological Cooperation,* edited by R. C. Euler and G. J. Gumerman, pp. 45–51. Museum of Northern Arizona, Flagstaff.

Lee, R.

1969   !Kung Bushmen Subsistence: An Input-Output Analysis. In *Environment and Cultural Behavior,* edited by A. Vayda, pp. 47–79. Natural History Press, Garden City, New York.

Lekson, S. H.

1984   Largest Settlement Size and the Interpretation of Socio-political Complexity. Paper presented at the 49th annual meeting of the Society for American Archaeology, Portland, Oregon.

1988   The Idea of the Kiva in Anasazi Archaeology. *Kiva* 53:213–234.

1990   Sedentism and Aggregation in Anasazi Archaeology. In *Perspectives on Southwestern Prehistory,* edited by P. E. Minnis and C. L. Redman, pp. 333–340. Westview Press, Boulder, Colorado.

1991   Settlement Patterns and the Chaco Region. In *Chaco and Hohokam: Prehistoric Regional Systems in the American Southwest,* edited by P. L. Crown and W. J. Judge, pp. 31–55. School of American Research Press, Santa Fe, New Mexico.

1993   Ruins of the Four Corners, Villages of the Rio Grande. In *Ancient Land, Ancestral Places: Paul Logsdon in the Pueblo Southwest.* Museum of New Mexico Press, Santa Fe.

1996   Scale and Process in the Southwest. In *Interpreting Southwestern Diversity: Underlying Principles and Overarching Patterns,* edited by P. R. Fish and J. J. Reid. Anthropological Research Papers no. 48, Arizona State University, Tempe.

Levy, J.

1992   *Orayvi Revisited.* School of American Research Press, Santa Fe, New Mexico.

Lightfoot, K. G.
    1984   *Prehistoric Political Dynamics: A Case Study from the American Southwest.* Northern Illinois University Press, DeKalb.

Lightfoot, K. G., and R. Jewett
    1984   The Occupation Duration of Duncan. In *The Duncan Project: A Study of the Occupation Duration and Settlement Pattern of an Early Mogollon Pithouse Village,* edited by K. G. Lightfoot, pp. 47–82. Office of Cultural Resource Management, Department of Anthropology, Arizona State University, Tempe.

Lightfoot, K. G., and F. Plog
    1984   Intensification along the North Side of the Mogollon Rim. In *Prehistoric Agricultural Strategies in the Southwest,* edited by S. K. Fish and P. R. Fish, pp. 179–195. Anthropological Research Papers no. 33, Arizona State University, Tempe.

Lightfoot, R. R.
    1992a   *Archaeology of the House and Household: A Case Study of Assemblage Formation and Household Organization in the American Southwest.* Ph.D. dissertation, Washington State University, Pullman.
    1992b   Architecture and Tree-Ring Dating at the Duckfoot Site in Southwestern Colorado. *Kiva* 57(3):213–236.
    1993   Abandonment Processes in Prehistoric Pueblos. In *The Abandonment of Settlements and Regions: Ethnoarchaeological and Archaeological Approaches,* edited by C. M. Cameron and S. A. Tomka, pp. 165–177. Cambridge University Press, Cambridge.
    1994   *The Duckfoot Site, vol. 2: Archaeology of the House and Household.* Occasional Papers no. 4, Crow Canyon Archaeological Center, Cortez, Colorado.

Lightfoot, R. R., and M. C. Etzkorn
    1993   *The Duckfoot Site, vol. 1: Descriptive Archaeology.* Occasional Papers no. 3, Crow Canyon Archaeological Center, Cortez, Colorado.

Lightfoot, R. R., M. C. Etzkorn, and M. D. Varien
    1993   Excavations. In *The Duckfoot Site, vol. 1: Descriptive Archaeology,* edited by R. R. Lightfoot and M. C. Etzkorn. Occasional Papers no. 3, Crow Canyon Archaeological Center, Cortez, Colorado.

Lightfoot, R. R., and K. A. Kuckelman
    n.d.   Conflict in the Thirteenth-Century Pueblos of the Mesa Verde Region. In *Sand Canyon: The Last Decades of the Pueblo Occupation of the Mesa Verde Region,* edited by R. H. Wilshusen. In preparation.

Linton, R.
    1936   *The Study of Man.* Appleton-Century-Crofts, New York.

Lipe, W. D.

1978   The Southwest. In *Ancient Native Americans,* edited by J. D. Jennings, pp. 327–401. W. H. Freeman, San Francisco.

1989   Social Scale of Mesa Verde Anasazi Kivas. In *The Architecture of Social Integration in Prehistoric Pueblos,* edited by W. D. Lipe and M. Hegmon, pp. 53–72. Occasional Papers no. 1, Crow Canyon Archaeological Center, Cortez, Colorado.

1994   Material Expression of Social Power in the Northern San Juan, A.D. 1150–1300. Extended version of a paper presented at the annual meeting of the Society for American Archaeology, Anaheim, California. Ms. on file, Crow Canyon Archaeological Center, Cortez, Colorado.

1995   The Depopulation of the Northern San Juan: Conditions in the Turbulent 1200s. *Journal of Anthropological Archaeology* 14(2):143–169.

Lipe, W. D., ed.

1992   *The Sand Canyon Archaeological Project: A Progress Report.* Occasional Papers no. 2, Crow Canyon Archaeological Center, Cortez, Colorado.

Lipe, W. D., and M. Hegmon

1989   *The Architecture of Social Integration in Prehistoric Pueblos.* Occasional Papers no. 1, Crow Canyon Archaeological Center, Cortez, Colorado.

Longacre, W. A.

1985   Pottery Use-Life among the Kalinga, Northern Luzon, the Philippines. In *Decoding Prehistoric Ceramics,* edited by B. A. Nelson, pp. 334–346. Southern Illinois University Press, Carbondale.

Longacre, W. A., and J. E. Ayres

1968   Archaeological Lessons from an Apache Wickiup. In *New Perspectives in Archaeology,* edited by S. L. Binford and L. R. Binford, pp. 151–159. Aldine, Chicago.

Longacre, W. A., and J. M. Skibo

1994   *Kalinga Ethnoarchaeology: Expanding Archaeological Method and Theory.* Smithsonian Institution Press, Washington, D.C.

Lourandos, H.

1985   Intensification and Australian Prehistory. In *Prehistoric Hunter-Gatherers: The Emergence of Cultural Complexity,* edited by T. D. Price and J. A. Brown, pp. 385–423. Academic Press, New York.

1988   Paleopolitics: Resource Intensification in Aboriginal Australia and Papua New Guinea. In *Hunters and Gatherers 1: History, Evolution, and Social Change,* edited by T. Ingold, D. Riches, and J. Woodburn, pp. 148–160. Berg, Oxford.

Lowell, J. C.

1988   The Social Use of Space at Turkey Creek Pueblo: An Architectural Analysis. *Kiva* 53:85–100.

1991   *Prehistoric Households at Turkey Creek Pueblo, Arizona.* Anthropological

Papers of the University of Arizona, no. 54. University of Arizona Press, Tucson.

Marshall, M. P., J. R. Stein, R. W. Loose, and J. E. Novotny

1979   *Anasazi Communities of the San Juan Basin.* Public Service Company of New Mexico and Historic Preservation Bureau, Planning Division, Department of Finance and Administration of the State of New Mexico, Santa Fe.

Martin, P. S.

1936   *Lowry Ruin in Southwestern Colorado.* Anthropological Series, vol. 23, no. 1. Field Museum of Natural History, Chicago.

Matson, R. G.

1991   *The Origins of Southwestern Agriculture.* University of Arizona Press, Tucson.

Matson, R. G., and B. Chisholm

1991   Basketmaker II Subsistence: Carbon Isotopes and Other Dietary Indicators from Cedar Mesa, Utah. *American Antiquity* 56:444–459.

Matson, R. G., W. D. Lipe, and W. R. Haase IV

1988   Adaptational Continuities and Occupational Discontinuities: The Cedar Mesa Anasazi. *Journal of Field Archaeology* 15:245–264.

Matthews, M. H.

1986   The Dolores Archaeological Program Macrobotanical Data Base: Resource Availability and Mix. In *Dolores Archaeological Program: Final Synthetic Report,* compiled by D. A. Breternitz, C. K. Robinson and G. T. Gross, pp. 151–183. Bureau of Reclamation, Engineering and Research Center, Denver, Colorado.

McGuire, Randall H.

1984   The Boserup Model and Agricultural Intensification in the United States Southwest. In *Prehistoric Agricultural Strategies in the Southwest,* edited by S. K. Fish and P. R. Fish, pp. 327–334. Anthropological Research Papers no. 33, Arizona State University, Tempe.

1992   *A Marxist Archaeology.* Academic Press, San Diego.

McIntosh, R. J.

1974   Archaeology and Mud Wall Decay in a West African Village. *World Archaeology* 6:154–171.

McKenna, P. J., and H. W. Toll

1992   Regional Patterns of Great House Development among the Totah Anasazi, New Mexico. In *Anasazi Regional Organization and the Chaco System,* edited by D. E. Doyel, pp. 133–143. Anthropological Papers no. 5, Maxwell Museum of Anthropology, Albuquerque, New Mexico.

McMichael, E. V.

1960   Towards the Estimation of Prehistoric Populations. Indiana Academy of Science, *Proceedings* 69:78–82.

Miller, D.

1985 *Artifacts as Categories.* Cambridge University Press, Cambridge.

Mills, B. J.

1989a Integrating Functional Analysis of Vessels and Sherds through Models of Ceramic Assemblage Formation. *World Archaeology* 21(1):133–147.

1989b *Ceramics and Settlement in the Cedar Mesa Area, Southeastern Utah: A Methodological Approach.* Ph.D. dissertation, Department of Anthropology, University of New Mexico, Albuquerque.

1994 Community Dynamics and Archaeological Dynamics: Some Considerations of Middle-Range Theory. In *The Ancient Southwestern Community: Models and Methods for the Study of Prehistoric Social Organization,* edited by W. H. Wills and R. D. Leonard, pp. 55–65. University of New Mexico Press, Albuquerque.

Montgomery, B. K.

1993 Ceramic Analysis as a Tool for Discovering Processes of Pueblo Abandonment. In *Abandonment of Settlements and Regions: Ethnoarchaeological and Archaeological Approaches,* edited by C. M. Cameron and S. A. Tomka, pp. 157–164. Cambridge University Press, Cambridge.

Montgomery, B. K., and J. J. Reid

1990 An Instance of Rapid Ceramic Change in the American Southwest. *American Antiquity* 55:88–97.

Morgan, L. H.

1985 [1877] *Ancient Society.* University of Arizona Press, Tucson.

Munro, N. D.

1994 *An Investigation of Anasazi Turkey Production in Southwestern Colorado.* Master's thesis, Department of Archaeology, Simon Fraser University, Burnaby, British Columbia.

Murdock, G. P.

1949 *Social Structure.* Macmillan, New York.

Murray, P.

1980 Discard Location: The Ethnographic Data. *American Antiquity* 45:490–502.

Naranjo, T.

1995 Thoughts on Migration from Santa Clara Pueblo. *Journal of Anthropological Archaeology* 14(2):247–250.

Neily, R. B.

1983 *The Prehistoric Community on the Colorado Plateau: An Approach to the Study of Change and Survival in the Northern San Juan Area of the American Southwest.* Ph.D. dissertation, Southern Illinois University. University Microfilms, Ann Arbor, Michigan.

Neitzel, J. E.

1994 Boundary Dynamics in the Chacoan Regional System. In *The Ancient*

Southwestern Community: Models and Methods for the Study of Prehistoric Social Organization, edited by W. H. Wills and R. D. Leonard, pp. 209–240. University of New Mexico Press, Albuquerque.

Nelson, B. A.

1981   Ethnoarchaeology and Paleodemography: A Test of Turner and Lofgren's Hypothesis. *Journal of Anthropological Research* 37(2):107–129.

1991   Ceramic Frequency and Use Life: A Highland Mayan Case in Cross-cultural Perspective. In *Ceramic Ethnoarchaeology,* edited by W. A. Longacre, pp. 162–181. University of Arizona Press, Tucson.

Nelson, B. A., and R. Anyon

1996   Fallow Valleys: Asynchronous Occupations in Southwestern New Mexico. *Kiva* 61(3):275–294.

Nelson, B. A., T. A. Kohler, and K. W. Kintigh

1994   Demographic Alternatives: Consequences for Current Models of Southwestern Prehistory. In *Understanding Complexity in the Prehistoric Southwest,* edited by G. J. Gumerman and M. Gell-Mann, pp. 113–146. Santa Fe Institute Studies in the Sciences of Complexity, Proceedings, vol. 16. Addison-Wesley, Reading, Massachusetts.

Nelson, B. A., and S. A. LeBlanc

1986   *Short-Term Sedentism in the American Southwest: The Mimbres Valley Salado.* University of New Mexico Press, Albuquerque.

Nelson, N. C.

1909   Shellmounds of San Francisco Bay Region. *University of California Publications in American Archaeology and Ethnology,* vol. 7, pp. 309–356. Berkeley.

Netting, R. McC.

1982   Territory, Property and Tenure. In *Behavioral and Social Science Research: A National Resource,* edited by N. J. Smelser, D. J. Tremain, and R. McC. Adams, pp. 446–502. Washington, D.C.: National Academy Press.

1990   Population, Permanent Agriculture, and Polities: Unpacking the Evolutionary Portmanteau. In *The Evolution of Political Systems: Sociopolitics in Small-Scale Sedentary Societies,* edited by S. Upham, pp. 21–61. Cambridge University Press, Cambridge.

1993   *Smallholders, Householders: Farm Families and the Ecology of Intensive, Sustainable Agriculture.* Stanford University Press, Stanford, California.

Netting, R. McC., R. R. Wilk, and E. J. Arnould

1984   Introduction. In *Households: Comparative and Historical Studies of the Domestic Group,* edited by R. M. Netting, R. R. Wilk, and E. J. Arnould. University of California Press, Berkeley.

Neusius, S. W.

1987   The Dolores Archaeological Program Faunal Data Base: Resource Availability and Resource Mix. In *Dolores Archaeological Program: Final Syn-*

thetic Report, compiled by D. A. Breternitz, C. K. Robinson and G. T. Gross, pp. 199–302. Bureau of Reclamation, Engineering and Research Center, Denver, Colorado.

Newell, H. P., and A. D. Krieger

1949   *The George C. Davis Site, Cherokee County, Texas.* Memoirs no. 5, Society for American Archaeology.

Nichols, D. L.

1987   Risk and Agricultural Intensification during the Formative Period in the Northern Basin of Mexico. *American Anthropologist* 89:596–616.

Nordenskiöld, G.

1979 [1893]   *The Cliff Dwellers of The Mesa Verde, Southwestern Colorado: Their Pottery and Implements.* Rio Grande Press, Glorieta, New Mexico.

O'Bryan, D.

1950   *Excavations in Mesa Verde National Park, 1947–1948.* Medallion Papers 39, Gila Pueblo, Globe, Arizona.

Ortman, S. G.

1995   *Escaping the Confines of Objective Analysis: Perspectives on the Type and Attribute Approaches to Ceramic Chronology.* Ms. on file, Crow Canyon Archaeological Center, Cortez, Colorado.

n.d.   Corn Grinding and Community Organization in the Pueblo Southwest, A.D. 1150–1550. In *Migration and Reorganization: The Pueblo IV Period in the American Southwest,* edited by K. A. Spielmann. Anthropological Research Papers, Arizona State University. In press.

Ortner, S.

1984   Theory in Anthropology since the Sixties. *Comparative Studies in Science and History* 26(1):126–166.

Orton, C.

1982   Computer Simulation Experiments to Assess the Performance of Measures of Quantity of Pottery. *World Archaeology* 14(1):1–20.

1993   How Many Pots Make Five? An Historical Review of Pottery Quantification. *Archaeometry* 35:169–184.

Pastron, A. G.

1974   Preliminary Ethnoarchaeological Investigations among the Tarahumara. In *Ethnoarchaeology: Archaeological Survey Monograph 4,* edited by C. Donnan and C. Clewlow, pp. 93–116. Institute of Archaeology, University of California, Los Angeles.

Pauketat, T. R.

1989   Monitoring Mississippian Homestead Occupation Span and Economy Using Ceramic Refuse. *American Antiquity* 54(2):288–310.

Pennington, C. W.

1963   *The Tarahumara of Mexico: Their Environment and Material Culture.* University of Utah Press, Salt Lake City.

Petersen, K. L.

1986   Climatic Reconstruction for the Dolores Project Area. In *Dolores Archaeo-logical Program: Final Synthetic Report*, compiled by D. A. Breternitz, C. K. Robinson, and G. T. Gross, pp. 311–325. Bureau of Reclamation, Engineering and Research Center, Denver.

1987a   Summer Warmth: A Critical Factor for the Dolores Anasazi. In *Dolores Archaeological Program, Supporting Studies: Settlement and Environment*, compiled by K. L. Petersen and J. D. Orcutt, pp. 60–71. Bureau of Reclamation, Engineering and Research Center, Denver.

1987b   Tree-Ring Transfer Functions for Estimating Corn Production. In *Dolores Archaeological Program, Supporting Studies: Settlement and Environment*, compiled by K. L. Petersen and J. D. Orcutt, pp. 216–231. Bureau of Reclamation, Engineering and Research Center, Denver.

1988   *Climate and the Dolores River Anasazi: A Paleoenvironmental Reconstruction from a 10,000-Year Pollen Record, La Plata Mountains, Southwestern Colorado.* University of Utah Press, Salt Lake City.

Peterson, K. L., V. L. Clay, M. H. Matthews, and S. W. Neusius

1987   Implications of Anasazi Impact on the Landscape. In *Dolores Archaeological Program, Supporting Studies: Settlement and Environment*, compiled by K. L. Peterson and J. D. Orcutt, pp. 147–184. Bureau of Reclamation, Engineering and Research Center, Denver, Colorado.

Pierce, C.

1998   *Explanation in Archaeology: A Case Study of Cooking Pot Change in the American Southwest.* Ph.D. dissertation, University of Washington, Seattle.

Pierce, C., M. D. Varien, J. Driver, T. Gross, and J. Keleher

1998   Artifacts. In *The Sand Canyon Archaeological Project: The Site Testing Program*, edited by M. D. Varien. Crow Canyon Archaeological Center, Cortez, Colorado. In press.

Plog, S.

1986   *Spatial Organization and Exchange: Archaeological Survey on Northern Black Mesa.* Southern Illinois University Press, Carbondale.

1990   Agriculture, Sedentism, and Environment in the Evolution of Political Systems. In *The Evolution of Political Systems*, edited by S. Upham, pp. 177–199. Cambridge University Press, Cambridge.

Polanyi, K.

1957   The Economy as Instituted Process. In *Trade and Market in the Early Empires*, edited by K. Polanyi, C. Arnsberg, and H. W. Pearson. Free Press, New York.

Powell, S.

1983   *Mobility and Adaptation: The Anasazi of Black Mesa, Arizona.* Southern Illinois University Press, Carbondale.

1988   Anasazi Demographic Patterns and Organizational Responses: Assump-
            tions and Interpretive Difficulties. In *The Anasazi in a Changing Environ-
            ment*, edited by G. J. Gumerman, pp. 168–191. Cambridge University
            Press, Cambridge.

1990   Sedentism or Mobility: What Do the Data Say? What Did the Anasazi
            Do? In *Perspectives on Southwestern Prehistory*, edited by P. E. Minnis
            and C. L. Redman, pp. 92–102. Westview Press, Boulder, Colorado.

Powers, R. P., W. B. Gillespie, and S. H. Lekson

1983   *The Outlier Survey: A Regional View of Settlement in the San Juan Basin*.
            Reports of the Chaco Center no. 3. National Park Service, Albuquerque,
            New Mexico.

Price, T. D., and J. A. Brown

1985   *Prehistoric Hunter-Gatherers: The Emergence of Cultural Complexity*. Aca-
            demic Press, New York.

Prudden, T. M.

1903   The Prehistoric Ruins of the San Juan Watershed in Utah, Arizona,
            Colorado, and New Mexico. *American Anthropologist* 5:224–288.

Rafferty, J. E.

1985   The Archaeological Record on Sedentariness: Recognition, Development,
            and Implications. In *Advances in Archaeological Method and Theory*, vol.
            8, edited by M. B. Schiffer, pp. 113–156. Academic Press, New York.

Reid, J. J.

1973   *Growth and Response to Stress at Grasshopper Pueblo, Arizona*. Ph.D.
            dissertation, University of Arizona. University Microfilms, Ann Arbor,
            Michigan.

Rice, G. E.

1975   *A Systemic Explanation of a Change in Mogollon Settlement Patterns*. Ph.D.
            dissertation, Department of Anthropology, University of Washington.
            University Microfilms, Ann Arbor, Michigan.

Rice, P. M.

1987   *Pottery Analysis: A Sourcebook*. University of Chicago Press, Chicago.

Robinson, W. J.

1967   *Tree-Ring Materials as a Basis for Cultural Interpretations*. Ph.D. disserta-
            tion, University of Arizona, Tucson.

1990   Tree-Ring Studies of the Pueblo de Acoma. *Historical Archaeology*
            24:99–106.

Robinson, W. J., B. G. Harrill, and R. L. Warren

1975   *Tree-Ring Dates from Arizona H-1: Flagstaff Area*. Laboratory of Tree-
            Ring Research, University of Arizona, Tucson.

Rocek, T. R.

1988   The Behavioral and Material Correlates of Site Seasonality: Lessons from
            Navajo Ethnoarchaeology. *American Antiquity* 53:523–536.

1996   Sedentism and Mobility in the Southwest. In *Interpreting Southwestern Diversity: Underlying Principles and Overarching Patterns,* edited by P. R. Fish and J. J. Reid. Anthropological Research Papers no. 48, Arizona State University, Tempe.

Rohn, A. H.

1963   Prehistoric Soil and Water Conservation on Chapin Mesa, Southwestern Colorado. *American Antiquity* 28:441–455.

1965   Postulation of Socio-economic Groups from Archaeological Evidence. In *Contributions of the Wetherill Mesa Archaeological Project,* assembled by D. Osborne, pp. 65–69. Memoir no. 19, Society for American Archaeology, Washington, D.C.

1971   *Mug House, Mesa Verde National Park, Colorado.* Archeological Research Series no. 7-D, National Park Service, Washington, D.C.

1972   Social Implications of Pueblo Water Management in the Northern San Juan. In *Zeitschrift für Ethnologie,* Band 97, Heft 2, Braunschweig, Germany.

1977   *Cultural Change and Continuity on Chapin Mesa.* Regents Press of Kansas, Lawrence.

1984   Lowry Settlement District. *National Register of Historic Places Inventory Nomination Form.* Document on file at the Bureau of Land Management, San Juan Area Resource Office, Durango, Colorado.

1989   Northern San Juan Prehistory. In *Dynamics of Southwest Prehistory,* edited by L. Cordell and G. Gumerman, pp. 149–177. Smithsonian Institution Press, Washington D.C.

1992   The Anasazi Northern Frontier. Paper presented at the 1992 Chacmool Conference, Calgary, Alberta.

Roper, D. C.

1979   The Method and Theory of Site Catchment Analysis: A Review. In *Advances in Archaeological Method and Theory,* vol. 2, edited by M. B. Schiffer, pp. 119–140. Academic Press, New York.

Rye, O. S.

1976   Keeping Your Temper Under Control: Materials and the Manufacture of Papuan Pottery. *Archaeology and Physical Anthropology in Oceania* 11(2):106–137.

1981   *Pottery Technology: Principles and Reconstruction.* Australian National University Manuals on Archaeology no. 4, Taraxacum, Washington D.C.

Sahlins, M.

1981   *Historical Metaphors and Mythical Realities: Structure in the Early History of the Sandwich Islands Kingdom.* University of Michigan Press, Ann Arbor.

Saitta, D. J.

1983   Comment on the Evolution of "Tribal" Social Networks. *American Antiquity* 48:820–824.

1990   Class and Community in the Prehistoric Southwest. Paper presented at the 2d annual Southwest Symposium, Albuquerque, New Mexico.

Sanders, W. T., and D. Webster

1978   Unilinealism, Multilinealism, and the Evolution of Complex Societies. In *Social Archaeology: Beyond Subsistence and Dating*, edited by C. L. Redman, M. J. Berman, E. V. Curtin et al., pp. 249–302. Academic Press, New York.

Schiffer, M. B.

1972   Archaeological Context and Systemic Context. *American Antiquity* 37:156–165.

1975   Archaeology as Behavioral Science. *American Anthropologist* 77(4):836–848.

1976   *Behavioral Archaeology*. Academic Press, New York.

1985   Is There a "Pompeii Premise" in Archaeology? *Journal of Anthropological Research* 41:18–41.

1987   *Formation Processes of the Archaeological Record*. University of New Mexico Press, Albuquerque.

Schiffer, M. B., J. M. Skibo, T. C. Boelke, M. A. Neupert, and M. Aronson

1994   New Perspectives on Experimental Archaeology: Surface Treatments and Thermal Response of the Clay Cooking Pot. *American Antiquity* 59:197–217.

Schlanger, S. H.

1987   Population Measurement, Size, and Change, A.D. 600–1175. In *Dolores Archaeological Program, Supporting Studies: Settlement and Environment*, compiled by K. L. Petersen and J. D. Orcutt, pp. 568–613. Bureau of Reclamation, Engineering and Research Center, Denver.

1988   Patterns of Population Movement and Long-Term Population Growth in Southwestern Colorado. *American Antiquity* 53:773–793.

1990   Artifact Assemblage Composition and Site Occupation Duration. In *Perspectives on Southwestern Prehistory*, edited by P. E. Minis and C. L. Redman, pp. 103–121. Westview Press, Boulder, Colorado.

1991   On Manos, Metates, and the History of Site Occupations. *American Antiquity* 6(3):460–474.

1992   Recognizing Persistent Places in Anasazi Settlement Systems. In *Space, Time, and Archaeological Landscapes*, edited by J. Rossignol and L. Wandsnider, pp. 91–112. Plenum Press, New York.

Schlanger, S. H., and R. H. Wilshusen

1993   Local Abandonments and Regional Conditions in the North American Southwest. In *The Abandonment of Settlements and Regions: Ethnoarchaeological and Archaeological Approaches*, edited by C. M. Cameron and S. A. Tomka, pp. 85–98. Cambridge University Press, Cambridge.

Schoenwetter, J.

1966   A Reevaluation of the Navajo Reservoir Pollen Chronology. *El Palacio* 73:19–26.

1967   Pollen Survey of the Chuska Valley. In *An Archaeological Survey of the Chuska Valley and the Chaco Plateau, New Mexico, Part 1: Natural Science Studies*, by A. H. Harris, J. Schoenwetter, and A. H. Warren. New Mexico Research Records no. 4, Museum of New Mexico Press, Santa Fe.

1970   Archaeological Pollen Studies of the Colorado Plateau. *American Antiquity* 35:35–48.

Schoenwetter, J., and A. E. Dittert, Jr.

1968   An Ecological Interpretation of Anasazi Settlement Patterns. In *Anthropological Archaeology in the Americas*, edited by B. J. Meggers, pp. 41–66. Anthropological Society of Washington, Washington, D.C.

Service, E. R.

1971   *Primitive Social Organization: An Evolutionary Perspective.* 2d ed. Random House, New York.

Shennan, S.

1988   *Quantifying Archaeology.* Academic Press, San Diego.

1993   After Social Evolution: A New Archaeological Agenda? In *Archaeological Theory: Who Sets the Agenda*, edited by N. Yoffee and M. Sherratt, pp. 53–59. Cambridge University Press, Cambridge.

Sherman, R. J.

1995   *Site Catchments and Satellite Imagery: An Ecological Analysis of Late Pueblo III (A.D. 1250–1300) Settlements in the Northern San Juan Region of the American Southwest.* Honors thesis, Yale University.

Shott, M. J.

1989   On Tool-Class Use Lives and the Formation of Archaeological Assemblages. *American Antiquity* 54(1):9–30.

1996   Mortal Pots: On Use Life and Vessel Size in the Formation of Ceramic Assemblages. *American Antiquity* 61(3):463–482.

Skibo, J. M.

1992   *Pottery Function: A Use-Alteration Perspective.* Plenum Press, New York.

Smiley, F. E.

1993   Early Farmers in the Northern Southwest: A View from Marsh Pass. In *Anasazi Basketmaker: Papers from the 1990 Wetherill–Grand Gulch Symposium*, edited by V. M. Atkins, pp. 243–254. Cultural Resources Series no. 24, Bureau of Land Management, Salt Lake City, Utah.

1994   The Agricultural Transition in the Northern Southwest: Patterns in the Current Chronometric Data. *Kiva* 60(2):165–190.

Smith, E. A.

1988   Risk and Uncertainty in the "Original Affluent Society": Evolutionary Ecology of Resource Sharing and Land Tenure. In *Hunters and Gatherers*

1: *History, Evolution, and Social Change,* edited by T. Ingold, D. Riches, and J. Woodburn, pp. 222–252. Berg, Oxford.

Smith, J. E.

1987   *Mesas, Cliffs, and Canyons: The University of Colorado Survey of Mesa Verde National Park, 1971–1977.* Mesa Verde Museum Association, Mesa Verde, Colorado.

Solheim, W. G. II

1960   The Use of Sherd Weights and Counts in the Handling of Archaeological Data. *Current Anthropology* 1:325–329.

Stark, B.

1985   Archaeological Identification of Pottery-Production Locations: Ethnoarchaeological and Archaeological Data in Mesoamerica. In *Decoding Prehistoric Ceramics,* edited by B. A. Nelson, pp. 158–194. Southern Illinois University Press, Carbondale.

Steponaitis, V. P.

1983   *Ceramics, Chronology, and Community Patterns: An Archaeological Study at Moundville.* Academic Press, New York.

1984   Technological Studies of Pottery from Alabama: Physical Properties and Vessel Function. In *The Many Dimensions of Pottery,* edited by S. E. van der Leeuw and A. C. Pritchard, pp. 79–122. University of Amsterdam, Amsterdam.

Stevenson, M. G.

1982   Toward an Understanding of Site Abandonment Behavior: Evidence from Historic Mining Camps in the Southwest Yukon. *Journal of Anthropological Archaeology* 1:237–265.

1991   Beyond the Formation of Hearth-Associated Artifact Assemblages. In *The Archaeological Interpretation of Spatial Patterns,* edited by E. Kroll and T. D. Price, pp. 269–300. Plenum, New York.

Steward, J. H.

1937   Ecological Aspects of Southwestern Society. *Anthropos* 32:87–104.

Stiger, M. A.

1979   Mesa Verde Subsistence Patterns from Basketmaker to Pueblo III. *Kiva* 44:133–144.

Stone, G. D.

1991a   Settlement Ethnoarchaeology. *Expedition* 33:16–23.

1991b   Agricultural Territories in a Dispersed Settlement System. *Current Anthropology* 32:343–353.

1992   Social Distance, Spatial Relations, and Agricultural Production among the Kofyar of Namu District, Plateau State, Nigeria. *Journal of Anthropological Archaeology* 11:152–172.

1993   Agricultural Abandonment: A Comparative Study in Historical Ecology. In *Abandonment of Settlements and Regions: Ethnoarchaeological and*

Archaeological Approaches, edited by C. M. Cameron and S. A. Tomka, pp. 74–81. Cambridge University Press, Cambridge.

1996   *Settlement Ecology: The Social and Spatial Organization of Kofyar Agriculture.* University of Arizona Press, Tucson.

Stone, G. D., R. McC. Netting, and M. P. Stone

1990   Seasonality, Labor Scheduling, and Agricultural Intensification in the Nigerian Savanna. *American Anthropologist* 92(1):7–23.

Tani, M.

1994   Why Should More Pots Break in Larger Households? Mechanisms Underlying Population Estimates from Ceramics. In *Kalinga Ethnoarchaeology: Expanding Archaeological Method and Theory,* edited by W. A. Longacre and J. M. Skibo, pp. 51–70. Smithsonian Institution Press, Washington, D.C.

Thompson, I.

1993   *The Towers of Hovenweep.* Mesa Verde Museum Association, Inc., Mesa Verde National Park, Colorado.

1994   *The Escalante Community.* Southwest Natural and Cultural Heritage Association, Albuquerque, New Mexico.

Treganza, A. E., and S. F. Cook

1948   The Quantitative Investigation of Aboriginal Sites: Complete Excavation with Physical and Archaeological Analysis of a Single Mound. *American Antiquity* 13(4):287–297.

Turner, B. L. II, and W. E. Doolittle

1978   The Concept and Measure of Agricultural Intensity. *Professional Geographer* 30:297–301.

Upham, S.

1982   *Politics and Power: An Economic and Political History of the Western Pueblo.* Academic Press, New York.

1984   Ecological and Political Perspectives on Labor Intensification during the Fourteenth Century. In *Prehistoric Agricultural Strategies in the Southwest,* edited by S. K. Fish and P. R. Fish, pp. 291–307. Anthropological Research Papers no. 33, Arizona State University, Tempe.

Upham, S., and F. Plog

1986   The Interpretation of Prehistoric Political Complexity in the Central and Northern Southwest: Toward a Mending of the Models. *Journal of Field Archaeology* 13:223–238.

Van West, C. R.

1994   *Modeling Prehistoric Agricultural Productivity in Southwestern Colorado: A GIS Approach.* Reports of Investigations 67, Department of Anthropology, Washington State University, Pullman, and Crow Canyon Archaeological Center, Cortez, Colorado.

Van West, C., and W. D. Lipe

1992   Modeling Prehistoric Climate and Agriculture in Southwestern Colorado. In *The Sand Canyon Archaeological Project: A Progress Report*, edited by W. D. Lipe, pp. 105–119. Occasional Papers no. 2, Crow Canyon Archaeological Center, Cortez, Colorado.

Varien, M. D.

1984   *Honky House: The Replication of Three Anasazi Surface Structures.* Master's report. University of Texas, Austin.

1994   *Demographic Cycles in Mesa Verde Region Settlement.* Ms. in possession of the author.

1997   *New Perspectives on Settlement Patterns: Sedentism and Mobility in a Social Landscape.* Ph.D. dissertation, Arizona State University, Tempe.

Varien, M. D., ed.

1998   *The Sand Canyon Archaeological Project: The Site Testing Program.* Crow Canyon Archaeological Center, Cortez, Colorado. In press.

Varien, M. D., K. A. Kuckelman, and J. H. Kleidon

1992   The Site Testing Program. In *The Sand Canyon Archaeological Project: A Progress Report*, edited by W. D. Lipe, pp. 45–67. Occasional Papers no. 2, Crow Canyon Archaeological Center, Cortez, Colorado.

Varien, M. D., and R. R. Lightfoot

1989   Ritual and Nonritual Activities in Mesa Verde Region Pit Structures. In *The Architecture of Social Integration in Prehistoric Pueblos*, edited by W. D. Lipe and M. Hegmon, pp. 73–87. Occasional Papers no. 1, Crow Canyon Archaeological Center, Cortez, Colorado.

Varien, M. D., W. D. Lipe, M. A. Adler, I. M. Thompson, and B. A. Bradley

1996   Southwestern Colorado and Southeastern Utah Settlement Patterns, A.D. 1100 to 1300. In *The Prehistoric Pueblo World, A.D. 1150–1350*, edited by M. A. Adler. University of Arizona Press, Tucson.

Varien, M. D., and B. J. Mills

1997   Accumulations Research: Problems and Prospects for Estimating Site Occupation Span. *Journal of Archaeological Method and Theory* 4(2):141–191.

Varien, M. D., and J. M. Potter

1997   Unpacking the Discard Equation: Simulating the Accumulation of Artifacts in the Archaeological Record. *American Antiquity* 62(2):194–213.

Vivian, R. G.

1974   Conservation and Diversion Water-Control Systems in the Anasazi Southwest. In *Irrigation's Impact on Society*, edited by T. E. Downing and M. Gibson, pp. 95–112. Anthropological Papers no. 25, University of Arizona, Tucson.

1984   Agricultural and Social Adjustments to Changing Environments in the Chaco Basin. In *Prehistoric Agricultural Strategies in the Southwest*, edited by S. K. Fish and P. R. Fish, pp. 243–257. Anthropological Research Papers no. 33, Arizona State University, Tempe.

1990   *The Chacoan Prehistory of the San Juan Basin.* Academic Press, New York.

Wallace, H. D.

1995   Ceramic Accumulation Rates and Prehistoric Tonto Basin Households. In *The Roosevelt Community Development Study: New Perspectives on Tonto Basin Prehistory,* edited by M. D. Elson, M. T. Stark, and D. A. Gregory, pp. 79–126. Anthropological Papers no. 15, Center for Desert Archaeology, Tucson, Arizona.

Watkins, J.W.N.

1968   Methodological Individualism and Social Tendencies. In *Readings in the Philosophy of the Social Sciences,* edited by M. Brodbeck, pp. 269–280. Macmillan, New York.

Watson, P. J., S. A. LeBlanc, and C. L. Redman

1980   Aspects of Zuni Prehistory: Preliminary Report on Excavations and Survey in the El Morro Valley of New Mexico. *Journal of Field Archaeology* 7:201–218.

Weigand, P. C.

1969   *Modern Huichol Ceramics.* Mesoamerican Studies: Research Records of the University Museum, Series 69M3A. Southern Illinois University, Carbondale.

West, S. M.

1992   *Temper, Thermal Shock, and Cooking Pots: A Study of Tempering Materials and Their Ethnographic, Archaeological, and Physical Significance in Traditional Cooking Pottery.* Master's thesis, Department of Materials Science and Engineering, University of Arizona, Tucson.

Whalen, M. E., and P. A. Gilman

1990   Introduction. In *Perspectives on Southwestern Prehistory,* edited by P. E. Minnis and C. L. Redman, pp. 71–75. Westview Press, Boulder, Colorado.

Whiteley, P. M.

1988   *Deliberate Acts: Changing Hopi Culture through the Oraibi Split.* University of Arizona Press, Tucson.

Wiessner, P.

1982   Beyond Willow Smoke and Dogs' Tails: A Comment on Binford's Analysis of Hunter-Gatherer Settlement Systems. *American Antiquity* 47:171–178.

Wilcox, D. R.

1996   Pueblo III People and Polity in Relational Context. In *The Prehistoric Pueblo World: A.D. 1150–1350,* edited by M. A. Adler, pp. 241–154. University of Arizona Press, Tucson.

Wilcox, D. R., and J. Haas

1994   The Reality of Competition and Conflict in the Prehistoric Southwest.

In *Themes in Southwest Prehistory,* edited by G. J. Gumerman. School of American Research Press, Santa Fe, New Mexico.

Wilk, R. R.

1984   Households in Process: Agricultural and Domestic Organization among the Kekchi Maya. In *Households: Comparative and Historical Studies of the Domestic Group,* edited by R. McC. Netting, R. R. Wilk and E. Arnould, pp. 217–244. University of California Press, Berkeley.

Wilk, R. R., and R. McC. Netting

1984   Households: Changing Forms and Functions. In *Households: Comparative and Historical Studies of the Domestic Group,* edited by R. McC. Netting, R. R. Wilk, and E. J. Arnould, pp. 1–28. University of California Press, Berkeley.

Wilk, R. R., and W. L. Rathje

1982   Household Archaeology. *American Behavioral Scientist* 25:617–639.

Willey, G. R., and P. Phillips

1958   *Method and Theory in American Archaeology.* University of Chicago Press, Chicago.

Wills, W. H.

1988a   *Early Prehistoric Agriculture.* School of American Research Press, Santa Fe, New Mexico.

1988b   Early Agriculture and Sedentism in the American Southwest: Evidence and Interpretations. *Journal of World Prehistory* 2:445–488.

1990   Cultivating Ideas: The Changing Intellectual History of the Introduction of Agriculture in the American Southwest. In *Perspectives on Southwestern Prehistory,* edited by P. E. Minnis and C. L. Redman, pp. 319–332. Westview Press, Boulder, Colorado.

1992   Plant Cultivation and the Evolution of Risk-Prone Economies in the Prehistoric American Southwest. In *Transitions to Agriculture in Prehistory,* edited by A. B. Gebauer and T. D. Price, pp. 153–175. Monographs in World Archaeology no. 4, Prehistory Press, Madison, Wisconsin.

1995   Archaic Foraging and the Beginning of Food Production in the American Southwest. *Last Hunters—First Farmers: New Perspectives on the Prehistoric Transition to Agriculture,* edited by T. D. Price and A. B. Gebauer, pp. 215–242. School of American Research Press, Santa Fe, New Mexico.

Wilshusen, R. H.

1986   The Relationship between Abandonment Mode and Ritual Use in Pueblo I Anasazi Protokivas. *Journal of Field Archaeology* 13:245–254.

1988a   Abandonment of Structures. In *Dolores Archaeological Program, Supporting Studies: Additive and Reductive Technologies,* compiled by E. Blinman, C. J. Phagan, and R. H. Wilshusen, pp. 673–702. Bureau of Reclamation, Engineering and Research Center, Denver.

1988b   Architectural Trends in Prehistoric Anasazi Sites during A.D. 600 to

1200. In *Dolores Archaeological Program, Supporting Studies: Additive and Reductive Technologies,* compiled by E. Blinman, C. J. Phagan and R. H. Wilshusen, pp. 599–633. Bureau of Reclamation, Engineering and Research Center, Denver. 12.

1991   *Early Villages in the American Southwest: Cross-cultural and Archaeological Perspectives.* Ph.D. dissertation, University of Colorado, Boulder.

1995   *The Cedar Hill Special Treatment Project: Late Pueblo I, Early Navajo, and Historic Occupations in Northwestern New Mexico.* Research Papers no. 1, La Plata Archaeological Consultants, Cortez, Colorado.

Wilshusen, R. H., M. J. Churchill, and J. M. Potter

1997   Prehistoric Reservoirs and Water Basins in the Mesa Verde Region: Intensification of Water Collection Strategies during the Great Pueblo Period. *American Antiquity* 62(4):664–681.

Wilshusen, R. H., and S. H. Schlanger

1993   Late Pueblo I Population Movement in the Northern Southwest: The Big Picture. Paper presented at the 5th Anasazi Symposium, Farmington, New Mexico.

Windes, T. C., and D. Ford

1992   The Nature of the Early Bonito Phase. In *Anasazi Regional Organization and the Chaco System,* edited by D. E. Doyel, pp. 75–85. Anthropological Papers no. 5, Maxwell Museum of Anthropology, Albuquerque, New Mexico.

Winterhalder, B.

1986   Optimal Foraging: Simulation Studies of Diet Choice in a Stochastic Environment. *Journal of Ethnobiology* 6(1):205–223.

1990   Open Field, Common Pot: Harvest Variability and Risk Avoidance in Agricultural and Foraging Societies. In *Risk and Uncertainty in Tribal and Peasant Economies,* edited by E. Cashdan, pp. 67–87. Westview Press, Boulder, Colorado.

Yanagisako, S. J.

1979   Family and Household: The Analysis of Domestic Groups. *Annual Review of Anthropology* 8:161–205.

Yellen, J.

1977   Intracamp Patterning: A Quantitative Approach. In *Archaeological Approaches to the Present,* by J. Yellen. Academic Press, New York.

INDEX

Numbers in italics refer to figures.

abandonment: and anticipated return, 113, 118–121, 223; and artifact curation, 113; and burned timbers, 115–121; and de facto refuse, 122; of kivas 114–121; of Mesa Verde region, 137–138, 188, 191–192, 201–202, 229; and middle-range research, 112–114; of pit structures, 114–121; ritual abandonment, 120–121; and salvaged timbers, 113, 118–121, 126, 199, 223; of sites in Sand Canyon locality, 116–125; strategies of, 47; studies of, by Dolores Archaeological Project, 47. *See also* abandonment process; roof treatment

abandonment process, 112–114; conditioning factors, 113–114; and distance of move, 113, 115, 118, 121, 223, 197–198; and formation processes, 113–115; general models of, 112–114, 122; gradual, 113, 118–121, 223; and historical factors, 114; inclusive scales of, 114; and middle-range theory, 113, 197; planned and unplanned, 113, 118–121, 223; rapid, 113, 118–121, 223; and roof treatment, 113–121. *See also* abandonment; roof treatment

accumulation rate: annual rates, 6, 77, 86–87, 89; confidence intervals for, 93; of cooking vessels, 6, 77, 85–87, 89, 195; of corrugated vessels, 85–87; for Dolores sites, 78–79; for the Duckfoot site, 76–77, 79; and ethnographic data, 70–72; factors affecting, 80; and

frequency of use, 71; per household, 6, 86–87; and occupation span estimates, 86–89, 93–96; of plain gray vessels, 85–87; for pottery, 78–80; in Sand Canyon locality, 79–80, 86–89; simulation of, 72–73, 219; and systemic number (household inventory), 64–65, 71–73; and vessel use-life, 71–72, 195. *See also* accumulations research; cooking pots; discard equation; Duckfoot site

accumulations research, 6–7, 62–64, 195, 217–218; and artifact discard, 63; and artifact use-life, 63–64; assemblage formation, 63–64, 217; and cooking pots 62, 66–79; at Duckfoot, 73–80; ethnoarchaeological studies of, 64–65, 69, 219; and frequency of vessel use, 65; history of, 62–64; and occupation span, 63–66, 70–73; and population size, 62–63; and pottery accumulation, 64–73, 78–80, 195; and simulations, 63–64; summary of methods, 73; and systemic number (household inventory), 64–65, 71–73; vessel breakage, 65–69. *See also* accumulation rate; cooking pots; discard equation

Adler, Michael, 21, 58–59, 144–145, 148, 209

agency, 25–28, 207–208

agents, 26–28; and rational and nonrational motivation, 26–27

aggregation, 48, 50, 148–149, 212–213

ABOUT THE AUTHOR

Mark D. Varien has conducted archaeological fieldwork in Mesoamerica, the South Pacific, throughout the western United States, and in various parts of the North American Southwest. His primary research focus is the Mesa Verde region, where he has worked for almost 20 years. He received his B.A. and M.A. from the University of Texas, Austin, and his Ph.D. from Arizona State University. His recent publications include *The Sand Canyon Project Site Testing Program,* "Unpacking the Discard Equation: Simulating the Accumulation of Artifacts in the Archaeological Record" (in *American Antiquity,* with James M. Potter), and "Accumulations Research: Problems and Prospects for Estimating Site Occupation Span" (in *Journal of Archaeological Method and Theory,* with Barbara J. Mills). Varien's current research interests include site formation processes, settlement patterns and landscape archaeology, community organization, and social theory. Other primary interests include archaeology and public education and Native American involvement in archaeology. He is presently Director of Research at the Crow Canyon Archaeological Center in Cortez, Colorado.

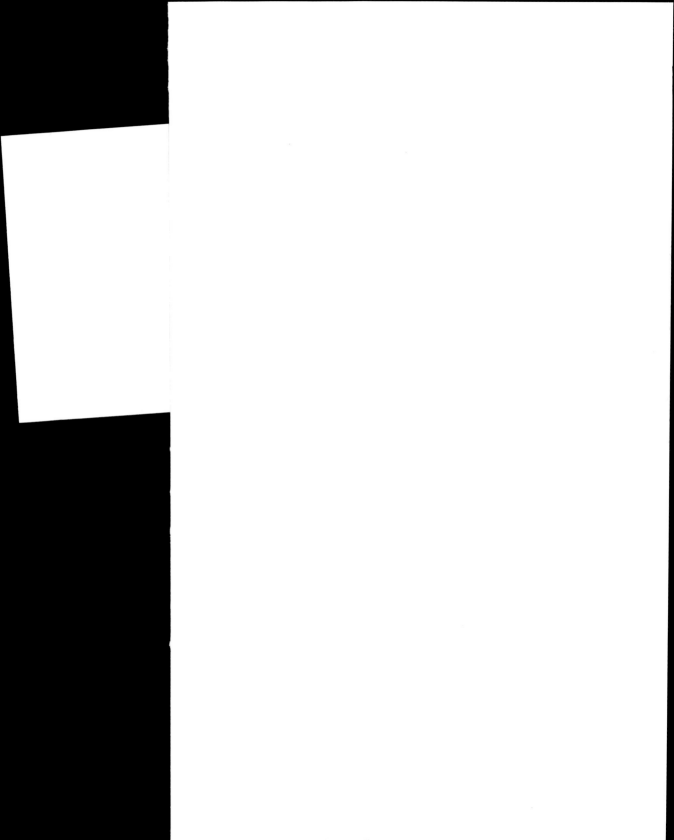

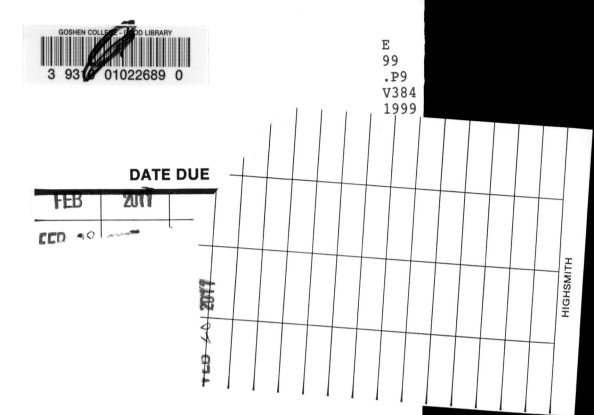